SEEDS OF TOMORROW

Seeds of Tomorrow

NEW AGE

COMMUNITIES THAT WORK

Oliver and Cris Popenoe

1817

Harper & Row, Publishers, San Francisco

Cambridge, Hagerstown, New York, Philadelphia
London, Mexico City, São Paulo, Singapore, Sydney

FIRST EDITION

Designer: Jim Mennick

Library of Congress Cataloging in Publication Data

Popenoe, Oliver.
SEEDS OF TOMORROW.

Bibliography: p.
1. Collective settlements—Case studies. I. Popenoe, Cris. II. Title.
HX632.P67 1984   335′.9′09048   83-48425
ISBN 0-06-250680-3

---

84 85 86 87 88 10 9 8 7 6 5 4 3 2 1

Contents

Introduction

This is a book about intentional communities: communities formed by groups of people who share a commitment to some common purpose and usually to some transcendental value.

Communities such as the ones we are writing about have existed throughout history. Most have had a spiritual basis. Since the early nineteenth century, however, a number have developed along secular lines, usually following an ideology of communalism or anarchism. All forms of communities share a belief that the larger society is failing to deal adequately with the important issues of people's relationships to each other, to their work, and to the world around them. Some communities are concerned primarily with the inner development of their members; others are very much involved in work in the world. There have been times when communities were the isolated repositories of some of the important values of civilization, and other times when they acted as agents of social change.

The world is again in a period of social chaos. We are witnessing an explosive growth of human population accompanied by an unparalleled destruction of our natural environment. The economic ramifications, for those of us in the affluent industrialized nations, suggest that sooner or later we will need to learn to live lives of voluntary simplicity because we will run out of the resources that we have so selfishly squandered. Seers from Nostradamus to Edgar Cayce have predicted that catastrophes will occur around the end of the twentieth century either as the result of cosmic changes, or of our inability to control the vast powers that our technology has unleashed.

Perhaps because of this, intentional communities assume greater importance. The 1960s saw a flowering of communes in the West associated mainly with the counter culture and the alienation of young people. Most of these communes lasted only a few years at best, but they were a part of the growing experience of a generation and they remain a part of our consciousness.

Throughout history, communities have frequently had an influence far beyond their numbers—whether it was the Essenes, who are believed to have provided much of Jesus' experience and ideas; or the Christian monasteries, which held the light of civilization in the Dark Ages and helped to reilluminate society at the end of that period; or the Owenites of New Harmony, Indiana, whose community lasted only 18 months, but who influenced American culture for the next 50 years. In Israel today, though only slightly more than 3 per cent of the population live in intentional communities, they play a disproportionately large role in Israeli life.

If we are indeed entering some new Dark Age, or facing some great cataclysm, it may be that those people who are devoting their lives to creating new communities have an important role to play. Perhaps they are the "seeds of tomorrow." It behooves us then, to examine their communities closely, not as little utopias—which they certainly are not —but as serious efforts by committed individuals to find better ways of living. But before we look to tomorrow, let's take a look at the past to see the links that join the new communities in a living chain with the old.

A group of young men, weary of the world, remove themselves to the desert where they establish a communal life based on brotherhood. They call themselves the Children of Light. They are searching for moral certainty at a time when old values have succumbed to new ideas and laxer ways of living. They love learning and gather together to have the Scriptures read and expounded to them. They are celibate, generally banning women from their midst as too distracting for those dedicated to the Spirit. They yearn to live without greed, anger, jealousy, or lust. One observer wrote

Everyone looks up to them as free by nature, and not subject to the frown of any human being. There is no buying and selling between them. Not a single slave or servant exists among them, and the members have several occupations at which, like rivals, they engage in with untiring energy, making neither heat, nor cold a pretense or excuse. . . . They avoid the cities, because they well know the iniquities which have become inveterate among city dwellers. . . . They stand almost alone in the whole of mankind because they have become moneyless, by deliberate action, rather than by lack of good fortune.*

The observer was Philo, writing in the first century A.D. about the Essenes, a community best known today as the writers of the Dead Sea Scrolls. Their contemporaries might have called them cultists or escapists, running away from the pressing problems of the time. History views them as an important link between unorthodox Judaism and Christianity, and possibly even the most important source of Jesus' teachings.

---

*Quoted in Herbert Russcol, *The First Million Sabras* (New York: Dodd Mead, 1970), 60, 63.

The Essenes were not, of course, the first group to remove themselves from the centers of civilization to try to live their lives according to higher and more demanding standards. But in terms of the Judeo-Christian world, they mark a good beginning. As the early Christians were persecuted, first by the Romans and then by fellow Christians of somewhat different persuasions, substantial groups continued to move to remote areas to create their own intentional communities. In the early centuries of the Christian era, tens of thousands fled eastward to what is now central Turkey, where they had underground cities in the large caves that abound there; others fled westward to the deserts of Egypt and Libya.

Later, during the Dark Ages following the collapse of the Roman empire, the monasteries played a new and crucial role. In the sixth century St. Benedict established the rule that governed most of Christian monasticism in the centuries that followed. He stressed the obligation to serve the world and to care for people, first through hospitality and then through service to the surrounding community. The Benedictine monks and the other orders that arose under the influence of his rule were concerned with the reestablishment of agriculture. They also started schools, because the schools of the Romans had largely collapsed.

Similar developments took place later in Islam. When the Seljuk empire broke down in the fourteenth century, Sufi orders, devoted in earlier times to removing themselves for self-perfection, became active in providing education, medicine, and other necessary services.

The Christian tradition, throughout its history, is filled with examples of groups that opposed the corruption of the establishment and started utopian communities. Usually their attempts to build a heaven on earth led ultimately to their execution by the authorities. During the period following the Protestant Reformation, many such groups fled to the New World to escape persecution and, from the Pilgrims on, they constitute an important element among the founders of the United States. (The story of Father Rapp, founder of Harmonie, Indiana, is told in Chapter 3.)

The present-day Hutterites—the oldest, largest, and most thriving of all communal societies in North America—survived the persecutions of the Reformation, the Thirty Years War, the efforts of the Hapsburg empire to convert them back to Catholicism, and many other trials. They were one of the groups of Anabaptists, originating in the Austrian Tyrol and Moravia during the sixteenth century, who rejected baptism and formed "communities of love." Private property was abolished, with possessions being surrendered voluntarily by newcomers, and through Christian pacifism they hoped that wars would come to an end. They were driven by war and persecution from Moravia into Hungary and finally into the Ukraine. After a hundred years there, about 400 persons emigrated to the United States in 1874 and settled in South

Dakota. Today they have over 220 agricultural colonies in the region of the Dakotas, with a population of over 22,000.

The nineteenth century was particularly rich in the development of utopian communities. Robert Owen's story, at the beginning of the century, is told in Chapter 3. A few years later, the Frenchman Charles Fourier wrote an influential treatise on a science of human relationships based on his theory of passional attraction. "A passional attraction," he explained, "is the drive that is given to us by nature prior to any reflection, and it persists despite the opposition of reason, duty, or prejudice."* He felt that nature intended the passions to be satisfied and that harmony would be found in a system that best permitted this. He developed plans for his society in great detail, calling it the Phalanx. Ideally, it would consist of 1,620 people divided into 16 tribes and 32 choirs—a large enough group to provide an adequate variety of passions. After Fourier's death in 1837, many of his followers went to America, popularized his ideas, and developed a number of short-lived communities. The most successful were the North American Phalanx in New Jersey, which lasted 12 years until devastated by fire, and the Wisconsin Phalanx. The latter began in 1844, flouished, and in 1849 was sold off, leaving many wealthy individuals instead of one wealthy community.

Another Frenchman, Etienne Cabet, studied the ideas of Owen and Fourier and wrote his own utopian tract, *Voyage to Icaria*. This utopia was total communism and took mass production to its logical conclusion, with uniformity of product, consumption, and social life. In 1848 Cabet and 69 followers bought 100,000 acres in Texas to establish Icaria. Unfortunately, many were struck down by yellow fever and the rest fled back to St. Louis. Cabet made a second start, buying the town of Nauvoo, Illinois, from the Mormons and populating it with around 1500 people, mostly former French tradesmen. Industries and a progressive school were started, and an orchestra, a band, and a theater group were set up. Although the community began well, dissension soon developed when Cabet tried to ban alcohol and tobacco and to introduce a strict sexual morality. In 1855 Cabet was expelled from the community and he left with 160 followers, establishing a smaller community outside St. Louis. Both groups went through difficulties and splits, but were fairly successful economically and eventually sold out at a profit in 1886 and 1898 respectively.

One of the most famous communities in America was the Oneida community, a group that combined spiritual and communal ideals. It was started by John Humphrey Noyes in Putney, Vermont, as a religious sect devoted to "Perfectionism." When its members began to live together on Fourierist lines, the local community drove them out and,

---

*Quoted in Ian Tod and Michael Wheeler, *Utopia* (New York: Harmony Books, 1978), 88.

in 1848, they bought a farm near Oneida, New York. Thanks to about $100,000 in capital supplied by the members, who had turned over all their assets to the community, they quickly established a broad economic base and bought more land. They manufactured chains, silk thread, woolen goods, and a popular animal trap. They also operated a canning mill, blacksmith's shop, sawmill, and flour mill. They built a large neo-Gothic mansion in which they all lived, complete with landscaped grounds, a theater, a progressive school, and a sauna. By the late 1870s they had grown to more than 300 people and had several branch communities.

Their way of life was similar in many ways to communal life today. They wore simple clothes, were mostly vegetarian, and avoided alcohol and tobacco. Women wore trousers and cut their hair short. They maintained harmony through self-criticism and group criticism, and many decisions were made at meetings of the whole community. If a decision could not be reached unanimously, it was put off until everyone could agree.

The Oneida community is best remembered for its system of "complex marriage." Noyes regarded monogamy as a "form of spiritual tyranny" in which men and women have power over each other on the basis of religious rules rather then love. Just as all property was shared communally, so all people should share themselves. They avoided having any children for about 20 years by making love without male ejaculation. Then, convinced that their system was sound, they began a practice of eugenic breeding called "stirpculture," under which 52 children were born to selected parents and raised as children of the whole community.

As time went on, the community faced a great deal of hostility from the external world over its sexual "license," and there was internal dissension over Noyes's increasingly authoritarian methods and his desire to pass the leadership to one of his sons. A crisis raged over who would initiate female virgins into complex marriage—a duty that for a long time was Noyes's alone. Then charges of statutory rape and adultury were brought against Noyes, and he fled to Canada. In 1879 the group gave up the practice of complex marriage. In 1881 the community was reorganized into the Oneida Community, Ltd., a joint stock corporation, bringing an end to the communal experiment. Today the company is a thriving capitalist enterprise that manufactures silverware. Many descendents of the original perfectionists work there or live in the vicinity.

It is hard to say which of the communities that are blossoming today will be remembered a century from now. Styles and concerns have changed from those of the nineteenth century. Today Eastern religions and ecumenical spirituality are more influential. The human potential movement has had its effect on the way of life in many communities, and there is a greater concern for consciousness raising and individual expression and development, as well as for women's rights. The psychedelic drug culture of the 1960s has had a profound influence in shaking people free of their socialized values and opening them to spirituality and a greater love for others and nature. Nevertheless, virtually all successful communities ban the use of illegal drugs, and many ban alcohol. Most communities today relfect the new ideologies on the edge of change: feminism, responsible sexual freedom, environmentalism (including alternative energy sources), and voluntary simplicity.

In this book we have chosen 21 intentional communities to examine. Among the topics we consider are how they came to be, what they believe, how they live, how they support and govern themselves, how membership is determined, and how they relate to the world around them. Most of these communities have a spiritual basis, and a survey of the history of communities shows us that spiritually based communities have been, on the whole, the most successful.

We have chosen a variety of communities in eight different countries to show a range of forms and experiences. The communities we discuss have been in existence for as few as 5 years and as long as 80 years. Many of these communities have been beset with problems. Success is not just a matter of longevity—just as in life there is a natural process of birth, the exuberance of youth, the achievements of maturity, the rigidity of old age, and finally death, communities go through similar stages. The way they were ten years ago is not the way they are today. The best of them are continually evolving.

Before you turn the page and begin reading the stories of these communities, let us make one more comment. Much concern exists these days about cults and the brainwashing of psychologically susceptible young people by clever gurus. In general, we steered clear of communities that we felt were excessively narrow. Among the communities we visited, we met many sensible, loving, committed people. Most of them came from middle-class backgrounds, were mature, had a good deal of education, appeared psychologically balanced, and knew what they were doing and why they were doing it. As pioneers they have frequently had a hard life, but generally it has been rewarding and satisfying. Intentional communities are not for everyone. But we all need to find some commitment to make our lives worthwhile, and living in communities has been an inspired choice for many.

Part I

UNITED STATES

Ananda's new community center with large assembly hall, dining room, and kitchen.

CHAPTER 1

Ananda Cooperative Village: The First World Brotherhood Colony

In 1976 a forest fire swept through the Ananda Cooperative Village in the Sierra Nevada foothills of California. In a few hours much of what had been painstakingly built up over the preceding eight years was gone. Some 21 homes—practically all of the homes in the community, were destroyed, and 450 of Ananda's 650 acres were charred.

As the wind fanned the flames, the members had only a few minutes to save their most precious possessions. John Novak, the village manager, got to his house just ahead of the flames. Someone said, "Go in and take anything that's important to you." Novak ran in, looked around, took a couple things off the altar, and ran out. His wife, Devi, had gone into town with their ten-day-old baby. When she returned she saw the roadblocks and pushed past them to get to their house. It was a pile of ashes. Her husband met her where the front door used to be, took her in his arms, and said, "Well at least that solves the problems we were having with leaks."

Miraculously, the fire missed the public buildings, as well as the monastery and retreat, located some distance away. Nevertheless, the fire was a great financial disaster for this small community struggling to survive. Ananda had no insurance. But everyone who lived at Ananda pitched in to rebuild. The charred trees were sold for timber, raising about $60,000, and letters sent to other communities for help elicited donations. The people of the county also made donations, bringing food, clothing, furniture, and other necessities to a gigantic box at the entrance to the property.

Rebuilding Ananda was the focus of the entire community's energies for a few months. Now, however, when the members think back on the fire, they laugh. They realize that it did a lot for the community. Materially, the fire cleared out the overgrown land, leaving a few large, strong trees and some new, beautiful vistas. The new houses that were built were better than the ones that were destroyed. Socially, the fire served to weed out the membership. Ananda had attracted many members who did not share the spiritual vision of its founder, Swami Kriyananda. Differences had been growing among the membership over Kriyananda's leadership and over the use of their limited resources. Questions such as: "Should we spend the $3,000 we've set aside on gravel to repair the muddy roads or on publication and distribution of Kriyananda's new book?" were debated. The fire ended the controversy. Those who viewed Ananda as simply a comfortable place to live left, but those who were spiritually motivated stayed on. In all, about 40 people left; a few on request, the others on their own initiative. As best it could, the community paid those who left for what they had lost.

The fire became a symbol for a much-needed renewal of, and recommitment to, the spiritual ideals of the community. About a week after the fire, it was learned that it probably had been started by a spark thrown onto the land by a county road grader with a faulty spark arrester. Some of Ananda's neighbors who also had been burned out got together to sue the county and eventually reached an out-of-court settlement. Ananda considered this course of action. It had $2 million to $3 million in potential claims and was facing the possibility of bankruptcy. After much discussion, however, Ananda decided to accept the responsibility itself and not lay the financial burden on other taxpayers in the county.

The story of Ananda really begins in the 1940s, with Paramahansa Yogananda, author of *Autobiography of a Yogi** and founder of the Self-Realization Fellowship headquartered in Los Angeles, California. Yogananda considered himself to be the last of a line of six great religious leaders, including Krishna and Christ. He saw the practice of yoga as a means to form a closer relationship with God. He stressed the ten precepts of Patanjali (200 B.C.): to avoid violence, lying, stealing, sensuality, and greed, and to promote cleanliness, contentment, austerity, introspection, and devotion to God. He was accepting of other forms of worship, calling his fellowship the *Church of All Religions*. In the last years of his life, Yogananda often expressed concern for the economic and social upheavals he believed were coming, and he spoke of a type of community he said was destined to become a basic social model: world brotherhood colonies.

"The day will come," he predicted, "when this idea will spread through the world like wildfire. Gather together, those of you who

---

*Paramahansa Yogananda, *Autobiography of a Yogi* (Los Angeles: Self-Realization Fellowship, 1946).

share high ideals. Pool your resources. Buy land in the country. A simpler life will bring you inner freedom. Harmony with nature will bring you a happiness known to few city dwellers."*

Among his disciples were two young novice monks, Norman Paulson and Donald Walters. Paulson went on to start the Sunburst Communities around Santa Barbara, and Walters later founded Ananda.

Walters was 25 when Yogananda died in 1952. He went on to become worldwide director of the Self-Realization Centers, then principal teacher and lecturer for the organization, and still later, international vice-president of the group. During this time he received full ordination into the monkhood and was given the name Swami Kriyananda, meaning "divine bliss in action."

In 1962 he was suddenly dismissed from the Self-Realization Fellowship, reportedly because it was feared his independent activities might lead to a schism. During the next five years he taught yoga in San Francisco, but was constantly on the lookout for a quiet retreat for himself. This goal was in conflict with his other goal, that of founding a world brotherhood colony. That goal led him to study and visit many intentional communities.

In 1967 he ran into Dick Baker, *Rōshi* (spiritual leader) of the San Francisco Zen Center, who had been looking for a piece of land to serve as a retreat for himself and his family. Baker Rōshi's choice was a tract of 172 acres in the Sierra Nevada foothills, available for $250 an acre, about half the prevailing rate. He was looking for six others to each buy 24 acres in this tract. Kriyananda expressed interest and accompanied Baker Rōshi on his next trip to the land, along with poets Gary Snyder and Allen Ginsberg, who were also interested in retreats for themselves.

As they neared the land, they passed through an area that had been the scene of hydraulic gold mining a century ago. The gigantic hoses had washed away whatever was loose to a depth of 50 feet or more, leaving rock outcroppings that looked like a moonscape. For the last three miles the deeply rutted dirt road wound through this ecological disaster, then rose up onto an undulating plateau covered with pines and evergreens, offering beautiful views of snow-capped mountains in the distance. Kriyananda knew at once that this was the retreat he had dreamed of. Each of the others also found a perfect site—and best of all, each chose a different parcel, so there was no conflict.

During the next year, while continuing to live and and work in the Bay Area, Kriyananda attempted to build a home for himself on his 24 acres. He wanted a dome. He settled for a geodesic dome, but he couldn't get it right. Three times he built one, and three times the wind blew it down. He took these experiences as a sign that he was not to have his own personal retreat, that he needed instead to build a com-

*Swami Kriyananda, *Cooperative Communities: How to Start Them and Why* (Nevada City, Calif.: Ananda Publications, 1968), 3.

munity. Nearly a year had passed and two adjoining 24-acre parcels had still not found buyers. Baker Rōshi was desperate to get them sold. Since the other buyers weren't planning to build for several years, Baker Rōshi agreed to let Kriyananda buy the other two parcels and start a community that would include families with children, provided it would return to retreat status within five years. An old friend put up the money, and Kriyananda had 72 acres on which to try to realize his dream.

Kriyananda held a meeting of interested people in San Francisco to discuss the idea of a new community. In an attempt to respond to the questions and doubts raised at the meeting and also clarify his own thinking, he wrote a short book entitled *Cooperative Communities: How to Start Them and Why*. It was originally mimeographed and later published, and has now gone through six editions. It served as a kind of charter for Ananda, and has been a useful guide to many others interested in starting communities.

At first, because of resistance to the idea of building a community, Kriyananda found only a few people to join him in building a meditation retreat center. Through 1968 he worked in San Francisco during the week to earn money and solicit contributions, and on weekends he supervised the carpenters in constructing a temple, a common dome for offices and eating, a bathhouse, and a home. By the end of the year construction was nearly completed and paid for, and several retreats had been held. By spring, 1969, a few families had moved in. Unfortunately their children were unusually noisy, which interfered with meditations. Baker Rōshi heard of this and wrote from Japan, asking them not to begin any further construction until he returned and could assess the situation in person.

The letter arrived on a Friday morning. That afternoon Kriyananda drove from San Francisco to the land, stopping off in Sacramento to see a friend. While there, a real estate agent came by, talking about the hottest land buy he'd ever seen. It turned out to be just six miles from the retreat. Kriyananda persuaded the agent to drive up with him that afternoon. He walked the property, was taken by its beauty, and asked the agent if he could hold several parcels—235 acres in all—over the weekend. The down payment was $13,500, which he didn't have, but he made several calls that evening, and by the next morning had the necessary financial backing. When he called the real estate office on Saturday, the agent told him that he had gone in at two o'clock in the morning and taken the parcels off the board. When the office opened the other agents were pleading with him to let them buy pieces for themselves.

The land was purchased and named Ananda (bliss) Farm (later, Ananda Cooperative Community and then Ananda Cooperative Village). This was the real start of the Ananda community. Word quickly spread that a new commune was opening and needed members. This was 1969, and thousands of people from the Bay Area wanted to move to the country and get away from it all. People began arriving from everywhere. The driveway was always crowded; one afternoon there were seven cars parked there filled with people seeking admittance. Many of this horde were dropouts, seeking an easy life rather than a spiritual one. They ate the fledging community's food, ran up its phone bill, and told the members how they ought to be living. The members reacted by spreading word that Ananda was not "where it's at." Soon they developed a reputation in certain circles for being uptight and materialistic. But others saw them as dedicated, responsible, and sincere, and they began to attract these kinds of people.

Kriyananda's own struggle during that early period was to see to it that the community developed in ways that would make it both spiritually and financially stable, while adhering to the principle that no member would have more than one vote. Some of the newcomers were people who had not been aware of the background of Ananda and had no particular interest in helping Kriyananda fulfill his dreams for it. From the start he had decided that he wanted to be a spiritual leader, but not a manager of the community. Partly by working personally with those members who showed a willingness to take responsibility, partly by offering sound reasons for his proposals, and partly by laying constant stress on their spiritual directions, he was able to accomplish his objectives.

One of the first struggles was over the question of drugs, which every newcomer promised not to take, but which often exercised a renewed attraction during times of difficulty. Marijuana growing is a major industry of Nevada County, where Ananda is located, so plenty of drugs were available. A few people had to be asked to leave, but by and large, the growing spiritual force in the community solved the problem. Another problem was the community's self-identity. Many members wanted it to develop into a close-knit family or tribe. Kriyananda, however, emphasized the importance of privacy and individuality, saying they were conducive both to spiritual development and communal harmony, and gradually the community evolved into an intentional village rather than a commune.

There were financial problems also. Mortgage payments on the farm amounted to $1750 a month. While they were a heavy burden at first, in time these payments came to be one of the principal factors in drawing the community together. "Money" was a bad word to many members. It represented the materialism they had fled. Speaking of this problem, Kriyananda said:

Many of our people had yet to learn that lethargy, too, is a form of materialism —far worse so, in fact, than money madness; that a non-productive life is destructive to spiritual consciousness; and that money is only a form of energy: it can be used wisely, as well as misused. As I consider the (for me) immense amounts of money that I had to make or raise in getting Ananda started, I am continually astonished at the fact that my real gain from those painful struggles has been inward, not outward. To work hard to materialize a high ideal is not materialism.*

In 1974 an adjoining farm of 350 acres was purchased. At the same time the community decided it needed more land, the owner independently decided that he wanted Ananda to have it. Having no money for a down payment, Ananda got it on a very generous lease-to-purchase basis. They leased it for two years at $1000 a month, and were able to buy it after that.

Today the Ananda community in Nevada County is made up of some 250 adults and 70 children. About 110 adults live on the properties of the community, 60 more live in the immediate neighborhood, and the balance are scattered around the county. Of those living on the property, one-third are monastic, one-third are single, and one-third are married. The monastery area, which includes Kriyananda's house, is located a couple of miles away from the rest of the community. The monastics, male and female, make a commitment to this way of life for an unspecified period of time. Their vows include celibacy, simplicity, and cooperation. Since they don't have responsibility for a family, monastics are more free to devote themselves to serving the community. Each community member is encouraged to spend at least a year in the monastery. It provides spiritual training that helps to lay a foundation for a future stable, spiritually based marriage.

Most members of the Ananda community are whites from middle-class and upper middle-class backgrounds. There are currently three blacks and no Asians. People from Jewish and Catholic backgrounds are disproportionately represented. About two-thirds of the members have at least some college experience and the median age is nearly 40.

There are no stated standards regarding sexual behavior; it is thought of as a private matter. Because of their spiritual interest, most people give sex a relatively low priority, and there is less of a sexual undercurrent in male-female relationships than is usual in our culture. In the early years, unmarried couples were discouraged from living together. That is no longer the case, but most couples eventually do get married. Several divorces have occurred, after which both parties remained in the community.

Ananda has a hilly terrain, ranging between 2500 and 3000 feet in elevation. At the lowest level, in a sort of bowl just beyond the gate-

---

*Ibid., 97.

house, is the social center of the community, called Ananda Village. One unpaved street runs through the village, with offices, a market, an auto repair shop, a high school, and a bathhouse lining it. The bathhouse is for residents who live in tepees or other temporary housing nearby. Along one edge of the village is the garden, including a solar greenhouse. Most of this area is surrounded by a high fence to discourage the many deer in the area from nibbling the plants. Farther up the hill is the dairy, with cows and goats. In other directions up the hills are the publications building and a new community center, which is under construction. At the time of our visit only one large building of this center had been completed. This contained a circular temple-assembly hall, about 100 feet in diameter, adjoining a similarly large dining hall with attached kitchen. The dining hall was used for the first time during Christmas, 1981, enabling all the members of the community to at last sit down for a meal together. Eventually a complex of buildings will be completed on this site, at a cost of $2 million to $3 million, providing housing and facilities for guest programs. Up the road is the primary school, which attracts children from outside the community as well as children of the members. Beyond this are many of the private family houses, with lovely views of the countryside.

Most of the houses are quite substantial. Well finished and comfortable, they incorporate both solar heating and wood heating. They have modern plumbing and electricity, although some had these conveniences installed fairly recently. The land belongs to the community; prior to 1976 the houses were individually owned. After the fire, the new houses were built sufficiently to provide shelter with community funds, and then finished with private funds. Technically and legally, all the houses belong to the community. In practice, however, their occupants think of them as theirs. If a couple is ready to build a house, they pick out a site from about 30 that have been developed, design the kind of house they want to live in, and then share in the work and cost of its construction. An Ananda housing bill of rights provides that no one will lose the money he or she puts into a house. If a couple leaves the community, they can sell their "right" to it to another member at the replacement—not profit—value of what they spent on it.

There are several levels of participation and membership at Ananda. People anywhere in the world can be part of Ananda's spiritual family and receive a monthly newsletter, correspond with people at Ananda, telephone on Sunday afternoons for spiritual advice or just to chat, and be in touch with other Ananda members in their own area. Spiritual family members who lend financial support to Ananda by tithing become part of the circle of joy. Those who wish to be even more active distribute books, hold meetings in their home, and work in other ways to introduce people to Ananda.

Newcomers who wish to live at Ananda usually take one of Ananda's training courses for at least a month, usually for several months, and then are placed into an orientation class that lasts for a year. Each class forms a sort of small family, naming a mother, father, aunts, and uncles drawn from senior members of the community. Meeting once a week, it provides an environment in which newcomers can ask questions and establish friendships with other newcomers and some old-timers. After three months applicants discuss with the family (which is also the membership committee) whether they should become members. If so, they pay a nonrefundable fee of $350 ($500 for couples and families), plus $15 a month ($20 for couples and families) to be lay disciples. Lay disciples at Ananda engage in daily meditation following Yogananda's teaching and techniques. The next stage, disciple, is an even deeper commitment to this spiritual path, and requires a fee of $1500 for individuals and $2500 for couples and families. These fees help to provide capital for the community and represent an investment in the property of the community. They are deliberately priced high enough to make applicants think seriously about the decision. The final stage, membership in the yoga fellowship, occurs only after members have been disciples for at least five years, and is by invitation of its membership at their annual meeting. About 70 people belong to the fellowship and they are the ones who legally own the property.

In addition to its community in Nevada County, Ananda has several other centers in California, following Kriyananda's belief that it is better to have a number of smaller world brotherhood colonies rather than let one get too big. Ocean Song, a growing community on 450 acres, is near Bodega Bay, north of San Francisco. With about 30 members, Ocean Song is developing a healing institute and also has its own garden, dairy, school, and guest programs. There are ashram city centers in Sacramento, Nevada City, San Francisco, and Atherton. The San Francisco center occupies a 45-room mansion and the Atherton center operates East-West Books, a well-known bookstore in Palo Alto that was purchased by Ananda in 1980.

Ananda has been quite successful in building its business base. It has developed a mixed economy of community-owned and privately owned small businesses. Each has been run with its own accounting and a strong emphasis on profitability. This includes all of their nonprofit educational activities which aim to achieve a surplus each year. The mixed economy reflects again the viewpoint of Kriyananda:

The great problem with total communal ownership is that it increases the need for communal discipline. People who receive everything without paying for it must be induced somehow to work for what they get. Without the motive of personal profit, the only solution, if the community is to be productive at all, is to stress either group "spirit" or the beauty of holy obedience. Advantage is too often taken of the resident's good will. He comes for a life of peace, and in the name of group spirit finds himself launched on all sorts of glorious projects: the construction of a new library, a hospital, a recreation center—and not just any kind of buildings, but, for the sake of the community's good name, the best imaginable. A communuty I know in India, seized with this noble motive, has devoted decades to building a temple that is intended to become more beautiful than the Taj Mahal. To what purpose?

Kriyananda goes on to point out that in Russia, where only 3 percent of the cultivated land is privately owned, this tiny portion supplies fully half of the nation's meat, milk, and produce. He concludes:

The soundest course, it seems to me, would be to follow the pattern to which people are in any case accustomed: Let them work for wages, and in turn pay for what they receive. Let them save what they like for the future. The simplest management is simply to give people the incentive to manage themselves. When they must look for their own needs, they will bestir themselves enough to produce.*

At present there are 27 businesses at Ananda. Together they gross about $2 million a year. Ananda is always prepared to help new businesses get started whenever someone is motivated to start one, even though some will fail. As Kriyananda told us, "An oak drops many acorns; if only a few produce new trees its purpose has been achieved." In the following list of businesses at Ananda, those with an asterisk are privately owned:

book publishing company
graphic design firm
blacksmith shop*
dairy
roasted nuts company*
hot air balloon repair shop*
pottery studio*
weavings shop*
auto repair shop*
construction company*
electric company*
general store
restaurant
health food store

public relations firm*
general services company*
music store*
book store
health clinic*
Institute of Cooperative Spiritual
   Living
Ananda Spiritual Family
meditation retreat
craft store
Earth-Sky, educational workshop
   group*
school
garden
record company

*Ibid., 30–32.

The largest businesses are East-West Books and the guest programs, each grossing about $250,000 a year; Master's Market general store and Earth Song health food store, each grossing about $240,000 a year; Mountain Song Craft Store, grossing about $200,000 a year; and Ananda Publications, grossing about $80,000 a year.

The community-owned businesses pay a salary of $400 to $500 a month at the minimum, plus the monthly residence fee. But salaries are based on need, not position. Managers make their own decisions as to what their employees are paid, taking into consideration back debts, car costs, family, and other needs. A person with a family, for example, might get $1000 a month. People often change jobs. Ananda's employment counselor is aware of the positions needing to be filled and tries to match them to member interests and skills. If a person gets burned-out in one job, another person may volunteer to switch positions.

In 1978 the practice of tithing back to Ananda was adopted as a general principle. Most individuals tithe 10 percent of their net income; a number of businesses, however, cannot afford such a large tithe. The guest program and Ananda Spiritual Family though, both tithe 10 percent of their gross, not net, income.

There are about 70 children in the community, 50 of whom are of school age. The community has private schools, called how-to-live schools, with grades from preschool through high school. Starting in 1971 with 8 pupils in a renovated chicken coop, the schools have grown to more than 70 students whose classes are in three large, comfortable, and attractive buildings. In addition to children from the Ananda community, the schools have a few boarders and others who come in daily from outside the community. Some people have moved close to Ananda just to send their children to its schools.

In addition to the regular academic curriculum, the how-to-live schools teach the skills of centeredness, inner harmony, and attunement with God. Children are taught that right behavior feels harmonious and wrong behavior feels disharmonious. Once they learn to make that basic discrimination, they respond attentively to the simple discipline of the question, "How does that feel?" Virginia Heline went to town with her six-year-old daughter, Shayma. They saw a woman spanking her little boy and screaming at him. Having seen only examples of calm, kind adults at Ananda, Shayma asked, "Mommy, why is that little boy's mommy behaving so badly?"

The schools operate on the theory that children develop in six-year stages. During the first six years they can be taught most easily by making appropriate adjustments in the environment, since this is the period when they are putting tremendous energy into learning about the physical plane. For example, children are likely to grow up to be neat adults if their home and classroom are neat and tidy during this period.

Between the ages of six and twelve, children are most strongly developing their capacity to feel. They are greatly influenced by music, color, rhythm and tales of heroes and heroines. Without well-developed feelings, children have no strong sense of right and wrong, or strong enthusiasm for doing something constructive with their lives. Between twelve and eighteen, people develop their willpower and perseverance. At this stage they can then be taught to apply sustained effort to accomplish worthwhile goals.

To round out their program and make the best use of their facilities, the schools offer occasional training seminars and workshops for teachers and parents, and also offer live-in summer camps for children from all over.

Before he started Ananda, Kriyananda expressed his ideas about government in *Cooperative Communities*. In large measure his notions have worked out well in practice. In the book he noted that the successes and failures of countless communities showed that a strong community government is necessary. At the same time he sided with Thoreau in viewing the best government as one that rules the least, that encourages personal initiative and responsibility, and that legislates on matters of communal convenience rather than personal outlook. Kriyananda added that, "No system can be any better than the people whose lives it directs. There can be no 'perfect' system, for its members will always be the determining factor in its performance.... A system can facilitate the expression of goodness in people; it cannot create goodness."*

Kriyananda started out with a strong vision of what he wanted. His goal was one of spiritual radicalism, not social radicalism. His challenge was to inspire people to share his vision. While most of the early members of Ananda were strongly individualistic, they also considered themselves disciples and this gave them a common point of reference and an understanding of the need to accept wise guidance. But disciples of whom? Some said, yes, they were loyal to Yogananda, founder of the Self-Realization Fellowship, but who was Kriyananda? Kriyananda answered this by saying that Yogananda was the spiritual master—guru—for both himself and Ananda members, but that there was also a need to respect the existing leadership. "I am the founder of this community," he said, "and if you are not in accord with the system I've set up, I think it is dishonest of you to be here." Some left, some changed, and Kriyananda himself learned how far he could push and when he should retreat gracefully and let people think things out for themselves. His philosophy of leadership is summed up in a booklet he published in 1980, *The Art of Creative Leadership*. In it he concludes:

---

*Ibid., 44.

The outcome of any project will subtly reveal the kind of energy that went into its development. A work of art reveals not only the skill, but also the consciousness, of the artist. A place of business reveals the general attitudes of its workers: their happiness or unhappiness, their confidence or frustration. A leader who leads truly, and never drives, will create in his subordinates the most constuctive possible attitudes, and will ensure the best possible results for his and their labors.*

The government of Ananda attempts to be as simple as possible. Decisions are usually made by those people most directly involved in a particular project or issue. There are only three rules: no illegal drugs, no alcohol, and no dogs. Dogs are banned because they often run in packs and may attack the deer. Smoking and meat eating are permitted, but only in private. Both are rare at Ananda. Behavior is guided less by rules and more by custom, based on respect for each other's rights. Kriyananda points out that in an intentional community, individual development and voluntary cooperation are interactive principles. Members who develop themselves inwardly are better able to cooperate with, and thereby help uplift, others.

Each year all resident members who have lived there for a year or more elect the village council. This is the board of directors for the community. It, in turn, elects officers from among its own members. These are spiritual director (comparable to president), general manager (comparable to vice-president), secretary, and treasurer. The spiritual director, Kriyananda, coordinates the spiritual and secular activities but remains detached from most secular details in order to maintain his perspective. In fact, he hasn't attended a council meeting in years. The general manager's function is similar to that of a town manager or the manager of a business corporation. At present the office of general manager is shared by a husband and wife team.

The village council appoints membership, planning, and housing committees. Usually a member of the council sits on each committee. The council also plans recreational, social, cultural, and spiritual events for the community. The village council meets twice a month and its meetings are open to any residents who care to attend. The yoga fellowship also has a coordinating council, which includes leaders from all of its different branches and city houses.

As Ananda has grown over the years, relations with the surrounding community have been essentially harmonious, but there are periodic difficulties in dealing with neighbors and with county officials. Surprisingly, perhaps, some of the greatest controversies with neighbors have been not with the so-called straight community, but with hippies and former city dwellers getting back to the land. Many fled from the San

*Swami Kriyananda, *The Art of Creative Leadership* (Nevada City, Calif.: Ananda Publications, 1980), 16.

Francisco Bay Area seeking a haven where the living is easy and the laws few. Some see this dream as being threatened by Ananda's high profile and steady growth. And because of Ananda's strict no-drugs policy, its emphasis on economic development, and generally demanding way of life, the community is sometimes perceived as being uptight. At times Ananda has trouble with county authorities in getting planning permission for various development schemes and approval of its buildings and public works. No convenient category exists in county regulations for a cooperative spiritual community. Hammering out a compromise is not always easy. Ananda is not alone in its difficulties. An estimated 75 percent of new developments in the area flout the county general plan and building codes. But Ananda is highly visible and highly motivated and is therefore less free than many of its neighbors.

Accordingly, in 1980 Ananda decided to seek incorporation as a municipality under California law. Two members spent four months researching the plan, concentrating particularly on whether it was possible to incorporate a religious community as a town. They decided it was. It had been done in Missouri in 1948 by Unity Village, headquarters of the Unity Church.

The problem that they then faced was how to maintain religious exclusivity on their own land while at the same time being a town that did not discriminate. First they persuaded a few of their non-Ananda neighbors to join with them in their effort. This was necessary anyway to connect Ananda's two principal pieces of land within the town boundaries. Then they proposed establishment of a housing corporation that would own all housing on the Ananda land and lease it to its members. It was decided that an applicant must meet these criteria in order to become a member of the housing corporation:

1. Be committed to the principles of the United States constitution.
2. Respect the ideas, values, culture, and religious beliefs of others.
3. Be committed to work to create and sustain a healthful, wholesome, positive, safe environment for people, animals, and plants.
4. Manifest cooperation and harmony in interpersonal and business relationships and community activities.
5. Make decisions by considering moral issues rather than just following desires or habits.
6. Be actively committed to self-improvement by being willing and open to observe and analyze oneself, to consider one's faults and to strive to overcome those faults, and to consider one's strengths, talents, and good qualities and strive to develop them as fully as possible.
7. Not use alcohol.
8. Not use illegal drugs.
9. Be willing to assume responsibility for one's own financial welfare.

The community hired outside consultants to prepare an environmental impact statement at a cost of $13,000. This statement was accepted by the state commission that decides on incorporation. But the problem of getting public support was a much greater one. Many neighbors expressed fears about a spiritual community incorporating: some cited the example of Jonestown; controversy raged in the local press. One very negative former resident of Ananda said, when interviewed by the *San Francisco Chronicle*, that even with an elected town council, the real power would remain in the hands of a select few. "There is an inner circle who will be the council, the commission, and everything else," he charged. "Ananda is not just a group of people who want to become a city. It is the direct projection of one man's insatiable appetite for personal power and worldwide fame."*

To counter this opposition, Ananda embarked on a massive public relations campaign that did more to spotlight the community than anything it had done in prior years. They put on talks and slide shows at every service club in the county. They arranged tours for county officials and their spouses, for the League of Women Voters, for every organized group they could find that was interested. They put on a fair in Nevada City. They arranged letter writing campaigns to newspapers and county officials. They learned a lot about how the outside world works.

They learned enough, in fact, that after going through several public hearings, in the summer of 1982 they dropped their proposal to incorporate as a municipality. They had observed the bad relations the Rajneesh group had with its neighbors in Oregon and the bad press that grew from that. And they saw that they were creating dissension in Nevada County and expending a great deal of energy for a proposal that wasn't crucial to their survival. The idea has been dropped for now, but it is probably not dead. As Ananda continues to grow, and to build on the better relationships it has established, another opportunity to become a town will doubtless present itself.

The whole movement, including its other centers around California, is growing. Kriyananda looks forward to the establishment of more branch communities, more how-to-live schools around the country with a training program at Ananda for the teachers, a ministerial training program, an annual Festival of the Joyful Arts, a music conservatory, and a program to explore solutions to the energy problem, including a study of solutions discovered by earlier civilizations.

Yogananda had predicted, "The day will come when this idea will spread through the world like wildfire." That day is not yet, but Kriyananda still believes that day will come. If it does, Ananda is likely to be in the forefront of the movement.

---

*Dave Carter, "Commune's Fight to Become a City," *San Francisco Chronicle*, 4 Jan. 1980.

One of the monks outside the large headquarters building at the Zen Center of Los Angeles.

CHAPTER 2

The Zen Center of Los Angeles: Enlightenment in the Inner City

> While Buddhism in the East has traditionally emphasized the enlightened one and his teachings, American practice seems to express itself especially in communities in which we manifest the enlightened life. I welcome this wonderful development, and believe that it will enrich the lives and practice of all who follow. The challenges involved are numerous and difficult; the opportunities seem unlimited.
>
> —TAIZAN MAEZUMI, RŌSHI
> Founder and president of the Zen Center of Los Angeles

The challenges involved in running the Zen Center of Los Angeles are numerous and difficult indeed. Most of the communities we have visited are located in rural, indeed idyllic, places where the members can pursue their destiny with few distractions from the outside world. The Zen Center of Los Angeles, however, is located in the heart of the inner city, where police helicopters often hover overhead at night, shining their searchlights down on the drug dealers in the park across the street.

Located just a five-minute walk south of Los Angeles's glossy Wilshire Boulevard, the Zen Center occupies nearly a whole city block in the decaying neighborhood known as Korea City. It has been a port of entry since the early 1900s, where people of various ethnic backgrounds arrive, stay a while to get their bearings, then move on to permanent homes elsewhere. Among the earliest inhabitants of the area were the Japanese, many of whom moved south after the San Francisco fire of 1906. During the 1950s and 1960s came a large influx of Mexicans, joined by Cuban refugees and immigrants from Central and South America. Then in the 1970s the Koreans arrived in Los Angeles in vast numbers—150,000 to 170,000 people, the largest Korean population anywhere outside of Korea. They are centered in this neighborhood. Crammed in a 1.2-square-mile area are large banks and tiny bars, luxurious department stores and Buddhist spiritual centers, vintage townhouses and shabby tenements, high-rise chain hotels and unique, hole-in-the-wall ethnic restaurants.

For anyone seeking spiritual growth or enlightenment amidst the clamorous realities of everyday life, this should be a fertile field indeed. And it has been. Since 1967 the Zen Center has grown to a live-in community of about 100 adults and 15 children, a total membership of more than 400, a net worth of more than $1.5 million, and branch or affiliated groups in a dozen other locations in the United States, Mexico, and England.

Zen is a form of Buddhism that has had a strong appeal in America, particularly among intellectuals, during the past several decades. It presents a simple vision of life as essentially good. It makes no esoteric or otherworldly claims and has no focus on supernatural beings or paranormal powers. It asks only that its followers learn to see clearly. Zen teaches that the only reality is the present moment and that its followers must grasp the moment and experience it wholly, avoiding the usual tendency to dream about the past and worry about the future. The very ordinary human way of life is the Way; it is perfection itself. If one looks for something outside of the self and one's immediate situation one goes astray. But one's experience is that of dissatisfaction: the Way and one's life seem irreconcilably separate.

Zen practice is the key to bridging this illusory gap. In a narrow sense, "practice" refers to the activity of sitting meditation, called *zazen*, concentrating with all one's effort until the gap between oneself and others is eliminated. In a broader sense, "practice" refers to the activity of completely involving oneself in whatever one is doing or experiencing so that there is no gap or separation between oneself and that activity or experience. It is the extension of *zazen* into one's life from moment to moment.

The Zen Center of Los Angeles has its origins in the early 1960s when a group of Americans interested in practicing Zen gravitated to the old Zenshuji temple in the Little Tokyo district of Los Angeles. The prime mover behind this group was Bernard Glassman, an aeronautical engineer with a Ph.D. in applied mathematics, who worked at McDonnell Douglas Astronautics Company. He had first begun to read about Zen in 1958, and began *zazen* in 1963. At first the group would meet one night a week for *zazen* and a lecture, with further meetings at one of the member's homes. By 1966 the group was meeting twice a week at the temple and the members had found a teacher, Taizan Maezumi, then resident priest at the Soto Zen mission of the temple.

Born in his father's temple in 1931, Maezumi was ordained a Soto Zen monk at the age of 11. Soto is one of the two major schools of Zen

Buddhism. After receiving degrees in Oriental literature and philosophy from Komazawa University in Tokyo, he underwent further training at one of the principal Zen monasteries and in 1955, at the age of 24, he was approved as a *sensei*, or "teacher." The next year he was invited to come to America as a missionary at the temple in Los Angeles. He worked initially with Japanese-Americans, but then began to extend his teaching to non-Japanese. Maezumi decided that he would spend the rest of his life in the United States. He worked hard to learn English and, after five years, became an American citizen. He was just what the young American students were looking for.

By 1967 the group, then around 15 strong, was ready to move out of the Zenshuji temple and create its own center. The group rented a house on Serrano Street with room for a *zendo* (meditation room or sanctuary) that could seat about 30 people, and residential quarters upstairs for Maezumi and his wife and several students. Here *zazen* was held daily, morning and evening. For a period the group considered itself a branch of the Zen Center of San Francisco. Because of technical difficulties in preparing the bylaws and financial statements, however, the group decided to remain legally independent.

At this time Maezumi was a *sensei,* but not yet a *Rōshi,* qualified to lead a Zen community. To establish a fully independent community, Maezumi called on his father in Japan to be the titular head. His brother, also a priest, came to America for a year to help get the new center established. With some financial help from Japan and several larger donations from members of the group, the first property was purchased on South Normandie Avenue for $26,000, with $5000 down and a mortgage for the rest. This house became, and still is, the *zendo.* In 1968 the Los Angeles Zendo was officially recognized as a Soto Zen Temple and training center by Soto headquarters in Japan. During the next couple of years several other priests came over from Japan to help in leading the practice, allowing Maezumi to return to Japan in 1969 to complete his studies. In 1970 he was approved as *Rōshi,* or spiritual leader, of the community. Henceforth he was known as Maezumi Rōshi.

During his absence the center underwent considerable growth, putting great pressure on the *zendo's* limited facilities. This led Glassman and one of his colleagues to conclude that they should follow the San Francisco example once again and start a rural monastery like San Francisco's Tassajara Zen Center in Carmel Valley, California. They began a search and examined some 30 sites from as far south as San Diego to as far north as Lake Isabella. They finally settled on a 228-acre site near Santa Barbara, costing $500 an acre. Its purchase and development would require raising about $125,000 immediately and $200,000 within the following two years. To carry out this undertaking, Glassman and his friend gave up their lucrative jobs in the aerospace industry to devote full time to fundraising, planning, and all the concomitant tasks. But the undertaking proved too large for them, and when Maezumi Rōshi returned from Japan he persuaded them to drop it in favor of a slower rate of growth at their existing location.

Growth was more gradual over the next several years. A few groups in nearby communities affiliated with the Zen Center. In 1971 the number of resident students doubled from five to ten and the house next door was purchased. Another at the end of the block was bought in 1974. By 1975 the pace picked up. Three more houses were purchased and a group in San Diego established ties with the center, giving it a more distant outpost. The next year the Center started its educational wing—the Institute for Transcultural Studies—and began publishing books of classical and contemporary Zen writings. In 1977 it acquired three more buildings on the block, two of them large apartment houses. Once again there was a strong push for growth, now coupled with the idea of owning an entire city block. While it is true that this expansion required constant fundraising, the number of people living at the center placed constant pressure on the space available. Space is still inadequate because even though the center has purchased apartment buildings, it has not realized the full benefits of ownership because it follows a policy of avoiding evictions and only taking over space as it becomes available through normal turnover.

Since 1977, the center has purchased three more buildings on the block, leaving only four properties, two large and two small, in other hands. With the continuing appreciation of the properties, the Zen Center now has real estate assets of nearly $3 million, offset by mortgages of a little more than $1 million.

About 125 adults live at the Los Angeles Zen Center, along with 30 children. Around 30 of the adults are monks (male and female, married and single). The monks are people who have dedicated their lives to the advancement of Buddhism; their shaved heads symbolize this dedication. About 10 monks are on staff at the center and it is from among them that the new teachers of Zen are created. About 10 staff people are laypeople who do not shave their heads as the monks do. Most of the residents, both monks and laypeople, work on the outside.

Most members are between the ages of 25 and 40, with a mean of around 33 years of age. About 15 of them are non-Americans, mostly British and Canadian, some of whom have married American members. Membership is fairly evenly divided between the sexes. A considerable percentage—perhaps one-third—come from Jewish backgrounds, while Catholics are also well represented. Because Zen is a practice that does not need to displace any other religion, some members follow it in tandem with another spiritual tradition. For example, Bernard Glassman, who now heads the affiliated Zen Center of New

York, is a Jew who keeps a kosher home and observes the traditional Friday night *Shabbas* meal with his family. On the other hand, the fact that Zen makes no claims about the existence or nonexistence of God makes it attractive to intellectuals who are seeking some spiritual practice, but cannot accept the theology of the religions in which they were raised.

The members of the Zen Center have probably the highest intellectual level of any community we visited, with at least three-quarters of them holding college degrees and many of them holding advanced degrees. Among its present officers, for example, one is a CPA and a lawyer, one has a Ph.D. in biology and had a distinguished teaching career, one has degrees in economics and educational administration, and one spent 17 years in research on molecular structure before turning to full-time photography and publishing. Few had any prior experience with intentional communities; most were attracted to the Zen Center because of its teachings, not because it is a community.

Actually the residents make up only about a third of the membership of the center. In addition to the residents, there are about 200 practicing members who live elsewhere—usually close enough to come by for *zazen* at least occasionally, plus 60 affiliate members and 60 corresponding members. Practicing members are those who wish to maintain a regular *zazen* practice, participating at the center when possible. They make a monthly financial pledge of $40. To become a practicing member one usually attends one or more of the introductory programs and then fills out an application and talks it over with the director of membership. The application asks about education and work experience, religious experience, and also whether the applicant has had any health or psychiatric problems. Affiliate membership is similar, but costs only $20 a month and is for people living too far away to participate much in center activities. Corresponding members, at $20 or more per year, are people who simply want to help support the center and receive its publications.

The line between being a practicing member and being a resident is somewhat blurred. People arrive to attend lengthy retreats and decide to stay on, or people move into the neighborhood and as they become more and more caught up in its activities, decide to become residents of the center. If they are coming from overseas, they may move in immediately. Turnover is low. About 10 percent drop out the first year; another 10 percent or so after that. Some have left to start affiliated groups such as the Zen Center of New York—which now has 190 members of its own—or the Zen Arts Center at Mt. Tremper, New York, which has 130 members. In 1976, after the center began its big expansion, a number of members were alienated by the growth and dropped out. They missed the family feeling when everyone would have tea with Maezumi Rōshi after a *zazen* sitting. There are also some people who remain practicing members of the center but who have moved out of the community because they have found more comfortable quarters elsewhere.

In 1983 about 20 people left with Joko, one of the senior teachers, to start a center in San Diego. Their places were quickly taken by new people. The center always manages to find some kind of space for people who want to live there, often by doubling up. If a single person is lucky enough to get his or her own room, it is usually a very small one. On the other hand, members with more seniority or members with families may have comfortable apartments or even, in a couple of cases, houses.

People on the staff receive room and board and a monthly stipend of about $135. It can be more in cases of particular need. Those not on staff who live at the center pay an average of $425 a month, which covers room, board, and all privileges of the center. Food is vegetarian, primarily natural food, with fish once every two weeks. It is served communally to all residents. Families with children may opt to prepare their own. While the communal food standards are fairly high, there is no objection to members eating or drinking what they want on their own.

The way of life is that of voluntary simplicity, but not fanaticism. In the *zendo*, clothing must be plain and shoulders and legs covered; otherwise it does not matter. In their free time, residents may watch the communal television, sit in the hot tub in one of the backyards, or play a little volleyball. Some who can afford it slip out to take in a movie or go out to dinner.

There are no specific restrictions on sexual behavior. Rōshi's attitude is that whatever people do they should do responsibly and mindfully. Quite a few unmarried couples live together and this often leads to marriage, which is a cause for great celebration in the community.

The question of taking a vow of poverty, at least for the monks, is one that has been debated at length. Some people feel that a true practicing Buddhist should be poor, without property or attachments. Others say that "attachment" is the key word. There is nothing wrong with having possessions so long as one is not attached to them. And some need to own property, such as those who need to accumulate capital for their business. In general, those who have a commitment sufficient to be on the staff, want their resources to be used for the center. In some cases people with money give the center the use of it, so that while the money is still theirs, the center receives the interest on it. Cars tend to be semi-private. One member lets the center use her car by day, while she has the use of it by night. In return, the center pays for the insurance on the vehicle. In other cases, four or five people may join together to support an automobile. At present, staff members are asked to take a vow renouncing the goal of accumulating material possessions. It is revocable when they leave the staff position.

Staff members get three weeks of vacation a year. Some of them are able to save enough to go away during this time, some take a job for a week through a temporary agency to make enough to go away for the other two weeks, and some get money from their family to go back home. There is also a welfare fund, made up of income from the coin-operated washing machines and interest on money lent by some members. If there is a special need, such as a family emergency, a staff member can borrow from this fund. Staff members also receive a yearly bonus in December, usually amounting to about $100. The finance office suggests the amount to the chief administrator, depending on what seems reasonable and how much money is in the bank.

Because many of the staff members have advanced degrees and professional skills, they are often able to earn some money on the outside as consultants. Michael Soule, the biologist who heads the Kuroda Institute for the Study of Buddhism and Human Values, and his wife Judith, a physician in the Center Clinic, have three school-aged children. Since the public school in the neighborhood is like inner city schools elsewhere, they have chosen to send their children to private schools, and they each do some consulting work to pay the tuition.

While the parents at the center are vitally interested in the moral and educational development of their children, they generally feel that they should not try to indoctrinate them in Buddhism. This does not mean, however, that the children are not involved in center activities. Most celebrations have some religious character and some are especially for children. In the annual celebration of the birth of the Buddha each April, children have the most important role. In front of the altar is a beautiful little pagoda made of fresh flowers, sheltering the figure of a baby Buddha. Each child offers a flower and pours sweet tea over the figure to nourish the growth of the Buddha. Immediately after the ceremony there is a party for the children with cake, ice cream, and a small gift for each. The result of all this is that some children manifest a considerable interest in Buddhism and some don't. Out of 20 to 25 adult offspring who spent some part of their childhood at the center, to date only a couple have become Buddhists. It remains to be seen whether those who spend their entire childhood and teenage years at the center will become Buddhists.

In recent years the Zen Center has been governed in a fairly authoritarian way, though it appears this may be changing. At its head is a board of directors elected at a yearly meeting of the voting members. The 25 voting members, all chosen by Maezumi Rōshi, are senior members who have been practicing for five to fifteen years. Thus the control is securely in the hands of those stable, senior people who can be relied upon to work together harmoniously.

The board elects the president (Maezumi Rōshi), seven vice-presidents, secretary, and treasurer. Each vice-president is in charge of a major activity. The list of officer candidates is drawn up by Maezumi Rōshi and Genpo Merzel Sensei (his chief assistant and appointed successor), based upon their experience with the jobs to be filled, time at the center, and maturity in their practice.

In the early days of the center a more democratic approach was employed, with a wide committee system. Out of this came the decision to buy land near Santa Barbara to start a monastery. When Maezumi Rōshi put a stop to that plan, he put a stop to the committee system as well, causing some discontent and the departure of a few people who didn't want to operate his way. But Maezumi Rōshi believed in "little by little"; a slow progress of maturation and growth. As this progress has taken place, he has played a less and less active role, imparting the purpose and vision, and letting people work out the details for themselves.

By 1982 discontent was growing among members who wanted to play a larger role in running the community, and they showed signs of being capable of undertaking such a role. Some felt alienation or frustration in not having more access to the board of directors. A series of town hall meetings was held to explore new avenues of participation. The scheme developed was one of setting up advisory teams to deal with specific problems. If a member wishes to work on a problem or area of interest, he or she must spark an interest in enough others to form a team. A town hall meeting is then held to empower the team, the team elects a chairperson, researches the problem, and writes a report with recommendations. These then go back to the town hall meeting. It remains to be seen how this system will work in operation.

Keeping so large an organization financially afloat is a problem. The annual turnover is about $900,000. Of this, 20 percent goes to meet principal and interest payments on mortgages and loans, 12 percent goes to support the medical clinic, and 60 percent is spent on building maintenance, community food, capital improvements, personnel stipends, and other administrative expenses. As for income, 58 percent comes from monastery and temple functions, primarily membership and training fees, but also the bookstore, stitchery (which makes meditation cushions and clothing), and retreats; 15 percent comes from the medical clinic; 3 percent comes from publications; 8 percent comes from fundraising and contributions; and the balance from borrowing and other nonoperating receipts such as interest.

The first business to be started was the Stitchery, in the early 1970s. It began making meditation cushions for the community and to sell through the bookstore. Later it expanded to making *futons* (sleeping mats) and some articles of clothing. It has done some mail order business by advertising in the center's newspaper. Its sales are small and it is regarded as more of a service than a source of profit.

The *ZCLA Journal* was begun in 1971. Some 750 copies were published to give away to members and friends. In 1976 the *ZCLA Journal* became *Zen Writings*, and Center Publications, a full-fledged publishing house, was born. Over a period of about five years it produced 15 books, both contemporary books about Zen and some Zen classics. The books were beautifully produced and many received positive critical acclaim. Unfortunately, however, the market for Zen books in English is not a large one. The center found that its publishing activities were overextending it in both personnel and finances. It was losing money and could not afford to tie up a lot of capital in maintaining inventory. So in 1981 the center eliminated most of its publishing activities and transferred distribution of what remained to Great Eastern Books in Boulder, Colorado, a book distribution company associated with Chogyam Trungpa's Vajradhatu (a spiritual community that follows Tibetan Buddhist practices).

The publication department continues to produce a journal three times a year in tabloid format. Called *Ten Directions*, this 20-page paper serves as the house organ, with news of center activities along with articles and stories about Zen. It is sent free to 8000 people on the center's computerized mailing list, and breaks even from the sale of advertising, primarily to center-related businesses.

The ZCLA Bookstore was started in 1977 when the center bought its headquarters building. It grew gradually to a level of about $1500 gross per month, much of it by mail through ads in *Ten Directions*. In 1983 it, too, was considered economically unviable and closed.

The largest business at the center is its medical clinic. It was started in 1978 by Judith Soule, M.D., and Julie McNitt, R.N. At first they had only a small examining room with a kitchen and a bathroom. Soule recalls, "We had only a desk and chair for Julie and a *futon* on the floor as an exam table. Every time we had a patient, we had to bolt the door so someone wouldn't mistakenly walk in." In 1979 they got a bank loan to buy examination tables and lab equipment and turned the kitchen into a combination examination room and kitchen. The space was so small it was hard to examine anyone taller than five feet, ten inches. The clinic staff spent half a day each week scouring the neighborhood looking for business. They visited health food stores, religious communities, and retirement homes, letting people know about the new nonprofit medical clinic offering conventional and alternative therapies (such as acupuncture and homeopathy) and a sliding fee scale.

Originally, most of the patients were people connected with the center. By 1982, however, a tabulation showed that only 6.3 percent were connected with the center. Some 42.8 percent were white, 24.7 percent were Hispanic, 9.9 percent were black, and 3.2 percent were Asian. Since fees are based on ability to pay, many pay little or nothing. With no state or private funding, the center only breaks even, and is seeking more higher-income patients to help support its low-cost care for the needy.

The clinic faced a problem in 1980 when it needed a zoning change to operate legally. The center hired a consultant who suggested that they get the whole block rezoned. They cultivated the neighborhood's city councilman, got him to speak at a joint meeting with Vietnamese, Korean, and Japanese Buddhist groups, and persuaded him to introduce a proposal in the city council meeting to create a qualified commercial zone for the block. This specified certain commercial activities that could be performed—that is, the ones that already were being performed. The center drummed up support all over the neighborhood and got hundreds of residents to sign a petition for the change. It was approved.

Another important activity of the center is its Kuroda Institute for the Study of Buddhism and Human Values, founded in 1976. Its object is to document and encourage the development of Buddhist thought in the West. It is authorized by the state to grant higher degrees, and offers courses on the history, texts, and philosophical foundations of Buddhist traditions. It has appointed 18 Buddhist scholars as fellows, and holds periodic conferences with psychologists, scientists, and leaders from other religions to examine the connections between Buddhism and their work. These conferences have been on such diverse topics as Zen and Christianity, the mindful practices of American Indians, Japanese papermaking, and Zen in the performance of music. Many of the proceedings are published by the University of Hawaii Press.

The center's landscaping business started in 1970 when cash was short and a number of its residents were asked to find work outside. They soon decided that for tax and insurance purposes it was better for the business to be private. At one time it employed as many as eight members of the community, but at the time of our visit it employed its two partners. In 1983 it won several citywide awards for excellence in landscape design.

Other small businesses include carpentry, with three to four members involved; house painting, with two members; and electrical work, with two to three members. At one time two members did plumbing.

One of the problems in running these businesses is occasional conflict with *zazen* practice. This is partly a matter of where the individual's primary interests lie and partly a matter of time, since *zazen* may take several hours each day, as well as occasional periods of a week or more.

The Zen Center of Los Angeles is a rapidly growing organization, though it is growing primarily in its outreach rather than as a live-in community. It has affiliated centers and meditation groups in five other cities in California, two in Oregon, two in Arizona, one in Utah, one in England, and two in New York that have been mentioned.

The next independent center that the Zen Center will establish will probably be in Mexico City, where there are about 80 students already. In the past several years there has been more contact with the San Francisco Zen Center. The centers share ideas on the spiritual level and the material level—that is, how to make ends meet.

In the summer of 1980 the center bought 160 acres near Idyllwild, California, in the mountains above Palm Springs. The land had been owned by one of the members, who offered it at a very good price— $120,000 with $40,000 down. With its present facilities the mountain center can accommodate up to 50 people for short retreats. With the great success of retreat programs in 1982 and 1983, the community has begun to envision a parallel development at the mountain center, which would provide strong, and perhaps stricter, training than in the city.

In the spring of 1984 the board of directors voted to put its city property up for sale and to look for an alternative site somewhere in the Los Angeles area. This decision grew out of a continuing concern about the crime level in the area and the financial difficulties of carrying the properties, coupled with a belief that such an assemblage so close to Wilshire Boulevard would be attractive to a developer.

So the Zen Center is now in a state of transition. The early dream of moving to the country is being partially realized. At the same time, city life will go on, but in some new form that cannot yet be foreseen.

Culture is important at Stelle. Here violinists play at a picnic.

CHAPTER 3

Stelle: An End or a Beginning?

About 75 miles south of Chicago, in the heart of the great American corn and soybean belt, lies a small community of 44 houses and around 125 people. If it were lifted up out of the farmland that surrounds it and relocated in the suburbs of almost any American city, it would look as if it belonged. The houses are typical of the suburban middle-class, set in sweeping lawns and connected by curving paved streets and side-walks.

This community is Stelle, Illinois. A closer look at Stelle reveals that it is very different from a typical suburban community. It was started in 1973 by Richard Kieninger—a man who rejects traditional religion and says that he was directed to build his city by invisible "Brotherhoods" in preparation for a doomsday in the year 2000 that would destroy 90 percent of humanity. Following Kieninger's detailed instructions, Stelle has been building a community of people who hope to survive this holocaust and play a key role in bringing about a subsequent "Kingdom of God." Stelle has attracted an able group of people, devoted to the cause of human perfection, who have developed unique and effective methods of educating their children and done some interesting research into survival technology.

All has not gone as planned, however. Personality conflicts and economic setbacks have caused a considerable reduction in the size of the group which reached 216 people in 1974. By 1982 the leaders of Stelle modified their demands that all residents commit themselves fully to the principles and practices of their founder, and they opened the community doors to any others who wanted to live there. This new development casts doubt on the community's cohesion and purpose.

Some 200 miles farther south, and 150 years further back in time, a similar experiment began in New Harmony, Indiana. Although it lasted only 12 years, it was the most famous utopian community in nineteenth-century America. It, too, was started by a man who rejected traditional religion and who was preparing his followers for the second coming of Christ—which he expected to see in his lifetime. New Harmony was remarkably successful in its early years, but later switched to a utopian agnostic vision that emphasized human perfection and focused on innovative educational methods and scientific research. It, too, dissolved as a result of personality conflicts and differing approaches. But when New Harmony became just another town, it retained a remarkable group of people who, for the next 50 years, made a contribution to the United States far beyond that of any other town of equal size.

The parallels between Stelle and New Harmony cannot be pushed too far. But sometimes we can get a better perspective on what is happening today by looking at what happened before. And so, before we get into the details of the Stelle story, let's look at the history of New Harmony.

In 1803 Father Rapp, an apostate Lutheran from Württemberg, Germany, arrived in the United States with the vanguard of some 700 of his followers. They came to the land of freedom and opportunity to escape harassment by the church authorities in Germany. The group first located about 25 miles north of Pittsburgh, where they created a town called Harmonie. They entered into a pact in which all members agreed to give all of their property to the group for the common good, obey all the rules of the community, work unselfishly for its well-being, and not demand a reward for their labor or services if they later withdrew from the community. They soon introduced the practice of celibacy, as an economic and social necessity, as well as for religious reasons. Since the millennium was believed imminent, there was no need to produce children. The members were thus loath to lose the time that pregnancies and child rearing would take from women, and the lack of children would help overcome the divisions within the community that were created by blood relationships. The aim was unity of the whole community, not unity of family groups.

An observer wrote: "There is no vicious habit among them. There is not an instance of swearing, or lying, or debauchery of any kind, and, as to cheating, so commonly practiced in civilized society, they have no temptation to it whatever. As individuals they have no use for money—and they have no fear of want."*

By 1814 the community had outgrown its location and the members decided to move farther west. Rapp found 7000 acres of wilderness on the banks of the Wabash River in southwestern Indiana, bought it, and moved the whole community there. The community stayed in Harmonie, Indiana, for ten years. During this time the members built a very impressive town with well-constructed brick and frame buildings (some

---

*Don Blair, *The New Harmony Story* (New Harmony, Ind.: New Harmony Publications Committee, n.d.), 20.

prefabricated), two churches, and a number of successful small-scale industries. The coopers made barrels and other containers, the tinsmiths manufactured tinware, blacksmiths tended six forges, and the workers in the oil mill made oil from linseed, hemp, walnut, and peach stones. Chandlers made 1000 candles per day, ropemakers made 6000 pounds of flax and hemp rope per season, the stocking weavers wove 16 pairs of stockings per day, brick kilns turned out thousands of bricks, and the grist mill ground 56 barrels of flour per day. Harmonie was not only self-sufficient, it produced a surplus of products that it sold. It even produced a very good whiskey, which the members didn't drink, but sold as far away as New Orleans.

The community was a success materially and spiritually. Members believed it was their destiny "to set an illustrious example of harmony of human relations, the natural cooperative economy of the community of good and the peaceful reign of Christian fellowship under such conditions, so that other communities observing this marvel of communal life, would gradually be led to adopt a similar policy."*

In 1824 Rapp decided to move his community back to Pennsylvania. Life was getting to be easy and quiet, with leisure time for thought, and Rapp found it difficult to keep his people in order, except during the hard work that attended a new settlement. Also the West had not developed as quickly as he had hoped, and he wanted to be nearer to the markets.

He put the entire town up for sale, advertising it as far away as Great Britain, and eventually found a buyer in the person of Robert Owen, who was looking for a place to carry out his own utopian ideas.

The Rappites then built a new town 16 miles north of Pittsburgh, which they called Economy. With commercial success came a gradual shift of attention from mysticism to developing a heaven on earth, with music, books, and objects of art to make life more pleasant. With more free time for the members, differences over the governing of the community occurred, with many regarding Rapp as a dictator. Large groups left to follow other leaders. Despite his vow of celibacy, Rapp became involved with a woman, which again split the community. During the 25 years after the move back to Pennsylvania the society gradually withered away, a victim of its own success.

The second stage of community at New Harmony, as Robert Owen called it, was even shorter. Born in Wales, Owen was a self-directed and self-made man who left home at the age of 12, saying to his father, "But don't you see that I have to go? I am finished here." In the next few years he held a variety of jobs, which taught him about people as well as about management. He began to doubt organized religion and came to the conclusion that people should not be praised or condemned for

*Ibid., 29.

what they believe or disbelieve, for they have little choice in the matter. He felt that people are molded by circumstances and are not entitled to praise or scorn for being the people they cannot help being.

He became superintendent of a large Manchester cotton mill at 19, then was made a partner. He soon persuaded his partners to buy a textile mill in New Lanark, Scotland, where he undertook a series of reforms in working conditions that earned him the opposition of both the clergy and his business associates. He treated his employees like human beings, not like pieces of machinery; encouraged cleanliness and good deportment; set up a company store with low prices, attempted to control the use of alcohol, put children into uniforms so none would feel inferior because of his or her attire; and continued paying his work force during a period when it was necessary to close down for lack of raw materials. The reputation of his experiments spread widely, and many came to see them for themselves. Not only did he improve the lot of his employees, but he also produced profits greater than similar traditional mills.

In 1824, while casting about for new ways to carry out his social ideas, Owen learned that a town was for sale in America. He sailed to the United States, saw the town, and bought it for $150,000. Here was the opportunity to develop his perfect society in a new land that had few established ideas and customs. His wife, however, did not share his spirit of adventure and refused to go along. The marriage broke up; she and one daughter stayed in Scotland, and Owen brought his four sons and two other daughters to America.

Once in America, Owen interested a number of other important intellectuals in joining him in his experiment. Preeminent among them was William Maclure, a wealthy businessman and president of the Academy of Natural Sciences. Both Owen and Maclure were followers of the Swiss reformist educator Johann Heinrich Pestallozi, who advocated education "by leading from dim precepts to clear ones," and who believed that any experience could be used as a textbook.

Owen and his group of intellectuals and idealists arrived in New Harmony in the spring of 1826, aboard a flatboat called the *Philanthropist*, to begin their great experiment. Their stated principles were equality of rights among all adults, community of property, freedom of speech and action, courtesy in all intercourse, preservation of health, acquisition of knowledge, and obedience to the laws of the United States.

The principles were indeed noble and Owen's followers planned to dedicate not only their personal fortunes but their lives to carrying them out. Within the community all work was to be equal and all were to receive the same compensation. But the idea of equality of work was troublesome from the very beginning. Some complained that the musicians were having too easy a time of it. Owen himself volunteered to be the baker and his effort with this enterprise became the town joke.

The quarreling among the members as to whose work was the most important soon became a serious threat to the smooth running of the community. Owen was asked by the governing committee to take over, in the hope that with the power in the hands of one person he would be able to reestablish harmony. But Owen became a dictator, bringing to an end the democratic hopes of the community. He also continued to travel a great deal to spread his utopian ideas, and so was not there to lend the strength of his personality to the community in its formative period. As dissension grew, some of the members broke away to establish small offshoots. In March 1827 the community was officially dissolved. The stated reason was that the experiment had been premature. Owen believed it failed because too many people were idlers, lacking the character necessary to make the experiment work. Others felt that Owen's absence was itself the greatest problem.

Nevertheless, most of the people who had gathered for the utopian experiment stayed on in New Harmony, and their influence was felt in many ways. Their most far-reaching influence was in education, particularly early childhood education. Pursuing the idea that people's characters are made for them and not by them, they developed an infant school where, almost from birth, children were surrounded with as perfect a set of circumstances as possible. The infant school was the physical manifestation of Owen's view that "children are the guests of humanity and should be treated with all honor, care, and kindness."* The children were given as many basic facts as they could understand, and learning was presented as a pleasure, not a chore.

In terms of its stated goals, New Harmony failed as a community. As a collection of able and idealistic people, however, New Harmony succeeded admirably, and was the birthplace of many American institutions. Among their innovations were the introduction of the first infant school in America, first kindergarten in America, first trade school in America, first free public school system in America, first women's club in America, first free library in America, first civic dramatic club in America, and first geologic survey in America.

In 1939 Richard Kieninger was a boy of 12 living in the suburbs of Chicago. He tells the story of his life from then on in the book that is central to the Stelle Group's existence, *The Ultimate Frontier*—which he wrote under the pen name of Eklal Kueshana.** Kieninger relates that he was approached one day by an elderly gentleman named Dr. White, who seemed to know a lot about him, and who proceeded to tell him about the Brotherhoods. As White explained it, the Brotherhoods (who are also seen as guides by communities in Australia and France that we discuss in later chapters) were established by Christ to help protect and

*Ibid., 41.
**Eklal Kueshana, *The Ultimate Frontier* (Stelle, Ill.: Stelle Group, 1982).

guide the people of the world and to prepare the way for the perfect Kingdom of God. White told Kieninger that the Kingdom of God was soon to be established, that its future inhabitants were incarnating now, and that: "It's you, Richard, who have been appointed to begin that nation."

Kieninger says that he saw White only infrequently after that meeting, but that over the years he met a number of different guides who further initiated him into the mysteries of the Brotherhoods, advancing both his knowledge and his sense of purpose. Outwardly his life was normal. He went to college, majoring in chemistry, but says that he was told by his guides to leave in his final year. They wanted him to go out into the world to learn about people and develop his personality. They told him that when he was in a job long enough to learn the routine and be offered a promotion, that would be his signal to move on to another job. Over the next 15 years Kieninger held many jobs: assistant office manager, life insurance sales representative, hardware salesperson, aircraft die maker, cabinetmaker, small business owner.

In 1963 he published *The Ultimate Frontier* and, with his second wife, Gail, started The Stelle Group as a nonprofit corporation. (*Stelle* means "place" in German.) For the next ten years the group operated out of the Kieninger home in Chicago. It grew very slowly at first, from 3 members in 1963 to 16 in 1966 and 30 in 1967. During this period the members were undergoing initiation and training under Kieninger's direction. They were also accumulating capital to purchase land and working out the principles and concepts for the design of their future community. As new people joined they would usually move into the immediate neighborhood of the Kieningers so that they could work more closely together. In 1968 the group established an elementary school in the Kieninger basement, directed by Gail Kieninger. By 1969 the group numbered more than 70 members, and a second step was taken with the establishment nearby of the Stelle Woodworking Corporation. Seven members each put up $1000 to provide the initial capital of a business that later could be moved to the new community. Kieninger took over the management. As its demands claimed more and more of his time, much of the running of the group devolved on Gail Kieninger and the trustees.

During this period the first of several schisms occurred, this one between what Kieninger says were the *doers* and the *discussers*. The latter included a considerable number of members who were demanding more say in how the group was run. Kieninger turned them down on the ground that he was an emissary of the Brotherhoods carrying out the instructions of his superiors. As a result, about one-third of the membership resigned from the group and moved away.

In 1970 the group finally purchased 240 acres of farmland, some 75 miles south of Chicago, as the site of their future community. This is near the southern edge of the Canadian Pre-Cambrian shield, geologically a very stable area, considered likely to withstand the severe earth changes the group believes will occur around the turn of the century. Well away from Chicago, it is still close enough to have economic ties to this major trading center. Members of the group volunteered their labor to build a modern 20,000-square-foot factory on the land, and construction began in the fall of 1970. More members joined and more donations and tithes were received to pay for the cost of materials. In November 1972 the Stelle Woodworking Corporation moved into the new factory, and by March 1973 the first two homes were built and occupied. The offices of the group and the school were moved to the new site at the same time and the community of Stelle, Illinois, had its official beginning. By this time there were about 150 members, though few could actually live in the new community. Many lived in surrounding communities; a few commuted from Chicago.

During the next 12 months, 11 more homes were built and streets and sidewalks were installed. A water purification plant and pumping station were completed, as well as a sewage treatment plant. All this work was designed and installed by members of the group. The water purification plant was unique, using a reverse osmosis method of purification. The first municipal plant of its kind in North America, it was built to handle the needs of up to 450 people. Many men were trained in the construction trades. A new corporation was established, Stelle Industries, Inc., of which the Stelle Woodworking Corporation, renamed the Stellwood Company, was made a division. New businesses were started as additional divisions: an automatic screw machine company, an injection-molded plastics company, and a printing operation. The construction of homes and utilities was also brought under this new corporation, and thereafter all profit-making activities were jointly owned by those members who controlled Stelle Industries, while the nonprofit functions were owned by The Stelle Group. As president of both corporations, Kieninger coordinated all their activities. Morale was high, growth was rapid, money flowed in as needed, experts joined as required, and people worked long hours with a great sense of satisfaction. They felt that they were helping to fulfill Dr. White's prediction that, before 1985, "The growth of the community near Chicago will be phenomenal. By various means, the Brotherhoods will influence the right persons to seek you out and to desire entrance into your budding city. It will be almost exclusively from among these citizens that the Brothers Themselves will select the persons qualified to colonize the Kingdom of God."*

But by 1974, membership in the group reached its all-time high—216 people. While the material gains had been substantial, personal prob-

---

*Ibid., 129–30.

lems were beginning to multiply. For some time, Richard and Gail's relationship had been breaking down with the result that they often were on opposite sides of issues, each vying for authority. The difficulties in his marriage led Richard to look elsewhere in the community for feminine companionship and this, in turn, created a situation that was more and more uncomfortable to all concerned. Finally Richard resolved the situation by making a sudden decision to leave the community totally and move to Texas. He resigned from virtually all of his offices and James, a long-time trustee and also a confidante of Gail's, was made president of both corporations. The animosity between Richard and Gail had by this time become so intense that Gail convinced the trustees to issue an edict that Richard thereafter could not set foot in Stelle or talk to any members except James and herself.

After six months in Texas, Kieninger returned to the Stelle area and showed up unannounced at a general meeting being held in a hall in a neighboring town. Addressing only James, Kieninger told the group that he had been barred from Stelle, discussed the events leading up to the barring, and called for a reform of the decision-making process at Stelle that would take power away from the trustees and give it to the members.

Several months of maneuvering followed, in which Kieninger was permitted back after he had first agreed to work under the trustees' direction; then Kieninger called for the resignation of the trustees; they countered by expelling him from membership. Finally a petition was signed by a majority of the members calling for an early meeting to remove the trustees. The group was polarized: one faction supported the trustees in their claim that they had acquired the authority to run Stelle on behalf of the Brotherhoods; the other faction (which included Kieninger) supported a democratic structure under which matters affecting the lives of individual members would be voted on through a referendum process. And the man who had started it all, and who had run it in an authoritarian manner for years, was now on the side of democracy.

In August 1975, before the recall meeting could be held but after it was clear that they no longer had the support of the community, the trustees resigned and Gail and James led an exodus of their strongest supporters—43 people in all—to Wisconsin, where they planned to start their own community. This, however, never developed.

About the same time Richard returned to Texas to work on starting another, smaller community east of Dallas, called Adelphi. After his divorce from Gail became final in November 1976, he applied for renewal of his membership in The Stelle Group. Since he no longer lived in Stelle he was not eligible to vote or hold office, but he was accepted as a teacher and emissary of the Brotherhoods, and he continues to return to Stelle several days each month to carry out these duties.

When Stelle was first started, a suburban community in the middle of Illinois farmland, it caused some raised eyebrows locally. At first the group kept its more esoteric aims quiet so as not to upset its conservative neighbors. In time, though, rumors about Stelle spread that were more upsetting than the truth. This led the community to broadcast its aims more widely. It holds an open house every year and occasionally holds informational meetings in other towns. This has resulted in a fairly widespread acceptance of the community in the area. When Gail and James left, along with most of the former managers, they left behind a large debt. The new president, Malcolm Carnahan, convinced a nearby businessman to take him around and introduce him to local bankers. He invited them out to see Stelle for themselves, and so was able to get a new loan to cover the debt.

Membership in the group reached its peak of 216 in 1974, hovered around 190 from 1975 to 1977, dropped to about 140 in 1978, then to around 125 in 1979, and has been fairly stable at that level ever since. Stelle has 44 houses, 28 of which are privately owned and 16 of which are owned by the group. The population includes three blacks and is predominantly middle-class to upper middle-class and well educated.

Stelle is a center for innovative ideas in social relations, education, and science and technology. Many of these ideas began with the blueprints set forth in *The Ultimate Frontier*, but they have developed beyond this as a result of the innovativeness of the members and their receptivity to new ideas extant in American society today.

Stelle is a curious mixture of a middle-class way of life combined with New Age values and practices. The men are all cleanshaven and they wear neckties in public or at any work for which neckties would not be inappropriate. The women similarly wear skirts. The residents' choice of attire illustrates the point, made in *The Ultimate Frontier*, that the physical environment is, to a large extent, the result of people's thoughts and actions and, conversely, people's thoughts and actions are, to a large extent, the result of the physical environment. Or, as one member said to us, "If you dress up, you feel up." The first homes, in addition to being earthquake proof, all had nine-foot ceilings since it was felt that high ceilings were more elegant. Stelle prohibits smoking in public (in fact, virtually no one smokes), abuse of alcohol, and use of illegal drugs.

At the same time, Stelle is a social workshop. Kieninger studied psychology in the course of his own self-education. He was particularly interested in Wilhelm Reich's concepts of body armoring: that people repress emotions by tightening their muscles, and must learn to release these muscles before emotions can be released. This has led to a community interest in Reichian therapy and Rolfing. Members have experimented with est, transcendental meditation, transactional analysis, and kinesiology (a form of diagnosis of health based on muscle tone). Each of these approaches elicits varying degrees of interest and discussion within the community.

In 1978 a number of the members took a variety of psychological tests in an internal research project to see what kind of people they were. Smarter, for one thing. The average IQ among the adults was 128; among the children, 130. The children in the early learning group tested at 135. The other tests, comparing the adult members with the general adult population of the United States, showed them to be more emotionally stable, trusting, self-motivated, creative, and tranquil, and less frustrated. They tested in the top 18 percent in heterosexuality— interest in the opposite sex, dating, kissing, being in love; in the top 23 percent for analyzing their own and other's feelings and empathizing with others; and in the top 28 percent for achievement—doing their best, solving difficult problems, meeting goals. They were in the lowest 20 percent in aggressiveness—criticizing and blaming others, and in the lowest 28 percent for self-abasement—feeling guilty or inferior.

The community spent two years in small group discussions of social and sexual issues. Members encourage responsible, caring relationships. Attitudes toward sex between consenting adults are pretty relaxed, however, partly as a result of the teaching of *The Ultimate Frontier* that it is desirable for a couple to live together for three years before marriage. As believers in reincarnation they have no religious objection to abortion, so there is no fear of unwanted children.

But children are usually desired and once they arrive they become the focus of much parental and community attention. Contrary to the current trend, the group places great emphasis on the role of women as full-time wives, mothers, and homemakers. The group is dedicated to working toward human perfection, and a proper upbringing of children offers the best chance to achieve this. Married women with children under six years of age are not allowed to work outside the home, except in part-time volunteer jobs. The group believes that all children should have at least one full-time parent or surrogate.

The group believes that mothers should teach their children to read by the time they are three years old and to write by the time they are four. The school started by Gail Kieninger in Chicago was a first effort to achieve this. No one, however, knew quite how to go about it, and both in Chicago and in Stelle there was a continuing search for the best method. They looked in many directions and eventually found help in the methodology developed by the Better Baby Institute of Philadelphia, founded by Glenn Doman, Ph.D., author of *Teach Your Baby to Read* and *Teach Your Baby Math*. The Better Baby Institute now regards Stelle as a practical workshop to demonstrate the validity of its theories.

The Stelle educational system is divided into two parts: the Mother-school for mothers of children from birth to age six, and the Learning

Center for older children. The Motherschool is specifically designed to assist mothers in teaching their very young children. As one educational expert, J. McVicker Hunt, Ph.D., of the University of Illinois at Champaign said: "It's much easier to foster development early, than to make up for lost opportunities later ... the highest rate of development is from birth to age two. That's the period of greatest plasticity. The longer you wait after that, the harder it is to make gains ... by four, it isn't easy."*

Motherschool consists of five early learning programs: the birth program, the MISPAH program, mothers' classes, the Montessori classrooms, and the parents' resource center. The birth program includes classes on nutrition, exercise, fetal development, and safe and fulfilling births. MISPAH stands for mother's individual staff person at home. Mothers receive regular visits from their MISPAH to help them create optimal educational activities for their children with the aim that they do school work on at least a third-grade level by age six. There are also special consultants on the home environment, physical development, and music. Music training involves learning to sing, read music, play an instrument, and have perfect pitch, and also includes the Japanese Suzuki method by which very young children are taught to play the violin. Mothers' classes are designed for mothers to share teaching ideas as well as their experiences as mothers, wives, and women. The main purpose of the two Montessori classrooms is to encourage character development in children. Each classroom is designed to promote the child's ability to experience life and learning as a joyous adventure, choose interesting work and concentrate on it, exercise self-discipline, and interact harmoniously with others. As much as possible, the materials enable the children to correct their own mistakes without waiting for a teacher to point out their errors. The parents' resource center is a cooperative that provides materials and experiences to help parents educate their children. It includes a large library of books on child development and education, music tapes and educational films, and sponsors weekly field trips for the children.

One of the most interesting and unusual methods developed by the Better Baby Institute is "bit cards." Each bit is an 11-inch square of cardboard with a picture of one item on it. Related pictures of items, such as North American birds, electronic symbols, sixteenth-century art, edible plants, and Baroque composers are quickly flashed to the children while mentioning what they are. In this way the child, almost subliminally, begins to become familiar with a wide variety of subjects. One Stelle family, while visiting their parents in Texas, went into a greeting card store with their three-year-boy. He looked across the room at a card on the wall, tugged at his father's sleeve, and said, "I

---

*"Education in Stelle," *Stelle Letter* 4 (1982):2.

want to go see the da Vinci." The picture was indeed a da Vinci, but not one that was included in a collection of bit cards of Renaissance art to which the child had been exposed.

The Stelle Learning Center is the academic equivalent of grades one through twelve. Children attend school all year, taking several short vacations. The objective is to assist the children to become balanced, confident individuals with a love for learning. With a low student-to-teacher ratio, the Learning Center uses mastery teaching, in which the student must master one concept before being introduced to the next. Thus students are able to progress at their own rate and there is no need to give grades. When the students are nine years old they begin to take part in the erdkinder (earth children) program, which includes boating, camping, skiing, hiking, the teaching of practical life skills, and survival experiences. Competition is downplayed.

This unique educational system is one of the most remarkable developments at Stelle and should be one of its strongest attractions in drawing new people to the community. At the time of our visit the Learning Center had 16 children, aged 6 to 14, enrolled, six of whom were from outside the community.

Stelle's pioneering innovations in science and technology relate to its belief that the earth will go through cataclysmic changes on or around May 5, 2000. This was originally predicted in *The Ultimate Frontier,* and the group finds a good deal of evidence to corroborate this prediction. Members point to the continental plates shifting in search of equilibrium, causing increased volcanic and earthquake activity in recent years; centrifugal aberrations in the earth's rotation because of lopsided polar ice caps; and finally, a particularly straight planetary alignment on May 5, 2000, which they say could trigger a major shift of the earth and its land masses.

This scenario dictates the development of a self-sufficient economy, alternative sources of energy, food storage, and other survival methods. It also means finding a way to airlift the community 14 miles above the earth for 14 days while the changes in the earth work themselves out. "What if this never happens?" we asked Tim Wilhelm, the group's vice-president and director of the office of technology. "We hope it never will," he replied. "Everything we've been doing makes this a better place to live and improves our lives and our children's lives. That's enough justification. But if the catastrophe does happen, we'll also be as well prepared as we're able."

Technological research and development to date has focused on housing, alternative fuel sources, and greenhouses. From the beginning Stelle's houses have been earthquake resistant; greater than usual amounts of reinforced concrete and complete sheathing with one-half inch plywood were used. In recent years many forms of energy-efficient houses have been built or retrofitted. Stelle's houses include examples of wood stove heat, active solar collectors, passive collecting walls added on to an older house, attached greenhouses, thermal envelope design, and earth bermed structures.

As yet, there is no effort to make Stelle completely self-sufficient. Rather, the aim is interdependency with the surrounding agricultural area, drawing on the farm resources of their neighbors and contributing their own special skills. Stelle has some organic vegetable gardens but does not presently have any livestock of its own. Since Stelle is surrounded by cornfields, it was logical that the group look at ways to use corn for fuel. The result was development of a plant that can produce about 50 gallons of alcohol fuel a day from corn. The U.S. Department of Energy gave them $50,000 to design a 1000-gallon-a-day plant. Stelle's own plant is not currently operating since the present cost of gasoline is too low to make alcohol fuel economical. But it is ready to start up whenever needed. Meanwhile the office of technology is exploring the possibility of using the plant to reprocess waste alcohol from a nearby cosmetic manufacturing plant to remove the contaminants in it.

In 1979 the group built a 1200-square-foot lean-to greenhouse against the south wall of its factory building. The growing beds rest on 55-gallon drums of water for heat retention. In winter the heat that rises to the factory ceiling is blown into the greenhouse and then circulates back into the factory through doors at each end of the greenhouse. The greenhouse can maintain overnight temperatures of 50 degrees or more when outside temperatures are below zero. It has been used to produce bedding plants for sale in the spring, as well as organic vegetables for the group's own use, sold to members through the Stelle Cooperative Food Mart.

In the fall of 1982, the group received a $59,000 grant from the Illinois Department of Energy and Natural Resources to build an even more imaginative prototype greenhouse. This one will have twin glazing of plastic with an air space in between, sitting over a trough filled with a foamable solution. At night air diffusers will convert the solution from liquid to foam, thereby increasing its volume about 200 times, and will blow it up into the glazed cavity to provide nighttime insulation. In the morning the air diffusers will be turned off and the insulating foam will drip back down into the trough.

The group is also engaged in basic energy research with the ultimate aim of finding an energy source suited to the massive airlift operation. This entails an analysis of prequantum physics, when scientists such as Michael Faraday and Nikola Tesla believed that the entire universe is filled with a substance called ether. Current electrical technology was largely conceived within the context of this ether-based cosmology, and the fathers of that technology believed that electricity was a condensate of the ether. Using this hypothesis, and working with outside consultants, a group at Stelle is experimenting to see if it can convert ether to energy instead of converting mass to energy via nuclear fission or the combustion of fossil fuels.

We have been describing a physically attractive community populated by sincere people doing worthwhile and interesting things. Why hasn't it grown?

The answers to this question seem to be a combination of the personal and leadership problems described earlier, its location and economic prospects, and the stringencies of membership in The Stelle Group.

Stelle's location in the middle of the American cornbelt is not ideal. It is flat and windy, cold in the winter, and too far from the cultural attractions of Chicago for easy access. There aren't many jobs in the area and Stelle has had difficulty creating its own. The Stellwood Company was the major branch of Stelle Industries, employing at its peak 50 people, 20 of whom were members of the community. It was sold to its employees in 1978 at the height of its success. Its major business was building component parts for large manufacturers. During the recession of the early 1980s these other companies took the work back into their own plants to provide continued employment for their own workers. Stellwood was unable to develop new markets and in 1982 it filed for bankruptcy. As the population of Stelle ceased to grow, the Stelle Construction Company no longer had work to do in the community and could find little outside, so it is no longer in operation. Stelle Plastics Company makes a modest profit, but it uses little of the community's large factory building. A private company, Matalanin Mold Company, owned by one of the members, uses some of the space, but at the time of our visit most of the factory was empty. In December 1982 a controlling interest in Stelle Industries was sold to Federal Chicago Inc., a Chicago-based manufacturing concern. It has since expanded the plastics capacity by 25 percent and brought in 4 aluminum die-cast machines. In the next year it expects to complete the factory building and add 100 to 150 jobs.

At the beginning of 1984, 77 employed people lived in Stelle. The group itself provided jobs for 10 people; Stelle Industries supported 15 people; 20 people worked at other businesses in the community, including the Cooperative Mart; Stelle Telephone Mutual, Stelle's own telephone company; and Metalanin Mold Company; and 32 people worked outside the community, some commuting 50 miles or more a day.

The Stelle Group, as principal owner of the community, had an income of about $660,000 in 1982, of which 17 percent came from member and resident donations and tithing; 33 percent came from outside donations and tithing; and 50 percent came from income-producing services. The largest portion of this was the grant for the experimental greenhouse. Some $80,000 was income from Stelle's 16 housing units, which rent for about $130 for a one-bedroom apartment, plus utilities. Nearly $50,000 came from the Office of Publications, which distributes *The Ultimate Frontier.* More than 200,000 copies have been sold to date. The Office of Publications also sells other inspirational and success-oriented books and tapes; puts out the *Stelle Letter,* which has a circulation of 5500; and publishes two specialized newsletters, *Parenting for Excellence* and *Personal Preparedness,* each with less than 500 subscribers. The latter assumes a collapse of the American economy and offers survivalist advice.

Possibly the greatest limiting factor in the growth of Stelle had been the requirement that residents become full members or resident associates of The Stelle Group. This did not mean necessarily accepting all of the beliefs set forth in *The Ultimate Frontier.* Indeed, the book and the group made a point of differentiating between information, which is what one reads or hears, and knowledge, which is what one learns from personal experience. Nevertheless, there had been a requirement for a personal commitment to the group's ideology and spiritual work.

There are three levels of membership: nonresident associate, resident associate, and full member. There are about 100 nonresident associates—people who have a strong interest in, but cannot move to, Stelle. A nonresident associate must have read the book, be in sympathy with the Brotherhoods' philosophy and committed to study and practice it, be willing to contribute skills and talents to the group and tithe to it, and attend guest week. Held three times a year, guest week gives interested persons and prospective residents a chance to live with a Stelle family, participate in community activities, and gain a better understanding of what Stelle is all about. Resident associates, of whom there are 29, must, in addition to the above, commit themselves to implementing the philosophy in their daily lives, furthering the work of the Brotherhoods' high personal and family virtues, participation in various courses, and the pursuit of excellence. Full membership is offered to residents who have completed the requisite course work and are considered to have the potential for achieving initiation into a Brotherhood in this lifetime. At present Stelle has 35 full members and the Adelphi Community has 24.

The homogeneity produced by these requirements has enabled Stelle to be, in some respects, a little utopia. The Cooperative Food Mart operates on the honor system. Residents take what they need and write down what they owe in a book on the counter. If something of value is found on the sidewalk it is likely to be pinned to a tree and left until the rightful owner comes along.

But while a lack of growth might seem utopian to some steady-state ecologists, it denies the premise of *The Ultimate Frontier* and undermines the effort to build a base for survival if Doomsday really comes. So in

1982 the group decided on a new strategy: to open the community to anyone who wanted to live there, without the requirement of participation in the group. Along with this was a plan to move the headquarters of the group to the smaller community of Adelphi in Texas where most of the more esoteric activities would be carried out. They hoped that the group members remaining at Stelle, along with the educational system, would be enough to maintain most of the ideals and atmosphere that have made Stelle unique. Like New Harmony after the dissolution of Robert Owen's experiment, there remain the seeds of a vital, innovative community. But as time goes on it will be less an intentional community and more a unique small town.

NEW AGE CITY. Intentional Community based on *The Ultimate Frontier* evolving into New Age City. Emphasis on personal & spiritual growth with varied transformational resources available in a mutually supportive environment. Innovative in education, self-development & technology. 125 residents, 42 homes, 240 acres, factory, businesses, schools, greenhouses, holistic health center. Free brochure. The Stelle Group, Box 312, Stelle IL 60919. (815) 256-2200.

This was one of a series of ads run in national magazines such as *New Age, Psychology Today, Mother Earth News,* and *Quest.* Stelle is now embarked on an all-out effort to create a new image and attract new blood. It uses the term New Age as defined by Kieninger: concerned with living in loving relationships with one's fellow men, working toward inner spiritual completeness, and being responsible for one's own life rather than yielding that responsibility to "experts."

Stelle is not technically a city—yet. Still an unincorporated village, it can become a municipality under Illinois law when its population reaches 200. That will give it more control over its environment than it now has, and it will allow it to keep more tax dollars in the community. It probably will also mean a public school system will be established alongside the private system.

Task forces are at work developing plans for many aspects of the new Stelle, including a package to attract new businesses to the community or the area. Residents feel that their way of life and world view make Stelle an attractive place for small businesses to locate. The community currently offers classes on entrepreneurship and prosperity, and is considering offering a variety of adult education courses to supplement those available at the community college, ten miles away. It is exploring the possibility of developing a residential and weekend growth center. A small holistic health center, started by a doctor who is a member of the group, is already in existence. In their most expansive dreams, members envision building a large educational center at Stelle—with perhaps a 3000 seat auditorium—and becoming the Esalen Institute of the Midwest.

A change in the population of Stelle necessarily means changes in the way that it is governed, since up through 1982 The Stelle Group governed the community. Under this government, members agreed to participate in all community business meetings, vote in all elections and referendums, and abide by the decisions of the majority. Any member could propose bylaws, resolutions, policies, or any other governing agreement. If a matter required more time than it could be given at a regular community meeting, it would be discussed at a public hearing, in small group discussions and task forces, or through written comments on the bulletin board in the mailroom. The executive function was handled by a board of trustees and a membership committee, both elected by the members for two-year terms. The judicial function was fulfilled by a panel of three mediators, also elected for two-year terms. If the parties in a dispute preferred other mediators, new mediators were drawn by lot from among all the adult members, and their decision was binding. The Bylaws provided that "failure by a Member to abide by a decision of a Review Panel as determined by a majority vote of the Mediators shall result in his automatic resignation from The Stelle Group.

Obviously this system would not work in a community in which members of The Stelle Group were in a minority. So at the end of 1982 Stelle worked out a transitional form of government, based on a Stelle Community Association. The Stelle Group itself was changed back to a more authoritarian structure, with Kieninger serving as Chairman for life. He was given the power to appoint the trustees, and the trustees were given the power to appoint the officers. The Stelle Community Association, on the other hand, includes as members all owners and occupants, divided into three classes. Class A members are individual owners, with one vote for each living unit they own. Class B members are adult occupants who have lived at Stelle for at least six months. The Stelle Group, as developer, is the class C member, with a vote for each platted vacant lot it owns. This gives The Stelle Group a dominant role at the beginning of the new community, but its role will gradually decline and finally cease when all lots have been sold, or by the end of 1987, whichever comes sooner. Only class A members can vote to establish the maximum annual assessments. On other matters affecting property, such as capital improvement assessments, a majority is required of both class A and class C votes. Both class A and class B members vote to elect directors and mediators and to enact resolutions not related to property.

A five-person board of directors was appointed by The Stelle Group, but at the end of their two-year terms the group will appoint two and three will be elected. When there are more class A votes than class C votes, The Group will continue to appoint one director every two years until all the lots have been sold.

The kind of rules that will be decided by majority vote of class A and class B members include those governing the keeping of animals; storage and use of vehicles and machinery; use of outdoor clothes drying lines, antennas, and trash containers; maintenance and removal of vegetation; and application of chemical or other kinds of fertilizers in accordance with pollution control standards. All such rules will be binding upon all members unless provided otherwise. Any member can challenge the appropriateness of any rule through a judicial process similar to the former one.

The intention, then, is to create a governing system similar to the earlier one, which, for a transition period, will be controlled by The Stelle Group. The members all hope that the new residents of the community will be of sufficiently like mind, and the process will be gradual enough, that many of their high standards will prevail in the future.

By the beginning of 1984, 35 people who were not members or associates of the group had moved to Stelle. Eight homes were sold during 1983, five of them to people not affiliated with the group. The Stelle Credit Union field of membership was expanded to include anyone who lives or works in six surrounding townships. The transition is underway. At this writing, we have no way of knowing what direction it will take. But we wouldn't be surprised if 150 years from now people who visit Stelle will hear about its contributions to our society, just as they do today in New Harmony.

Organic gardens at the Renaissance Community, with a large, multifamily house under construction at the rear.

CHAPTER 4
_____

The Renaissance Community: A Commune of the 1960s That Survived

> They make mistakes and they make big ones, but they make them fast
> so they learn fast.
> —PETER CADDY, one of the founders of Findhorn

During the 1960s a great many communes were established within the counterculture. Most of them waxed, waned, and died. Someone looking at the Renaissance Community during its first few years probably would have predicted a similar fate. It was a mob of teenage kids living together in squalid, cramped conditions, inviting all comers to join them, outraging the neighbors, and starting a series of businesses that promptly failed. In the summer of 1973 they had 365 members. They were so notorious that a national magazine ran an article about them entitled, "The Devil in Massachusetts."

But the Renaissance Community confounded its critics. As Peter Caddy later observed, it learned from its mistakes. In January 1984 it had 60 adult members and 45 children, was building a self-sufficient homestead on 80 acres in Gill, Massachusetts, and got along with its neighbors so well that its president was appointed to Gill's Finance Committee and its clerk was appointed clerk of Gill's Board of Selectmen. As with most young communities, a lot of coming and going has taken place. Nevertheless, the core is large and stable. Perhaps three-fourths of the current members have been with the community for eight years or more.

This is its story.

The year was 1968. Michael Rapunzel (he chose his own last name), then a strapping 17-year-old, had made the pilgrimage to California, been turned on by the Summer of Love in the Haight Ashbury, and come back to his hometown of Leyden, Masssachusetts. But back to what? What did a small, depressed factory town in northwestern Massachusetts have to offer a kid who had seen an entirely new way of life? Rapunzel went off to the woods and built a tree house to live in. He worked for some of the local farmers in exchange for part of their crop, and spent his evenings alone in meditation.

Soon a number of his friends joined him and the group grew to 8 people, all living in the tree house. The members began to realize the possibilities of what they could do together. They had strength, enthusiasm, openness, friendship, love, and excitement. One early member recalled, "If we went to town we were totally high; everybody else was down. They talked without any enthusiasm, as if they had nothing going for them, whereas we felt we had everything going for us, and yet, we had nothing physically."

The eighth person to come was a former girlfriend of Rapunzel's. She wanted to join the group even though she and Rapunzel didn't get along. This forced the members to look seriously at the nature of the group and decide how far the experiment should be allowed to grow. The members decided that if it was to be a family of people who shared ideals, it should be open to the world. The young woman was asked to stay.

As the group continued to grow, the conflicts between the values of the members and those of their parents' generation resulted in conflicts and confrontations between them and the outside community. Someone burned their tree house down while they were away at work. A month later, just before snowfall, they constructed a fifteen by thirty foot cabin using funds offered by a visiting psychologist. Over the next two years they moved a number of times within western Massachusetts and southern Vermont. It was a time of trying circumstances as they were confronted with both physical hardship and emotional conflict.

In the fall of 1969 the group rented a 17- by 40-foot bunkhouse at a summer camp in Heath, Massachusetts. It was uninsulated and heated only by a single wood stove. By midwinter 80 people were squeezed into this space. Sanitary facilities were primitive, the food was boring, but spirits were high. It was a combination love-in and encounter group all winter long. Visitors swarmed to Heath every weekend to share the experience.

Kathy Murphy was one of those people. She knew from early childhood that the world was not the way it was supposed to be. Guided by her inner awareness, she found herself a misfit at school and knew she could never settle into a so-called normal way of life. A friend had joined the community and suggested that she check it out. In July of 1969 Murphy did, and found the world she was looking for. She was particularly affected by Michael Rapunzel: "Michael has the ability to see into the deeper realities—what motivates people as well as what hangs them up. When I first met him we talked about things that really mattered to me. I had been waiting all my life to communicate with people on those levels."

Murphy joined the group in that early chaotic period. During the day the members took whatever jobs they could find, working for farmers, picking apples, and cutting firewood. The rest of the time they meditated, talked, and read. There was a core group of 12 people. Each of them led smaller groups, discussing problems at all levels from the personal to the cosmic. Rapunzel, who was the spiritual leader of the entire group, was helped in his own development by Elwood Babbitt, a well-known trance medium. Babbitt, the subject of a recent book by Charles Hapgood,* is known for his life readings, in which he looks back through a person's previous lives and offers advice based on his clairvoyant knowledge. In addition to working with Rapunzel, Babbitt gave several spiritual talks to the whole group and introduced the members to *The Aquarian Gospel of Jesus the Christ.*** This book, an esoteric treatment of Jesus' life and ministry, is now a principal text for the spiritual beliefs and practices of the group.

By the spring of 1970 the members of the group had chosen a name, the Brotherhood of the Spirit, and its period of explosive growth was underway. People came from all over; many from big cities such as Boston, New York, Philadelphia, and even as far away as Los Angeles. Sandy Howes, who now runs the office, was working in New York doing design for an urban planning firm. She decided one day in 1969 to abandon her career and head for Warwick. John Pollard, at one time president and now business consultant of the community, had just finished an M.B.A. at UCLA in 1970 when he dropped his career plans and came. People brought their skills, their enthusiasm, and what material resources they had. A couple of divorced women sold their houses. The funds were used to buy an old inn on ten acres in Warwick for $20,000. The group tore down old barns and used the materials to build a three-story dormitory. The size of the group peaked at about 365 people.

This was altogether too many kids for the small town of Warwick to absorb easily. While their labor was useful to the local farmers, they were also eager—some might say overeager—to demonstrate to the world their ideal of brotherhood. They sent teams down to the University of Massachusetts and the other colleges in Amherst on "teaching trips" to preach their principles and teach meditation to whomever would listen. It was during this period that they achieved their notoriety and a very active citizen's movement in Warwick was at work to force them out.

---

*Charles Hapgood, *Voices of Spirit Through the Psychic Experience of Elwood Babbitt* (New York: Dial/Delacorte, 1975).

**Levi, *The Aquarian Gospel of Jesus the Christ* (Marina del Rey, California: DeVorss & Co., 1907).

The group responded to this pressure in several ways. One was to disperse physically, buying properties over a 20-mile radius in nearby Northfield, Gill, and Turners Falls for its members. The second was for some to seek stable jobs and some to open their own businesses. They reasoned that these steps would both improve their image and give them a firmer financial base.

In 1974 one member found work in a nearby state institution for the retarded. Under an enlightened new director the school was undergoing a drastic change from its previous nineteenth-century character to a more humane and caring attitude. It made an excellent laboratory in which the group members could practice their beliefs, and they constituted a considerable pool of labor willing to take unglamorous jobs in an unglamorous place. During the next two years as many as 50 members at one time worked in all the departments there, their positions ranging from floor scrubber to administrator. It was a mutually beneficial relationship; each had profound effects on the other. The arrangement also helped many people in the nearby towns to view "those hippies" as responsible adults.

Many of the group members were musicians. Here was a natural asset to build on. In 1973 they formed several musical groups and played both locally and throughout the Northeast. Because of cost limitations, they built their own sound equipment. This led to the idea of renting it out to others, and the Burstin' Sun Sound Company was formed. They decided to record and produce their own music, and so the Renaissance Recording Studio was born.

One member went to work as a truck driver for a major rock group, an experience that led to another new business. Rock groups usually play one-night stands, requiring them to pack up their equipment as soon as the concert is over and hit the road for the next concert, driving through the night, and then spend several hours setting up at the new location. The pace is draining. Wouldn't there be a market, the truck-driving member reasoned, for a service that would provide a special bus equipped with beds in which the group and their support personnel could be driven quickly and comfortably? The result of this idea was Rockets, a business that buys old buses, guts their interiors, and completely rebuilds them as luxurious moving hotels, with bunks, bars, kitchenettes, and bathrooms. This business currently owns two converted buses that are rented out for about $4000 a week, complete with driver.

Most of the businesses were located in Turners Falls, where in 1972, the group bought an entire block of buildings, known as the *opera house block;* it had actually housed an opera house from the 1870s through the turn of the century. Later it was turned into a 500-seat movie theater. In the decline of this old factory town, it too had closed down. The

Renaissance Community (it adopted that name in 1975) thought it could bring about a renaissance in Turners Falls as well as in its own community. It gave the theater and the adjoining stores a complete overhaul. It built its recording studio in the balcony of the theater, complete with film and video equipment. In the stores it started many new businesses: a plumbing and refrigeration company, grocery store, pizza parlor, natural foods restaurant, and youth center, complete with pool tables and pinball machines. The latter was intended to attract the youth of the area so they could be befriended and counseled. As the kids grew up, the Renaissance Community would have an increasing body of influential local friends and supporters.

After several years of scattered living, the group felt the need to become more solidified again. Accordingly, in October 1975 it bought 80 acres in Gill that also included an old inn. Here it began the 2001 Center, intended to eventually become a self-sufficient homestead for all the members. The group has come full circle. Starting as a backwoods farm-working commune, it had evolved into a business and media community, and now has found a way to integrate the two on its own land.

During the past few years the emphasis has shifted away from the businesses and toward development of the 2001 Center. This reflects, in part, a failure to successfully operate most of its businesses. The community tried to do too much and overextended itself. And, as with so many other communities that we have visited, most of its members lack business acumen. For a while, almost anyone could get group support for a new project that he or she wanted to try. But Turners Falls just wasn't ready for the kind of renaissance the group had in mind. The businesses that were dependent on local clientele didn't make it. The Noble Feast Restaurant, for example, served good food and people came from Brattleboro and Amherst—each about 25 miles away—to enjoy it. But that was in the warm weather months. In the winter it was dead. In 1980 the group closed down the restaurant and its other businesses in Turners Falls, putting the opera house block up for sale.

The businesses that succeeded were those that didn't depend on local clientele: the buses and the Renaissance Greeting Card Company. The latter started very simply; a few cards were silk screened one Christmas to send to friends. The friends were so impressed that the following year they printed six different designs of black and white cards to send to friends, also offering them for sale to people on their mailing list. Again the response was good, so they moved on to full color cards, selling them wholesale to stores. In a few years the company was thriving, employing a dozen people and distributing cards throughout the United States as well as to the United Kingdom, Canada, and Australia.

But this too was not to last. The company is still thriving, but it is no longer a part of the community. In early 1981 most of the team that ran the company left the Renaissance Community and moved to Spring-vale, Maine, where they still run the company successfully, but do not live together as a community. The issue over which they separated was the way the community was run, particularly how it functioned finan-cially. It seems to us that the split was more a matter of personalities than principles. In any case, once the decision to leave was made, the people in the company negotiated an agreement with the community to buy out its assets. It was a fairly amicable separation; some of those who left still return to visit the community.

The town of Gill, with a population of about 2000 people, consists of a general store and a liquor store sandwiched between farms, large and small. At the north end of Gill, is Mount Harmon School, an excellent and prosperous prep school. Otherwise it is a fairly poor community that has little to hold its young people. The area has a typical New England look: rolling hills, a clump of woods here and there, and large old houses.

One-half mile north of the general store is a signboard on the right that announces: "The 2001 Center, School of the Ministry, All People and Visitors Welcome, 10–4." Behind it is a parking lot and the old stone building that was once an inn. Inside we are met by a gaggle of children taking a lunch break from the community's preschool. This building also houses many of the newer members and guests and some of them have gotten plates from the kitchen and brought them out to the tables in the front room.

Some 100 yards to the left is a large prefabricated metal industrial building where the buses are garaged. Inside is an extensive collection of metal and woodworking machines and tools, as well as the commu-nity laundromat. It is also the center for all vehicle repair.

A dirt road to the right of the old inn winds up around a hill that dominates the property. Passing the fledgling orchard one comes first to the "barn," a two-story building, about 30 by 80 feet, with nicely outfitted offices downstairs and a large hall upstairs that is suitable for meetings or dances. It was the first building constructed on the place and is now being retrofitted with solar heating panels.

Continuing on, one fork of the road ends in the woods, where two frame houses are under construction. Each will accommodate several couples and their children. The one we visit will have a separate room for each couple on one floor and rooms for the children on the floor above. The families will share a living room and kitchen. The quality of construction is good; the group is obviously building for the long haul.

On top of the hill two much larger dwellings are also under construc-tion, although the first of them actually has been in use for several years. It has a curvilinear look, with shingles that follow shapes of the building and its circular windows and doors in waves and swoops and drips. Its style is reminiscent of the architecture of the Spaniard Antonio Gaudi, or of Anthroposophist Rudolf Steiner's followers who design curves in everything to follow the patterns of nature. Around the south side of the building an arc of glass forms a solar greenhouse. It warms the house with the winter sun while permitting the occupants to grow winter vegetables and spring seedlings. The greenhouse edges into the large living room, separated by a glass wall that can be opened. The living room is dominated by a sunken area that is used for meetings and a gigantic free-standing fireplace whose chimney soars upward 30 feet to the ceiling. The wood furnace in the basement was designed by Richard Hill an engineering professor from Orono, Maine, featuring a fan that blows a jet stream of air across the fire to ensure rapid and complete combustion. The house, which accommodates about 30 people, is dramatic in its scope and thoughtful in its details. For example, a second-floor bathroom has a curved cubicle housing the toilet; at the eye level of anyone sitting on it is a six-by-ten inch window providing a view of the woods.

Beyond the house is a fenced organic garden; its neatness and raised beds indicate that the gardeners are practitioners of the biodynamic-organic and intensive French gardening methods first developed in Santa Cruz by Alan Chadwick and later disseminated through several popular books. The beds, carefully constructed of screened earth mixed with manure and compost, enable the community to grow two or three generations of crops each year.

On the other side of the garden is another house under construction, a huge frame some 60 to 70 feet high. Less curvilinear than the house on the hill, it is equally dramatic, with many split levels inside.

A Barre, Vermont, architectural firm, Sanford, Sellers and McClay, spent a year helping plan the new buildings and developing an overall site plan in exchange for $2500 cash and the community's labor to carry out the plan. A large model of the site plan is on display in the barn.

The group hopes ultimately to make the place entirely self-sufficient. After the houses are finished the members plan to install a large windmill to pump water and generate electricity for domestic use. About 40 solar panels already are installed on some of the buildings. One of the members snapped them up at a fraction of their value when a contractor building solar condominiums in Vermont went out of business. Although the group grows some of its own food it is still far from self-sufficient. Its members plan that it will be.

These plans, and the name 2001, reflect an awareness of the various prophecies of seers such as Edgar Cayce regarding earth changes and social chaos occurring at the end of this century. This center is intended to be a Noah's ark in preparation for that eventuality. But it is more than that. It permits a way of life that integrates the ideals of the group members. As one member, John Charamella, said, "We believe that we are moving into an age of spiritual change—away from a materialistic orientation toward a more spiritual one. Being self-sufficient allows you to live a more spiritual life. Being in touch with nature helps the spirit find its center."

It is easy to be overwhelmed by the massive amount of energy going into construction and overlook the spiritual basis of the group. A hand-out sheet given to people interested in visiting or joining the group says:

Our vision of the 2001 Center, is that of a self-sufficient community: an environment where people from different backgrounds can live together and learn about each other: where members can unfold the creative energies within themselves in an atmosphere of love, joy, and wisdom. We are incorporating as much alternative technology as possible, including passive solar design, under-ground design, gravity fed water with wind powered pumps and wood heating. Yet at the same time we are growing an awareness of a true spiritual technology, where through meditation and living communally in a close attunement with nature we are learning to be self-sufficient within ourselves, exploring the beauty of unlimited human potential that exists in each of us, to care for the earth, to love ourselves and others and to be truly sensitive.

The Renaissance Community is a community where people live and work together and share a common philosophy, the pinnacle of which is the desire for God consciousness.

We are an open community in that we welcome anyone who is willing to work with us in attaining this consciousness.

We believe that all people can live together in compliance with the seven immutable laws if that is their desire. (The seven immutable laws are: order, balance, harmony, growth, God perception, spiritual love, and compassion.)

While the Renaissance Community likes to call itself open, it is not a crash pad or drop-in center. Prospective members are interviewed carefully to see that they understand the purposes and the rules of the group and the fact that they are expected to work six days a week. Saturdays are devoted to group projects, working on the land or the houses. Visitors may stay for up to two weeks. At the end of that time they are usually ready to leave or settle in. Most new members are in their twenties; some have been as young as 16 (with their parents' consent); some are in their mid-thirties.

Most of the members of the community are in their twenties or thirties, with the average age perhaps 27 or 28. About 60 adults and 45 children are in residence. About 5 of the children are infants; about 20 are in the day care center; and about 20 are in school. The oldest child of members is a 16-year-old girl. Of the adults there are more couples than singles, though only about five couples are legally married. The general consensus is that it doesn't make much difference. On the other hand, when people do get married it is cause for much celebration. In two instances large weddings were held, with many of the town residents invited.

More members of this group have working class backgrounds than at many spiritual communities we studied. Perhaps 20 percent have a college education, and those that do usually work at skilled labor for the group; that is what is needed in this phase of building.

There is no membership fee. Every member takes a vow of poverty. In theory, members are expected to turn over all personal assets to the group. In practice, only major items, such as cars, are owned communally. People with a substantial bank account or real estate can wait six months or more before transferring these assets, to make sure that they really feel they want to be a full member of this group. Once an individual signs a vow of poverty, however, he or she signs over these assets. Should a member decide to leave, everything earned while having been a member remains with the group, but assets brought into the group may be returned.

The group is not doctrinaire about food. A few members are vegetarians and the cook is macrobiotic; but most eat meat. They also eat a lot of tofu, beans, and brown rice. For years drinking was banned, but a couple years ago Michael Rapunzel decided that was too strict. One night he arrived at dinner with a large jug of wine. Everyone had a glass and they decided it wasn't so bad after all. Now a moderate amount of beer and wine is drunk by many of the members. Marijuana and other drugs are banned, but this rule is somewhat flexibly enforced. We heard about one person who had been a heroin junkie. Now when he wants a little grass the group turns a blind eye, happy over the progress he has made.

The main sources of income for the group are a weekly donation for room and board, plus a monthly fee for utilities and taxes. Two service companies, the Renaissance Builders and Renaissance Excavating and Rockets (the bus company), bring in a large portion of the money. The builders take an expense allowance for weekly pocket money and put the balance of the money they make into the 2001 Fund to get new houses built. One of the women runs the Top-Notch Cleaning Service, which provides a way to use unskilled labor to bring in some money. No one is paid for work done in the community. Debbie Edson, the president, works for the group four days a week, gets free room and board, and then cleans house one day a week for pocket money.

The governing of the community operates largely by consensus. Because there is a high level of consensus among the oldtimers, the process often does not need to be carried out in any formal sense. Individual initiative is stressed: "Anybody can do anything if they can do it" or

"If you see it, you do it." This seems to work well on the whole, though difficulties do arise.

All meetings are opened with an "attunement," that is, a few minutes of group meditation. Usually they are chaired by Michael Rapunzel, or in his absence, by Kathy Murphy or Debbie Edson. Religious services are held on Sunday afternoons. Community meetings are held on Monday, Tuesday, and Thursday evenings and individual house meetings are held on Wednesday evenings. The meetings, which are mandatory, serve several purposes: to work out conflicts and make decisions, as well as provide a time for group meditation and socializing.

The Renaissance Community is unarguably a success, even though it has had a great many failures. It enjoys generally good relations with its neighbors. Steve Striebel, the chief of police in Warwick—once the scene of so much animosity—is now a close friend and spent three weeks helping the group build the massive chimney in one of the houses. Robin Paris, the community's clerk, is clerk of the Gill board of selectmen and writes a Gill newsletter that is given away in the general store and the liquor store. Rapunzel ran for selectman in Turners Falls and was badly defeated. But he, or others, will run again. Members are encouraged to vote and in a small community such as Gill their votes certainly count.

The good will of the larger community is also courted through various events, such as weddings and dances, which draw neighbors into the 2001 Center. And the neighboring farmers and homeowners appreciate what is being done to save energy and develop the land in an ecologically sound way. As one group member said, "We've tried to persuade the townspeople that, if we are weirdos, at least we're nice ones."

They are nice ones and they are very hard-working ones. When the year 2001 arrives, we expect to see them still going strong.

A universal worship service held on Sundays at the Abode.

CHAPTER 5

The Abode of the Message: Sufis in the Footsteps of the Shakers

THE SHAKERS

Here established, 1787,
First community in America,
A celibate order devoted to
"Hands to work, hearts to God."

—Signboard on the road to
the Abode of the Message

The Shakers began as a small branch of radical English Quakers who adopted the practices of shaking, shouting, dancing, whirling, and speaking in tongues. The American branch was founded by Ann Lee, an illiterate textile worker from Manchester, England, who, after experiencing persecution and imprisonment for noisy worhsip services, had a series of revelations that convinced her she was the female aspect of God's dual nature and the second incarnation of Christ. In the spring of 1774 she arrived in America with a band of eight followers, responding to a new revelation that she was to establish her church in the New World. Following Lee's death in 1784, the new leadership established the communal pattern that was to be the Shaker social organization for the next century and a half. Based on a belief in celibacy, equality of the sexes, and communal ownership of property, the Shaker faith taught its followers to "give hands to work and hearts to God." The exalting of this faith took the form of joyful singing and dancing, and was also expressed in the great skill and artistry that the Shakers brought to all their tasks. Their industry and ingenuity produced numerous inventions, of which the screw propeller, the circular saw, and the clothespin are but a few.

In 1787 Elder Joseph Meachum, the new leader, established the first organized Shaker settlement on the slopes of Mount Lebanon, New

York. From this location, far away from the temptations of the world, missionaries were sent out to begin other settlements throughout the country. At the height of the popularity of the faith during the 1840s, Mount Lebanon was home to nearly 600 Shakers, and about 6000 others lived in 18 communities in New England and as far away as Indiana and Kentucky. But the Shaker practice of celibacy was an obstacle to the group's continuation, since no children were born into the faith. The group declined after that period, dropping to about 1000 by 1900 and to just a handful of elderly survivors today. Shaker villages have become museums or have been converted to other uses. Some Shakers continued to live on Mount Lebanon until 1950. A number of the buildings were turned into a private school; others served as a summer camp. The latter eventually failed; the mortgage was foreclosed on, and in the mid-1970s the land and buildings were put up for sale.

In the early 1920s another spiritual movement began to assert itself in Europe. Called the Sufi Order in the West, it was started by a noted Indian musician, Hazrat Inayat Khan. Although Sufism traces its roots back to pre-Islamic faiths, it has much in common with the mystical aspects of Islam.

Sufism is a way of looking at the world and a way of living in the world. Ideally, it helps its practitioners understand the physical and spiritual relationship of the individual with both the self and with all things outside the self. Sufism, according to Inayat Khan, is a way for humanity to awaken to the true meaning of life and discover the divinity of humanity—not only within the individual, but in religion, science, energy, business, health, government, education, art—every aspect of life. As Inayat Khan wrote: "If there is any moral principle that the Sufi movement brings, it is this: that the whole of humanity is like one body, and any organ which is hurt or troubled can indirectly cause damage to the whole body."*

On his death, Hazrat Inayat Khan was succeeded by his young son, Pir Vilayat Inayat Khan, who was raised in Europe but has spent most of the past two decades in the United States. Thus the Sufi Order, which is international in scope, has its headquarters in the United States. The younger Inayat Khan has gained a following of thousands— mostly young people—who are attracted not only by Sufi ideals, but also by the practices, which include daily prayer and meditation, weekly worship that recognizes all major religions, whirling, sacred music, and dance.

In 1975 Pir Vilayat and some of his principal followers began looking for land on which to establish a community. The search began on the

*G. Coates, ed., *Resettling America: Energy, Ecology and Community* (Boston: Brick House, 1981), 137.

West Coast and then moved to the South Atlantic states, where the soil is good and the climate pleasant. His vision called for 100 people on 500 to 1000 acres. Just before final action was to be taken on land in South Carolina, the planners learned of the Mount Lebanon site—450 acres, mostly on the side of the mountain. The land was expensive, the area had a harsh climate and short growing season, the buildings had been neglected and were in need of repair. And yet, the leadership and Pir Vilayat felt some call. Perhaps here was where the Sufis were really supposed to be. Their practices and beliefs paralleled those of the Shakers in some ways, particularly the ideals of simplicity, work, perfection, daily prayer, whirling, and dance. The idea quickly took hold and the decision was made: the Sufis would resettle and rebuild the Shaker community. The property cost $350,000 with a big mortgage ballooning at the end of ten years. But it had to be done and it was done. Enough money was raised from a variety of large and small contributions to make the down payment and, in May 1975, the first crew of 20 people moved in and started preparing the new community for the 75 people expected there by the end of the summer.

As the Abode of the Message—as the new community was called—has developed its own history and spirit, the feeling of carrying on the Shaker tradition has abated. But it was strong in those early months, and the pioneers gave a lot of thought to how to work harmoniously with the spiritual tradition they had chosen to inherit. They had to work hard to restore the buildings to livable condition, plow and plant the fields, and plan for the governance and inner life of the community. The early days were far from easy. The adjustment to community life, lack of space and privacy, hard work, and lack of money all required a great deal of patience on the part of the members. Most of the new residents did not know each other initially, and many had conflicting views about the purpose and direction of the community. The principles of Sufism were put to the test as the residents worked their way through these problems.

Although Pir Vilayat served (and continues to serve) as president of the community, he was absent a great deal more than he was present. The day-to-day leadership fell primarily on Stephen Rechtshaffen, a young physician from New York City, and Taj Inayat, an American woman in her thirties who is Pir Vilayat's Spiritual Partner and the mother of his two sons. Working under Pir's guidance, Rechtshaffen, as vice-president, focalized the administrative and material leadership while Taj Inayat emphasized spiritual and esoteric leadership.

The history of the changes the Abode went through in working out its economic base illustrates very well the movement from egalitarian idealism toward a much more individualized approach that we have seen repeated in a number of communities. The goal of the residents of the Abode was to develop an economic structure that would allow each individual to meet financial needs while also contributing equitably to the community.

The basic components of the economic structure had been planned well in advance of the community's establishment. The system, which was intended to encourage cooperation and not competition, allowed for shared work as well as individual incentive. Initially, each community member was asked to donate $500 to the Abode as an admission fee, in addition to paying $500 for five months' rent and food. It was hoped that by the end of five months the community would achieve economic self-sufficiency. Because of the great financial need of the community (large mortgage, high taxes, building repairs, new businesses in need of financing), this goal was not achieved for 18 months.

Despite this, at the end of the first five months the community began experimenting with a credit system, with all work given one credit per hour. In addition, each person was expected to give some time to community service—the principle of karma yoga. The value of the credit was determined by dividing the total community income by the number of credits earned each month. Credits earned by each person were tallied, rent deducted, and the balance deposited in a credit pool bank from which it could be withdrawn, on demand, in cash. This didn't work well because there was so little money in the system. Total credits increased faster than total income. In order to earn enough credits to meet rent and basic living expenses, each adult had to work more than 50 hours per week and this wasn't feasible for parents with children.

The next step was to institute profit sharing. This allowed those whose outside work brought income into the community to keep a percentage of the gross amount earned. It encouraged people to bring in more money, since it benefited both the individual and the community. It also, however, reduced the incentive to perform those jobs that earned only credits and had no profit sharing, leading people to slack off on those jobs.

A problem with karma yoga also arose. Some people felt their work was so vital that extra time given to it should be considered their contribution toward karma yoga. This was allowed, but was later seen as a mistake that undermined the idea of selfless service to the community.

By the end of the second year the residents felt that the credit system had become hopelessly complex, and it was abandoned for a system that paid cash salaries for specific jobs. With this system all members donated, after payment of food, rent and medical expenses, 40 percent of their remaining incomes to the community. This splitting of income provided a source of support for the community and helped link members financially, while giving each member the primary responsibility for his or her own finances. Shortly after this system was instituted, the Abode experienced a substantial increase in income through a large influx of visitors, new memberships, stabilization of community businesses, and increased opportunities for community members to work outside in local private businesses. The ideal of karma yoga was restored and, as people ceased to view such jobs as sources of income, they were performed with greater joy.

A further step away from egalitarianism was taken in the summer of 1981, when the splitting of income was abolished. Members now pay just for food and rent and some make a small donation each month to support the religious activities of the community.

From the start, the Abode set a goal of developing several community businesses that would largely support the community. It planned to operate businesses that would offer products and services that benefit people while at the same time supporting the community. The profits accruing from each business were to be used by that business for reinvestment and wages. All were incorporated under a for-profit corporation called the Winged Heart Corporation.

The Reza Quality Bakery was the first of the Abode's cottage industries. At its height it supplied health food stores and supermarkets within a large radius of the Abode with seven kinds of whole grain breads and other products, as well as supplying the kitchen at the Abode with all its baked goods. Another early enterprise was the Heart and Wings Volkswagen Repair Shop. A member from Kansas had supported himself for several years with such an operation and wanted to do the same in the community. With funds from the community he set up shop in Pittsfield, Massachusetts, nine miles away, and developed a reputation for honest and reliable service.

In an effort to find a better way to heat and insulate the Abode buildings, some members began to study energy efficiency. This included research into wood burning heat, solar heat, methane, insulation, and fuel-saving devices, and led the community to establish the Winged Heart Energy Systems, a business that supplied and installed wood stoves, fuel oil-saving devices, wood splitters, and composting toilets.

Mount Lebanon Natural Foods was established as a food distributing company, distributing health foods to local grocers as well as supplying the Abode itself.

At the same time some members set up private businesses, which were privately capitalized. Stephen Rechtshaffen, M.D., established the Springs Health Center in Lebanon Springs, three miles away, as a holistic health center offering both members and townspeople a complete health care system. Abode artisans made and sold stained glass, weavings, jewelry, and clothing in their own private shops. Other members began an earthmoving operation, called Earthworks, a horseshoeing business, and several small importing businesses.

Today, other than the thriving Springs Health Center, and a few individual crafts operations, these businesses are no more. What went wrong?

The businesses suffered from undercapitalization, overexpansion, poor management, and a high rate of turnover—often holding people for only three months or so. A large part of the problem with the community businesses was simply that no one had a personal stake in them, so no one exerted the energy and care necessary to make them successful. After the man who started the garage went back to Kansas, the others had little interest in keeping it going. Car repair is not a natural mix with the contemplative life. It was the same with the bakery. There weren't many people who would wake up in the morning, ask themselves the question, "What do I want to do with my life," and then answer it with, "Be a Baker!"

The businesses also suffered from the antiprofit, anticapitalist attitude prevalent among the members of America's counterculture. As a result, the Abode members often didn't keep good books or know exactly where they stood financially.

The bakery and garage closed down in August 1980. The alternative energy business lasted a year longer. As many similar businesses did in 1980–1981, it overexpanded and then business dropped off precipitously, leaving it with a large inventory of slow-moving merchandise. The food distributing company was sold to one of the Abode members, who continues to operate it on a very small scale, primarily as a retail operation for the Abode. The Winged Heart Corporation, parent of all these failures, was left with a debt of about $20,000 that it probably will never pay off.

The Abode also went through other major changes in the years 1980 and 1981. In 1980 Stephen Rechtshaffen left the community. His holistic health clinic was thriving and he was giving more and more time to the Omega Institute, another Sufi organization, which puts on training courses and seminars in a variety of subjects. He still lives nearby, however, and feels close to the community. In 1981 Taj Inayat moved to Santa Fe with a group of members of the community to start a new Sufi retreat there. At the same time, the Sufi Order Secretariat also moved to Santa Fe. These moves led to a substantial reduction in the membership of the community, brought new leadership, and resulted in many changes in the operation and feel of the community.

Akbar Scott was a lawyer in Boston who had allowed his practice to dwindle while he and his wife Aziza, both Sufis, pursued their spiritual interests and ran an elementary school for 80 children. They were considering going to India so Akbar could study music in the town where Hazrat Inayat Khan had lived. They knew they were ready for a change. Then they got a call from Pir Vilayat Inayat Khan, asking them to come to the Abode and take over its leadership. They accepted and their vocations changed totally while the spiritual and material aspects of their lives were brought into greater harmony than ever before.

While Akbar and Aziza have maintained the basic governing pattern established by Pir Vilayat, they have changed some elements of the style of government. Prior to starting the community, Pir Vilayat had designed the basic administrative structure as a merging of democracy and hierarchy. He believed that, at its worst, a democratic method of governing can be tedious, ineffective, and encourage extreme individualism, while a hierarchical form of governing can be oppressive, encourage extreme conformity, and be damaging to the development of the individual. Pir Vilayat sought a balance between these two extremes.

The hierarchical structure of the Abode consists of the president, Pir Vilayat, who is ultimately responsible for the direction of the community, and two vice-presidents, the Scotts, who have the responsibility of running the community on a day-to-day basis. Akbar's duties include chairing the executive committee (the chief decision-making body) and the family meetings. Aziza chairs the esoteric committee and the admissions committee. Each attends the meetings of the other's committees, as well as any other meetings important to the overall governing of the community. In all aspects of their jobs they are expected to view the Abode in its wholeness and make decisions with the guidance of Pir Vilayat in mind.

During the leadership transition, Akbar and Aziza spent a good deal of time feeling out the community: learning to trust the members and gaining their confidence. Akbar views its method of governance as a lot like the British constitution: unwritten but strong nevertheless. As a musician, he thinks of governing as the art of creating harmony amidst counterpoint. He emphasizes that humility is the first quality of a good leader.

Controversial matters are first discussed at the family meeting, where all members of the community get together once a month. If a solution is not obvious, the matter is then discussed by the executive committee, a representative body of community members that meets weekly. Everyone expresses how he or she feels and usually a compromise is agreed on. Sometimes people agree to disagree. Akbar feels that the handling of the controversy is more important than the settlement.

One example of such a controversy concerned the problem of deer, who were eating the crops. The farm crew felt that something needed to be done about them. Some members wanted to shoot and eat the deer. Sun Bear, an American Indian, visited the community during that time and encouraged this course of action. On the other hand the community had been established as a wildlife sanctuary and many thought that they should not violate the animals' trust. Pir Vilayat sided with this view since the deer flesh was not really needed as food. After a long family meeting the members decided to wait a few days to make a decision. In the meantime the farm crew decided that the deer were not that much of a problem after all, so the issue evaporated.

The Abode occupies 450 acres. It has several large and several small old Shaker buildings. About a dozen private houses have been built. A great many improvements, funded partially with a federal historic preservation grant, have been made in the old buildings. The community cultivates 10 acres; 5 in vegetables and 5 in grains and beans. There is also 1 acre planted in fruit trees, 1 in strawberries and asparagus, and ½ acre in herbs. As the community expands its cultivated land, it hopes to raise more grains and beans and some cash crops. During the summer members eat mostly from the gardens and freeze and can as much as possible for the winter. The members have built a beautiful solar-heated greenhouse to extend the growing season, and a large root cellar for cold weather storage.

On the hill above the community is an area for summer camps and retreats with its own kitchen, bathrooms, and meditation huts. Retreats involving 20 to 60 outside people are held monthly and the summer camp may draw 200 or more people. On the very top of the hill is an imposing stone-and-wood sanctuary whose form suggests four Buddhas seated back to back, facing in four directions, while their bodies merge into one being. They symbolize both the enlightened individual and the unity of humanity in the ideal of perfection. Their heads form a glass turret whose light is the light of understanding.

Community vehicles include a four-wheel drive, ¾-ton truck with snowplow; a pickup truck; a 1½-ton truck for hauling wood; an old dump truck; a station wagon; a Volkswagen camper; two tractors; a hay bailer; a bean combine; and a crawler-loader with back hoe. Most members have their own private cars, but if a member wants to borrow one of the community vehicles for private use he or she pays about 40¢ a mile to do so.

The Abode community consists of about 60 adults and 20 children. About half the adults are single; the rest are couples and single parents. Most adult members are in their twenties and thirties; the oldest are in their sixties. Canadians and Europeans occasionally visit for short periods, but immigration laws make it difficult for them to stay. One black is in residence; the rest of the members are white. Probably 30 percent to 50 percent have college backgrounds and this percentage is gradually rising. But no one has ever really charted these differences, since one of the major objectives of Sufi teaching is to rise above the differences that divide people. One doesn't have to be a Sufi to live at the Abode; it is enough to be dedicated to a spiritual life and to have respect for the Sufi path.

Few of the members had experience living in other intentional communities, although many had lived in Sufi group houses, called *Khanqahs,* in different cities. This is one of the common ways in which people learn the principles and practices of Sufism. The Sufis also hold summer camps in the United States and Europe, where the Abode is publicized. Pir Vilayat sometimes sends people to live at the Abode.

Visitors may stay for a month. After three days they are invited to a meeting of the six-member admissions committee, chaired by Aziza, to get acquainted. If they become candidates for membership, they must pay rent and donate their labor for two weeks. There is usually a two- to three-month waiting period before a final decision is made, and during that time they continue to meet with the admissions committee monthly. The Abode expects people to make a 100 percent commitment of their energy and enthusiasm while they are residents, but there is no particular expectation about how long they will stay. They are asked to meet again with the admissions committee if they decide to leave.

Except for the large exodus of residents to Santa Fe in early 1981, the usual turnover has been about 10 percent to 15 percent per year. As the community businesses folded, the Abode began to attract fewer youthful seekers and more older, self-directed people. Akbar is pleased with this development and relieved not to have the businesses anymore: "When you don't provide employment for people, they need to take responsibility for themselves. They progress more that way."

The Abode does employ about 15 of its members as staff. They receive a basic salary of $480 a month, and more if they have children and need it. Salaried staff include Akbar, the farm manager, head cook, office administrator, and various maintenance workers including one who cuts wood full time. Aziza takes no pay from the community but gets about $200 a month from running its retreat program. The rest of the work is done by karma yoga and by apprentices during the summer months.

The apprentices work at the Abode through a program called the Earth Light Apprentice Program. It offers participants the opportunity to become proficient at a skill while taking part in community life and establishing regular meditation and spiritual practices. Apprentices pay $140 a week while they work and learn carpentry, herb and flower gardening, organic gardening, or nutrition and natural foods cooking and baking. The program offers four one-month sessions beginning each June.

The farming is done mostly to meet the Abode's own needs; it has neither the food surplus nor the marketing skills to sell much of it outside. In addition to raising, cooking, and storing food and repairing and maintaining the buildings, the Abode runs a small bookstore, which makes most of its sales to visitors. The books are also sold at conferences and sessions of the Omega Institute.

The community holds frequent spiritual retreats and seminars, which bring in visitors and income. It also plans to set up a more formal school for Sufi instruction, similar to Pendle Hill, the Quaker school near Philadelphia which runs a six-month residential course on Quaker ideas.

The Omega Institute was started by Abode residents, though there is no formal connection. Pir Vilayat Inayat Khan is chairman of the board and Stephen Rechtshaffen runs the organization. For several years the Omega Institute operated from rented school campuses not far from the Abode, making it easy for community members to help out and for persons attending its courses to also visit the Abode. In 1982, however, the institute purchased a summer camp about an hour away from New York City as the new location for its programs. While this made it easier for the institute to attract an audience, its link to the Abode became weaker.

Members of the Abode community are also involved in the operation of the Mountain Road Children's School, located about eight miles away in Stephentown, New York. All but one of its staff of five full-time and two part-time teachers are members of the community, and about half of its nearly 50 students come from the community. The school was founded in 1975 to provide an education through which children could develop mentally, physically, socially, and spiritually. It offers a pre-school for three-year-olds and four-year-olds, and kindergarten through sixth grade for older children. It owns its own building, a 16-room, 150-year-old Dutch Colonial on 22 acres, which served during the 1920s as a finishing school for young ladies. Sufi teachings are not emphasized in the curriculum; the intention is rather to offer a high-quality private education that incorporates a spiritual awareness into its program.

Daily life at the Abode includes considerable spiritual content. The day begins at 6:30 with morning meditation. Breakfast is at 7:00, and work usually begins between 8:00 and 9:00. Midday prayers are at 12:15 and lunch at 12:30. Evening meditation is at 5:30 and dinner at 6:00. Classes or meetings usually begin about 7:30. The group prayers and meditations are not mandatory and attendance at them fluctuates. Usually between 6 and 12 people show up for those in the morning and at noon, while the evening ones average 15 to 20. Two classes are offered each week. The esoteric teaching class is the more popular. The other class consists of music, dance, whirling, and selected readings.

Sunday is set aside for welcoming visitors and sharing in universal worship. This service was originated by Hazrat Inayat Khan and is an expression of reverence and gratitude for the light brought to humanity through all religions, both those they know about and those they don't. Each service involves participation in a reading and a practice—usually singing or dancing—from each of several of the world's major religions. Attendance at universal worship has grown over the years and usually includes 40 to 50 people. Many former members come back from time to time for these services, as well as neighbors and friends from miles around.

While the members of the community regard themselves as members of one large family, it is frequently difficult for all to feel connected. With busy schedules, buildings that were designed with few common spaces, and many families living in their own homes as much as one-half mile away from the center, it is often hard for all to feel fully involved with each other. They have found that if a conscious effort at getting together in a social way is not made, some members feel as if they are lonely in a crowd. One way of dealing with this lack of space and time for the cultivation of personal relationships is by following Pir Vilayat Inayat Khan's advice:

Sometimes one just has to find one's own rhythm and one's own vibrations, and that is very difficult when one is with many people, for one wants to be alone or to be able to do things that don't matter, not like meditating, which really matters. One wants to perhaps read a newspaper or play ball or let the children play horse on one's back, or even just laugh without any meaning, like the Tibetan and Christian monks who have a time in the day when they laugh for half an hour without any reason. We don't have to institutionalize laughter. I think that something that's called for is having a time during the day when it's not kosher to work. Much as we have things to do, we just do something else.*

Among the activities that bring people together are a family concert series in which members of the Abode "family" present an evening of music and poetry, and an Abode classical choir that meets once a week and performs at community celebrations. Several dramas are also performed each year. The Abode softball team is part of the Lebanon Valley Softball League, providing contact with the surrounding community, as well as exercise for Abode members.

The original scheme for building houses at the Abode was that the members would have help from the community in the construction work, and then the community would buy out their investment over a period of time. The community is rethinking this method, however, and may move to private ownership of houses. Some people have grouped together to live in communal houses or in clusters of houses. These people are thus able to be together in a peaceful, relaxed setting, without the constant pressure of the Abode's schedule.

Members living in houses away from the main complex may choose to remain on the Abode meal schedule and eat in the communal dining room, or they may prepare meals in their own kitchens. A rent reduction is given to those who prepare their own meals. All members, however, are encouraged to eat one meal a day in the communal dining room to maintain contact with the others. The communal diet used to be strictly vegetarian, but it is now "nonideological," with fish once a week and chicken once or twice a month. No red meat, white sugar, or white flour are used in the group cooking, and organic products are

*Ibid., 149.

used as far as possible. On their own, however, people can cook and eat whatever they want.

All in all, the atmosphere at the Abode is a free one. Within the context of a common spiritual orientation, the keynote is discretion and consideration of other people. Alcoholic beverages can be consumed privately but they are not served by the community. Members, however, cannot use illegal drugs or get drunk. A single person pays $235 a month, and is expected to work four hours a week and one-half day a month as karma yoga. For this the member gets a private room, all he or she can eat, and good company in a spiritual environment.

The Abode now often attracts people who have growing careers outside the community. This means that they spend time in, and have friends in, Albany or Pittsfield or New Lebanon. The Abode, as a result, is less isolated and more integrated into the surrounding community. And the Abode has now been in existence long enough that most people in the area have been there or know a resident personally. Several years ago the mother of a youthful visitor became concerned and called the state police. The police officer was not only reassuring; he told her that he encourages people to visit the community! Local newspaper articles have been favorable, frequently mentioning the Shaker connection. The Abode holds an open house and fair on its birthday every June so that its neighbors can see what it is all about, and looks for opportunities to put on plays or concerts in the surrounding area. At Christmas 1983 its choir sang in the local Catholic church. The Abode is a member of the Network of Light, a group of New England spiritual communities that meet four times a year, on the solstices.

While Pir Vilayat has spent little time in the community in recent years he plans to return and make his residence there in the Fall of 1984. Now in his late sixties, he seems ready to play a less active role in running the international Sufi order, leaving more of the leadership to Taj Inayat operating from the Secretariat headquarters in New Mexico.

The Abode of the Message is a community that has gone through its growing pains, changed its style, and settled down for the long haul. Since it does not demand as high a level of commitment as many other communities we have visited, it may in the future become more of a mainstream community and attract people who don't wish to become Sufis but enjoy living in the kind of atmosphere they create.

Members of the Rochester Folk Art Guild raising the wall for a new building.
RFAG photo.

CHAPTER 6

The Rochester Folk Art Guild: Creating Pots and People

There is an entire book of knowledge in a craft that parallels the laws of becoming a whole person. You can understand something through a craft that you couldn't get from a thousand books.

Here we have the chance, with the larger community, to make conditions for more hopeful human living together. By helping each other in the tasks of daily life and striving for better exchange, there comes more time. And with that, more freedom for creation.

As I work with the clay, I try to find a quiet place in myself. A much finer relationship can then begin to grow. Our wish is to carry this quality of attention to everything we do.

—MEMBERS OF THE ROCHESTER FOLK ART GUILD

In November 1982 the Renwick Gallery of the Smithsonian Institution in Washington, D.C., held an exhibition to celebrate the twenty-fifth anniversary of the Rochester Folk Art Guild. The voices above belong to some of these 45 artisans who live on East Hill Farm in the Finger Lakes Region of New York State, in a unique community.

The members of the guild work anonymously, as folk artists in traditional cultures have always done. Guild members feel that much of contemporary art has become a form of personal aggrandizement and is dominated by the belief that one has to constantly make something new and different. The guild pursues another aim: "We use the crafts as a tool for seeing, and persevering in the struggle with our egoism. The pot is not mine to sign. It is the result of my being fortunate enough to work under the conditions created by the guild. To put my name alone on it would not be true."

Most of the people here had no previous artistic training. What drew them to the community was the opportunity to learn and practice the principles of inner development formulated by G. I. Gurdjieff. It is his teachings that set the tone for everything that happens on this farm. We were very impressed with the beauty of the place, the people, and their products.

Gurdjieff was born in the Caucasus, in Russia near the Turkish border, in the 1870s, spent much of his youth seeking the sources of esoteric wisdom from the Middle East to Tibet, and finally began teaching in Russia just before the 1917 revolution. Driven out of Russia by the revolution, he and his followers eventually made their way to Paris, where he established the Institute for the Harmonious Development of Man, and where he continued to teach until his death in 1949.

The Work, as it is called, requires that the student use the experiences of daily life as the basis for self-study and self-development. The principles behind the Work are that as people are, they are not awake or conscious beings, but through a special kind of work on themselves it is possible for them to acquire much that they do not now possess. This, however, cannot be done alone. Gurdjieff taught that to escape from the emptiness of ordinary life requires the help of others who are more developed, some kind of organization, and a great deal of cooperation. Gurdjieff Work usually includes group meetings with a teacher, where the issues of self-observation, struggle with negative emotions, and work with bodily sensation are explored. The aim throughout is to develop simultaneously the three centers: intellectual, emotional, and moving-instinctive. Gurdjieff also taught what he called the movements. These are complex group exercises or sacred dances done to music, which requires a precise attention of the body, and leaves little room for mental chatter. Students frequently gather on weekends to do practical work, such as construction, manual labor, or crafts. This not only exercises faculties that may have been little used before, but also produces the kinds of friction and difficulty that lead to change. Creating these kinds of situations, in which a person's masks are temporarily stripped away, is an art of which Gurdjieff was an absolute master.

Gurdjieff's teachings were drawn from many sources, including esoteric Christianity, Sufism, and Buddhism, yet the way he worked with people was uniquely his own. He attracted a great many intellectuals and mature seekers, some of whom became Gurdjieff teachers. Until about a decade ago the Work was more or less hidden from public notice. In recent years, however, it has become more widely known, and several hundred books have been written about Gurdjieff and his ideas.

The guild's founder, Louise March, came to the United States from Switzerland in the early 1920s to do postgraduate work at Smith College. One night she was invited to a Carnegie Hall studio to hear some of Gurdjieff's music being played. She met Gurdjieff himself that evening and soon followed him to Paris to become his student. She spent the next few years with Gurdjieff, translating his writings into German, acting as his secretary, and accompanying him on his later trips to and from the United States. Eventually she moved back to the United States, married, and raised a large family on a farm near New York City.

In 1957 Mrs. March began visiting Rochester to meet with a few Gurdjieff students. She soon attracted a group of eager Gurdjieff followers. Gradually the group grew to about 20 people. That was the beginning of the Rochester Folk Art Guild. The exploration of the crafts began very simply. Working mainly in each other's homes on weekends, the members developed over the next decade a serious attitude toward the discipline and potential of crafts as a vehicle for inner work. They reached a point where they became willing to commit themselves full-time to crafts. A search began for a center where full-time work could be carried on.

Understanding the importance of nature and connection to the land, Mrs. March and a few others made many trips to the farm country south of Rochester, looking for the right place. In the words of one member:

We were in the Naples area one very hot afternoon, having gone down many back roads and come to many dead ends. It began to rain. Finally, we were told about a place nearby that might be for sale. As we approached the farm we noticed the vineyards, and the level of interest increased. By the time we got out of the car, there was a very strong feeling that Mrs. March knew we had found our place.

Though the owner was noncommital, and they weren't even shown around, that feeling persisted. In less than a week, on July 4, 1967, the agreement was signed to purchase the farm.

In the fall of 1967 the first group, 12 people, moved in. Others came on weekends. Among them they shared an immense task, and the intensity of the work stretched everyone far beyond what they thought they could do. Almost everything was started from scratch. Some learned farm work; in the beginning no one knew how to plow or what to do with the grapes. Others cleaned out the chicken coop and converted it to a pottery workshop. Still others built an addition onto the main house to serve as a meeting and movements hall. An addition to the main barn was also completed. Work continued day and night. People contributed what little money they could. Free labor and the use of salvaged materials held the cost down. Members of the guild offered to remove unwanted barns from their neighbors' farms, and in so doing harvested useful materials. It was by doing these jobs thoroughly and quickly, including a complete cleanup, that the guild established good relations with the other residents of the small town of Middlesex.

Building continued as the needs and directions of the community expanded. Many more people came to live. New residences were built, as were wood, weaving, iron, and glass workshops. As time went on, building and construction became recognized as a craft, and as this interest and understanding grew, the buildings became larger and more beautiful. By 1972 an overwhelming need was felt for a new meeting and movements hall. Intensive planning meetings were held every week, and work on the stone foundation began. Louise March spoke of that period:

How did this building get to this form? We had it on paper, we had it in a model, we had choices. We had a dome, we had a cross. We changed as we went along. We found also that our capacity wasn't for a dome; not yet. . . . Every weekend we met together and were flushed with red cheeks when we ended. We searched for this detail or that. And you know, you wring it from some fine substance in you, or from above you, to get to what you want to express. We tried to put into this building that something special, always realizing that it would never be the ultimate.

The new meeting hall is the most central and most impressive building on the farm. Completed in 1975, it consists of a main room, about 30 by 50 feet, with a cathedral ceiling, a semicircular apse at one end, and an anteroom at the other. The materials, details, and craftsmanship are all first-class. The beams are hand-planed and carefully joined without nails or screws. The massive cedar-shingled roof and stuccoed walls rest on a beautifully worked stone foundation. It is a remarkable building.

The building in which we stayed is one of the newer residences. Built in the style of a Japanese country house, it accommodates five or six residents, plus occasional guests. One enters through a large foyer, removes one's shoes, and steps up to a raised walkway that leads around the foyer to the five bedrooms and the bathroom. The bathroom has a composting toilet and a small wood hot tub. The building is heated by three large masonry tile stoves that provide an even, gentle heat long after the fire has gone out. The exposed woodwork, the handmade and decorative tiles, and other details show a quality of care that is quite rare in the United States. As in all the buildings on the farm, everything from design and installation of the tile stoves and the woodwork to the electricity and plumbing was done entirely by guild members.

The Rochester Folk Art Guild is a fine example of a community where people make very little money, yet their quality of life, both materially and spiritually, is very high. This emphasis on excellence can be found in everything the residents do. For example, most of the furniture and utensils they use are produced in their own shops. One member explained it this way:

If we have a real search and struggle, perhaps it can be felt in what we make. You know, what is exceptional in man is very small and needs repeated feeding, watering, and cultivation. It's not until you touch something and use it, that some of the more important impressions have a chance to come through. Quality is more than an idea. You can experience it.

Meals are eaten together, often in silence, though it can also be a time of lively exchange. The original addition onto the main house is now used as the dining room, but meals move outside whenever weather allows. The kitchen work is considered a craft, and the same level of attention and awareness is given to food preparation as to potmaking and glassblowing. When asked for a recipe, the cook replied, "I rarely make any dish the same way twice. Besides, you need more than recipes. You need a feel for what you're doing and how that's affecting the food." We were later introduced to the guild's four cookbooks, which do contain numerous recipes, some traditional, and many developed in the kitchen. The preface of their first cookbook, *One Pot Dishes*, says, "We cook not so much from the head (cookbooks) as from our instinct (taste) and the wish to maintain ourselves healthy and capable of much good work."*

At the guild, every small detail of life has significance. As one weaver put it, "Belonging to the guild is a discipline that goes beyond any of the crafts. The question is, can we make a craft of our lives?"

The guild currently includes about 45 resident adults and about 14 children, 9 of whom are preschool age. In addition, about 20 people come regularly on weekends. These include families with children, people who live close by, and people who drive long distances. Another 50 or so people who have been with the Guild in the past still maintain a connection with it. The original group was mostly composed of single people in their twenties. Now most of the residents are in their mid-thirties, and many are married. Members come from virtually every part of the United States, and several foreigners were residents at various times. Most members have college backgrounds, but the guild does not keep records of such things and attaches little importance to a person's personal history.

No particular emphasis is placed on recruiting new members. Rather, as in the old adage, "When the student is ready the teacher appears," the right people seem to find their way to the community. There are no set requirements of newcomers, but it is necessary that they have some sense of inner aim. Louise March often asks people to put down in writing why they wish to come and what they expect. The next step is usually an interview with Mrs. March and a trial visit. Visitors are asked to pay $20 a day and are assigned work according to their abilities and the needs of the guild. Often they are asked to maintain silence for the first week or so, except to speak with Mrs. March. "Silence is contagious," she says. "Silence is very interesting. You hear the birds, you

---

*Anon., *One Pot Dishes* (Middlesex, N.Y.: Rochester Folk Art Guild, 1975).

almost hear the flowers bloom. You hear the breath of another and know how he is."

Little formal distinction is made between visitors, newcomers, and members. If a person stays long enough, the community becomes home. Usually if people don't fit in, they come to their own decision to leave.

Where a person works depends on where help is needed and the capacities of the individual. Activities are organized into ten main departments: pottery, glass, weaving, sewing, wood, iron, graphics, construction-maintenance, farm, and kitchen. People tend to move around at first, working at several different pursuits, until they find the one that seems most right:

When I was first a member of the Folk Art Guild, I had an opportunity to explore many different kinds of work. I worked in the woodshop, in silk screen, in block printing. I washed dishes or helped with meals. Then one day I had a chance to try my hand at pottery. And when that happened, I felt a sense of life that I had never experienced before. With the centering of a pot, of a ball of clay on a turning wheel, for the first time in my life I felt that there was the possibility of a center in me. It's now been over ten years since I first felt that; I have stayed with it, and am sure that it is my life's work. The more I work in pottery the more order I see; and the more order I see, the more it's possible to see.

· The working of the 318-acre farm has been an important part of guild life from the beginning. Following the traditional view of farming as a craft and the principle of stewardship of the land, the farmers have worked to make the farm a solid foundation that supports, and is closely related to, the whole guild. The farm operation brings in $15,000 to $20,000 a year, primarily from the sale of grapes, and smaller amounts from the sale of hay and market lambs, which are raised on the farm each year. The lambs are born to the guild's flock of sheep, who keep the weavers supplied with high-quality wool. The farmers operate a small dairy, producing milk, cheese, and yogurt for the residents' consumption. They raise their own beef and lamb also, and a flock of chickens is kept for eggs. The large gardens supply the community with fresh vegetables in season, and much gets canned, frozen, or stored in the root cellar for the winter.

We were given a tour of all the workshops when we visited the community, and the range and quality of the work produced by each was truly impressive. In the pottery workshop we saw beautiful porcelain vases, stoneware mugs, tile tables, and fountains. In the weaving workshop we were shown wall hangings, rugs, and pillows, and in the sewing workshop we saw clothing of all kinds, including suits, hats, coats, vests, caftans, ponchos, and burnooses; all were exceptionally well made. The glass workshop had a striking display of decorated and colored pieces, as well as a line of crystal items. The woodshop makes fine furniture and traditional toys. Some items have been made since the early days of the guild, such as the rocking horse and the Noah's ark. The ark, which is hand carved and comes with 51 hand-painted animals, has become one of the hallmarks of the guild.

The thoroughness with which each craft is explored is also worth noting. Artisans in the glass workshop make their own glass, and designed and built the furnaces used for melting it. The residents also make many of their own tools. While the graphics workshop artisans don't make their own paper, they do make almost everything else. They have published close to 20 books, some original stories and some adaptations of folk tales. All the writing, editing, illustrating, pasting up, printing, and binding is done in the workshop. They also do all of their own photography, artwork, and printing for advertising and publicity.

The crafts produced by guild members are currently sold in about 100 shops and galleries throughout the United States. The guild puts on at least four major exhibitions and sales each year in Rochester and Syracuse, and also invites the public to the community once or twice a year for an open house, with demonstrations, exhibitions, and crafts for sale. Each workshop also sends its artisans to a number of craft fairs every year to market the workshop's wares.

Guild members see their relationship with the outside world as an important one, and not only from the financial view. One member speaks of a vital exchange that takes place between maker and user that can nourish both in a special way:

There are many things we do that do not have a great financial return because they take so much time. Yet we sense the importance of making these things and bringing them to people at our sales. This too has become a tradition with us. People expect us to bring things that others don't try because it is "unprofitable." The Jack-in-the-Box that the woodshop makes is an example of this. It charms people so much. We know we are not making money on it, but it is something that we need to pursue. And the world needs it too. When you hear the exclamations of delight as the Jack jumps out, you know . . . it just touches people.

No one is paid a salary. For many years everyone made regular financial contributions. Now, with the guild more established, the policy is more flexible. There has never been a requirement that members turn over their personal assets. How they support the guild financially is a function of how they value the experience of being a part of it, as well as what financial resources they have. Many of the basic necessities are provided, and people sometimes take part-time jobs if they need to earn money.

The guild is a tax-exempt, educational, not-for-profit corporation. It receives 15 percent to 20 percent of its income from contributions; about 10 percent from farming; and the remainder, close to $200,000, comes from the sales of its various crafts. The contributions come primarily from members, both on and off the farm, and, to a lesser extent, from parents of members and from other individual supporters. It has received grants of about $5000 each from the New York State Council on the Arts, the National Endowment for the Arts, and the Corning Glass Works Foundation. Contributions other than cash have come from Case-Hoyt, a large printing company in Rochester, which supplied paper, and Corning Glass Works, which supplied glass, machinery, and technical assistance. In 1980 the guild started an endowment fund, which now totals around $200,000. It hopes to build it to $500,-000 within five years.

Department heads are chosen by Louise March on the basis of their experience and level of understanding. A weekly meeting is held at which they discuss questions that concern the departments and are in need of a wider audience. Mrs. March, now in her eighties, works closely with these people to develop a strong leadership which will be responsible for continuing the work she has initiated. She described the way things are governed on a day-to-day basis:

We have a hierarchy here. Those who know say, those who don't know don't say. It is difficult to know at what tempo someone gets really useful here—overcomes his own small outlook and is capable of participating in what we all visualize as ideal. Participation opens doors and windows. Some drag; some become capable of doing things they never dreamed of.

A general planning meeting for the whole community to set priorities and goals for the coming year is held each January. Other meetings are held as needed, and can concern anything from coordinating work in the vineyards to a discussion of children's problems. Coming to decisions is not merely a matter of consensus. Each individual in the group must speak and listen with great sensitivity, always remembering that he or she is part of a larger organism. It is this sense of responsibility that underlies the organization of, and interaction between, the various parts of the guild.

This view of the guild as an organism is reflected in the close relationships between departments. Everyone helps with the farm work, for instance, and it is considered an essential part of each resident's education. Whether it's tying grapevines, working in the woods, hauling hay, or digging potatoes, when the call goes out people give as much help as they can to the work at hand. The weavers and farmers work together to develop better wool quality and a greater variety of natural colors in the fleeces of the guild's sheep. The blacksmiths and the glassblowers collaborate to produce the iron and glass lamps for which the guild is famous. Ideas and work within departments are constantly exchanged. In many cases the finished pieces are the result of several people's efforts.

There is a strong feeling among guild members that due to expected economic difficulties, community life will be, of necessity, the wave of the future. They hope that their experiment in creating a freer, less selfish way of life will be viewed as an example of what is possible. Though they live and work as a community, the family unit is considered very important. Many marriages have taken place within the community, with a few double and even one triple wedding. In addition to their commitment to each other, couples share a commitment to a shared struggle in the Gurdjieff Work, that provides a foundation for the whole relationship. They also feel that the community way of life allows for wider interests, and results in a healthier climate for marriages.

The influence of the community way of life is also felt in the rearing of children at the guild. Children get to know many different adults, which is considered essential to their growth. Many families have children (most of them born on the farm), and Louise March guides the parents in being both supportive and demanding of the child. She often quotes Mr. Gurdjieff: "Child small, get small place." Because they are not the center of attention, the children are nourished in a more natural way. They partake of community life, working with adults and learning through example and by experience. Mothers share child care responsibilities, so children get to see each other quite a bit. The possibility of opening a guild school is being explored. For the time being, children attend the local public schools, and this experience is considered valuable as well.

While the guild supplies nearly everything its residents need, members still retain personal property, such as clothes, some tools, musical instruments, and books. There are half a dozen personal cars in addition to those owned by the guild. The guild has its own gas pump; if members are using their cars for personal, rather than guild purposes, they pay for the gas.

Each department has a library of books on its subject. A general library of books on the inner life is also available and Mrs. March has a large collection of books that members often borrow. Sometimes important books are read aloud at mealtime.

The arts and leisure activities are pursued with a great deal of energy. A choir meets regularly, and many musical collaborations have taken place over the years. Three of the guild musicians produced a recording of original music in 1975, and last year compiled a collection of pieces from live concerts, which is on cassette. The music is unique and both the record and cassette are very popular. A lively interest in theater has resulted in original productions of the Chinese folk tale "Monkey" and "Pinocchio," as well as Shakespeare and Chekhov plays. Several feasts and celebrations are observed during the year, the largest of which is at the end of August to celebrate Mrs. March's birthday. One year guild members presented an entire circus that day, much to her surprise and delight. All these pursuits are undertaken in the spirit of participation and response, and always as a learning experience.

Health care is a matter of personal choice. While some members visit doctors in town, the community also gets help as needed from two physicians who are nonresident members of the guild.

While the guild displays a high degree of ecological consciousness, it is not at present striving for total self-sufficiency. It uses a large amount of propane, for example, in running its pottery and glass kilns. This has created economic problems, as the price of propane has risen from 20¢ to 80¢ a pound. If it were to become unavailable it would mean the end of the guild's glass industry. The guild has shifted much of its general heating from propane to wood, which it cuts from its own land.

Looking ahead, other buildings, such as a guest house, will be built when the guild has the resources. Also, some of the older structures are in need of repair and upgrading of the insulation. Because of the general economic recession, the past several years were financially difficult, but the guild seems to thrive on difficulty. Residents believe that much harder, more uncertain times are coming in the near future, but they believe a way can be found to continue to express the highest aspirations of human beings very simply and practically.

"To work concentratedly and to do something that speaks truly to another man is a miracle," says Louise March. "We have come to be convinced that mankind's supreme task is work. Every human being is a speck in the universe. This makes us more modest—on our knees and open to higher influences. This is the true value."

The Farm manufactures rooftop solar heaters. This one is being assembled by a Guatemalan Indian trainee.

CHAPTER 7

The Farm: A Third World Nation Surrounded by the United States

The hippies of the 1960s, born out of the alienation that stemmed from the Vietnam conflict and nurtured by psychedelic drugs, developed an alternative culture that to many of us seemed pure, loving, beautiful—and completely impractical over the long run. Hundreds of thousands tuned in, turned on, and dropped out, able to exist on the surplus of a rich society. In their rejection of the materialistic values of their parents, many of them set up communes in the city or the country. Thousands were established; most soon faded away.

One of the largest groups of hippies was a collection of several thousand in San Francisco who gathered on Monday nights at various theaters, or on Sunday mornings at Balboa Park to hear talks by a young San Francisco State University English instructor named Stephen Gaskin. Gaskin had taken LSD perhaps 150 times and in the process had a clear vision that spirit is energy. He wasn't satisfied, however, merely to travel through inner space. He was driven to teach others to see the truth as he had come to see it, and to help them apply it in the material world. His religion was eclectic. He once said that if you put all the principles of the world's religions on IBM punchcards, and made a big bundle of them, where the holes went straight through the bundle was what he was teaching. But his sermons were not so much about abstract theories as they were about practical life. He told the kids to grow up, be straight with themselves and each other, and take responsibility. It was an important and rare message in those love-in, flower-power days in San Francisco.

In 1971 Gaskin went on a national lecture tour. He converted a bus into a house on wheels for the trip, and about 270 of his students decided to do likewise and go along with him. Gaskin had several goals: to carry his message across the country, to enable many of his followers to visit their parents and help them understand their children's new lives, and to look for a place in the country for the group to settle in as a community. His goals were met. The group members ended up pooling their individual resources to buy, for $70 an acre, 1014 acres near Summertown, a small rural community 75 miles south of Nashville, Tennessee. They called their new home simply the Farm. They really didn't know what they were getting into. They'd spent all their money for the land, so they camped out that first winter in their buses and a few tents. They had wheat berries but no mill with which to grind them, so they just boiled them into a gruel. They had thought they might have to work one day a week to get by. Only one member had any previous farming experience. They learned the hard way.

During most of its history the Farm operated as a gigantic commune. Everyone had to take a vow of poverty and no money was used within the community. Cash expenditures in the larger economy were only about $400 per person per year. But as the years passed and families grew, the residents became less willing to put up with these hardships and many began drifting away. During 1982 and 1983 about half the members left, causing those remaining to reexamine their economic arrangements. In October 1983 they introduced a new system that allowed members to keep private property, paid them for their work, and required them to pay for food, housing and services on the Farm. The Farm has moved from commune to cooperative.

Today the Farm consists of 1750 acres and about 550 people. There are approximately 275 adults and an equal number of children. Some 50 of the adults are single, pretty evenly divided between men and women, and the rest are married. The Farm still lives in poverty but operates a variety of technologically advanced businesses. Since 1974 it has run its own outreach program to the needy in third world nations and the United States, called Plenty International. Plenty is recognized by the United Nations and has received about $1 million worth of grants from the Canadian government and more from other agencies both public and private. Its administrative and overhead costs are just 5 percent of its total costs, making it the most efficient foreign aid program in the world.

The hippies really came through. Of all the communities we have visited, the Farm not only has the most people, but it has the most heart, and is making the most impact on the world outside its boundaries.

As we approach the Farm we see how poor the countryside is. The woods are mostly scrub, the soil is worn out, and so are most of its inhabitants. The road narrows and finally at the end of Drakes Lane is the gatehouse of the Farm. The gate is the Farm's collective front door, staffed day and night by a group of four or more people, at least three of whom are men. They are friendly and they don't have guns (the community is pacifist) but they do control who goes in and out. The Farm has made a great effort to befriend and help its neighbors and has been generally successful. But there are Klansmen in South Tennessee and there are crazies and there are deadbeats who could quickly overload the Farm's capacity for hospitality.

A drive around the Farm does indeed remind one of a third world village in physical terms. The roads are dirt and the buildings—except for the schoolhouse—are unpainted frame structures made largely of salvaged materials. The clothing is largely hand-me-down and heavily patched. The vehicles are ancient. But there are crucial differences. The smiles, friendliness, and purposefulness of the residents suggest that they are healthy, happy, and feel good about their village and what they are doing in it. And the shortwave radio antennas, the parabolic disc to pick up television from satellites, the ambulances, and the solar water heaters, all indicate that there is more here than immediately meets the eye.

Why does the Farm look this way? Because it has been too busy trying to develop its businesses, has given a lot away to help others, and doesn't place a high value on consumption. A wish list has been drawn up of about $100,000 worth of public improvements to be made when spare funds are available: paving the main roads, bringing running water to those houses that still lack it, finishing the meeting hall, and putting in a swimming pool. But residents are fairly nonchalant about their physical environment, based on a conscious choice to demonstrate that one can indeed live very well on very little.

This 1750 acres is only part of the Farm's far-flung operations. Other Farm communities are legally separate but think of themselves as part of the same "family." Some 35 members live on a 350-acre farm in Franklin County, New York, and some 40 live on a 500 acre farm near Lanark, Ontario. The latter provides an official link with the Canadian government so that Canadian funding of Plenty is possible. The members travel around Canada planting trees for income. Three couples of mixed nationalities from the Farm are living in southern France with some European friends, attempting to start an international branch. A dozen live in Nashville where they run a restaurant. Other members of the Farm community are or have been involved in Plenty projects in the Bronx and Washington, D.C., and in Bangladesh, Guatemala, Lesotho, and several countries in the Caribbean.

When Gaskin calls the community a "third world nation surrounded by the United States," he's speaking not only of its standard of living and its ties to people of third world nations (including American Indian nations within the United States); he is also expressing a concept of sovereignty. This is obviously not a political or legal sovereignty. It is a practical sovereignty—the members' reclaiming of responsibility for their own selves in ways that most people in modern society have lost: growing and processing their own food, caring for their own health, building their own homes, conducting their own marriages, birthing their babies, educating their children, and burying their dead. And then going outside their "nation" to help others do likewise. About the only thing they don't have is an army, and that is something they are happy to do without.

Because the Farm is so well known, many people are interested in visiting it or joining it. Usually they write before they visit, though some just show up at the gate. Visitors stay at Visitor's Village, a small campsite just inside the gate. Visitors who are the most energetic get to know people and often find a place in one of the houses. People interested in membership talk it over with members of the board of directors, participate in the activities of the community for a few weeks, and then are either voted into membership or refused by the board. It doesn't cost anything to join but members must sign a vow of poverty and are expected to turn over what they own beyond personal items such as clothes, musical instruments, or tools of their trade. Since the changes made in October 1983, members can have their own bank accounts. Car titles must be transferred to the Farm but their previous owners can continue to use them. The change is too recent for anyone to be sure just how it will work. The existing members have little and they haven't yet had the experience of someone with substantial assets wanting to join and keep the assets.

While the founders of the community were largely college graduates and dropouts, this is less true of newcomers. On the whole, community members take a dim view of college educations, believing that they mold people in useless or wrong directions, and are a waste of time and resources. The Farm has sent some of its members to medical school, however, because it recognizes both the need for the specialized training and the value of the license that goes with it. On the whole, people at the Farm believe that any sufficiently motivated person can learn what he or she needs to know about a subject when it is needed. For example, Ina May Gaskin, Stephen Gaskin's wife, learned about midwifery on the job. She now heads the Farm's midwifery program; her book, *Spiritual Midwifery,** is widely used around the country; and she is invited to address professional groups. The Farm has trained a large number of midwives and emergency medical technicians (EMTs) both there and elsewhere through Plenty.

---

*Ina May Gaskin, *Spiritual Midwifery* (Summertown, TN: The Book Publishing Co., 1980).

The Farm has a few older members, some of whom are parents of members who joined earlier. Other parents have bought land just outside the community on which to retire. That land probably will come to the community on their death. One old Texan named Joe Silver, whose wife was senile and needed to be put into a nursing home, wrote saying how much he admired what the Farm was doing and asked that they be allowed to live there. The residency committee wrote back that they would put his name on the waiting list (at that time a wait of several months was usual because of the housing shortage). Silver began sending the community a number of small gifts, and then a color television set. One day the residency committee was going over the waiting list and asked Gaskin if they should let Silver in. He replied, "Why not? You let his television set in!" Silver was accepted, now performs a useful role helping to mow grass and maintain the grounds, and is able to keep his wife with him.

Children of the Farm don't become members until they are 18, but they are allowed to vote at 16. At 18 they are asked to apply for membership and take a vow of poverty if they want to stay. If not, they are helped to leave with the community's blessing. Some have been given bus fare to the coast and a sleeping bag as a parting gift. Some want to leave for good, some want to go out into the world for a while and then come back, but most elect to stay. This is a tribute to the community's sense of mission and its ability to inculcate this in the children, and it also reflects the growing opportunities for travel and experience that the community offers.

We met Katherine Moore, a lovely young woman of 19 who had been in the community since she was 11. At 15, Moore had been in charge of the horses and could plow a field with them better than most men. At 16, although she didn't run for the position, she received the fourth highest vote to become a member of the Council of Elders. When we met her she had recently finished emergency medical technician training and was about to go to the Bronx to work on the Plenty ambulance team. While there she also expected to work with the team that makes professional videotapes of Plenty activities. With the other Plenty projects, Moore will have many opportunities to develop a range of skills and see the world, all without leaving the Farm community.

Sometimes people are asked by the residency committee to leave for reasons such as dishonesty or violence. Since the Farm feels that this is like taking away a person's citizenship, every effort is first made to work out the problem. The Farm is a place where a lot of personal problems can be worked out because it is like an extended family, with a lot of love and a real effort by everyone to be straightforward. Gaskin says:

I see people get well all the time, from pretty nutty places. I don't mind being crazy. It doesn't even make me nervous. I've been crazy so many times it's like my backyard; you know, the front yard has this kind of garden and the back-yard has that kind of garden. If I wander around in there with somebody long enough, and attract their attention, we can walk in the garden together and remove fear and paranoia.

Nevertheless, some people have to be asked to leave. The residency committee talks to them and says, in effect: "You know you're not changing. You want us to serve you while you continue your destructive behavior. We're not going to do that." In such a case, however, the problem is usually sufficiently obvious that the person leaves without being asked.

During most of its history the Farm was governed more on the basis of what felt right at the time rather than by any formal system. In 1974 Gaskin was arrested on a drug charge because the community had been growing and using marijuana. Members called its use a sacrament of their religion, but that didn't stop the Tennessee authorities from put-ting Gaskin into the penitentiary for a year. In retrospect, Gaskins feels that the jailing was a good thing for the community, since it forced the members to learn to run their affairs without him. (Today, in addition to being teacher, counselor, and front man for the Farm, Gaskin works for its Book Publishing Company as author and editor. He also devotes a great deal of his time to Plenty but plays virtually no role in running the community.)

Aside from community town meetings every couple of months or so, telephones and cable TV are used for internal communication. The Farm has its own internal dial-telephone system, which it bought at a good price from a nearby town that was converting to a push button system. Instead of a dial tone, the caller gets a recorded voice with the messages of the day. Every home has a television set and they are con-nected in a cable system. In addition to broadcasting the latest movies and hit shows picked up off satellites by their Skyscanner antenna, members initiate their own programs when there is an issue to discuss. Whoever is most concerned presents the issue to the community and members respond with telephone calls to the studio.

The entire community gets together on Sunday mornings when Gas-kin gives a talk as its spiritual teacher. General problems were originally dealt with there, or in a specially called town meeting. But this was an awkward way to run such a large community and a few years ago Farm members decided to elect a council of elders. Since they really didn't know how to go about it, members were simply invited to vote for 20 people they thought should be on the council. There were no nomina-tions and no candidacies. From this, they drew up a list of all the people named in the order of the number of votes they received. A midwife, Mary Louise Perkins, got the highest vote, 268 out of 480. The next six were also women. As we have mentioned, Katherine Moore, who was 16 at the time, was fourth and two other teenagers were also elected. Gaskin excluded himself from consideration because he wanted the community to be completely self-governing, or, as he put it, he didn't want to "hog all the experiences." Laying out the results on a bell curve showed that 50 people had substantial support, and so the council of elders was set at that size.

After operating for a while it became obvious that some council members were honoraries—elected because people liked them, but not able or willing to do the job. So the council purged itself into a working body of about 35. New ones were elected later bringing the number back up to 50. The council met every two weeks to deal with general policy questions and problems. It appointed the residency committee of 12 persons, primarily from its own members.

Day to day management was the function of the management council, consisting of the city manager, treasurer, lawyer, and personnel chief, all elected by the elders; and the heads of the various businesses, elected by the persons working in those businesses. The management council made all the financial decisions for the community and even the major ones for the various businesses. With the exception of the job of lawyer, which requires a unique skill, the manager jobs turn over every year or two. It is not a matter of people vying for the positions, but rather one of finding the most qualified person for each job, persuading him or her to take it, and then seeing how long that person is willing to keep the responsibility.

In general, the aim of the community is to avoid entrenched social position. On the other hand, the heads of the businesses normally stay on as long as they are doing a good job. The businesses are usually headed by the people who started them and they continue to run them with full authority as long as they run them effectively.

The Farm's single greatest problem has always been the financial limitations on what it wants to accomplish. The human energies are there, but the money has not been. In 1981 these were their sources of gross income: The Book Company, $562,971; The Building Company, $270,884; Farm Foods Company, $246,145; Solar Electronics Company, $117,279; Solar Energy Works, $213,066; Tie Dye Tee Shirts, $42,762; Village Media Services, $33,076; The Truck Company, $82,-344; The Foundation (including contributions), $320,176; and other, $143,976. Total gross income was $2,032,679, cost of goods sold was $819,559, leaving a net income of $1,213,120. After taking out all the expenses of running the businesses and the Farm—advertising, buildings and equipment, vehicles, taxes, and so on—but not deducting personnel costs, the net profit was $482,748. Divide that by the number of people to be fed, clothed, housed, educated, and entertained—approximately 1200 at that time—and you come up with a figure of about $400 per person per year. Economically, this is what made the Farm a third world nation.

And this is what led to the growing dissatisfaction of many members. After ten years of very hard work and little noticeable advance in their physical comforts or ability to provide for their growing families, many members decided to give up the dream and go back to the outside world. Others wanted to hold onto the dream but that meant making some changes that would satisfy the membership generally and stop the erosion.

The council of elders felt that it was too large and unwieldy to make the changes and that the management council was too unrepresentative to do so. So in early 1983 it proposed a new form of government: the management council would be replaced as the active decision-making body by the board of directors of the foundation. This board—elected by all the members—had existed all along but had been inactive. A newly elected board with the mandate of the membership of the community would then make whatever changes were necessary to establish the financial health of the Farm.

In March 1983 nine members were elected to the new board of directors. They were generally people who had been in leadership roles before; the new chairman, Richard McKenny, was one of the founders of the Farm and is the head of the Solar Electronics Company. In the present system, the board's executive committee and key officers—the vice president, controller, farm manager, treasurer, lawyer and personnel chief—work together on a daily basis. The elders continue to meet occasionally to discuss general issues, but in an advisory rather than active capacity.

The change from collective to cooperative was developed over a period of six months and took effect in October 1983. Prior to that time, members received no pay and everything on the Farm was free. When the community store was open, residents simply went in and took what they needed. Signs were posted indicating what level of consumption was considered reasonable. Some used clothing was purchased by the bundle and patched as needed.

At present the land and houses are held in common but the services —community store, soy dairy, laundry, medical clinic, and so forth— operate as worker cooperatives, charging for their services and paying their employees from the proceeds. Each adult pays $34 a week (children are free) for housing and a share of the Farm's overhead. Hourly wages (which for legal purposes are thought of as a distribution of part of the foundation's earnings to members) are usually about $3.35 to $4.00 and weekly earnings range between $150 and $300, depending on the need of the person and the money available in each business. No general standards of need or equity have yet been established for the whole community.

The change to a "wage" economy has also affected the way the businesses operate. Before this, some of the businesses paid more to support the foundation than they now pay in wages. So they have come out ahead. But the new system requires all work to be cost effective and this has resulted in elimination of many jobs both in the businesses and in farm services. Some of the people who lost their jobs have found others and some have had to leave the community to seek employment elsewhere.

Members live in about 40 different homes scattered around the Farm, ranging from single family homes to a structure that houses more than a dozen people. A house may accommodate two or more families with children and several singles. Normally each couple has its own room, singles of the same sex share bedrooms, and children are grouped by family or sex or age—whatever suits the household. All the houses have outhouses, most have running water, and all have electricity. Both wood and solar heating are used. The Farm buys bundles of eight-foot lumber scraps from a nearby sawmill for $2 a bundle. These are cut to firewood length at the Farm's own sawmill and distributed to each household. Everybody in the house shares the common areas and takes turns with the cooking and cleaning. Mothers who work outside the home turn their preschoolers over to the "houselady" of the day. Although there are no strictures that limit the kinds of jobs performed by men and women, sex roles tend to follow traditional patterns with women predominantly concerned with children and home activities.

While the community does not place restrictions on adult sex life, members take the whole issue of relationships, marriage, and family more seriously than many outside the community. Few couples remain unmarried. The community encourages people who want to be together to get married, on the ground that it shows their commitment and will make their parents happy. Divorces are handled free by the community's lawyer. The local judge is cooperative. He respects the community because it has always insisted that child rearing and child support should be divided equally.

A few gays and lesbians live at the Farm. Stephen Gaskin has led meetings of the men and Ina May Gaskin has led meetings of the women to discuss homosexuality and encourage tolerance and understanding by the heterosexuals.

Although adults have the freedom to handle themselves sexually as they see fit, so long as they do not exploit others, teenagers are not given the same freedom. The rule for those under 18 is "No dope; no fucking." Stephen sometimes meets with the kids, agrees on how hard it is to follow this when they are biologically ready for sex, but points out that until they are able to take responsibility for any children that might be born, they don't have the right to inflict that problem on the community. Members believe that while this rule is not always honored, it probably is adhered to far better than in outside society. The Farm, after all, is a very small town, and informal social controls are strong.

The Farm produces most of its food needs, processing much of it in its own bakery, cannery, or soy dairy. The farming is not 100 percent organic, but it is moving in that direction as the composting becomes more effective. Between 60 and 100 tons of compost are generated each year. Each house has its own vegetable garden.

All of the members are strict vegetarians who consume no dairy products. The only animals used on the Farm are horses; the members reason that horses wouldn't exist very well on their own without their symbiotic relationship with people. Soybeans are the major source of protein: members consume a lot of tofu which is produced in a large soy dairy on the Farm. The Farm has developed its own soy ice cream, called Ice Bean, which is now its third largest business. A favorite dish is tortillas and beans, adopted after reading the study that helped inspire Frances Moore Lappe's work on protein complementarity.*

Originally, too, the Farm members eschewed sugar, white flour, and margarine. They started a sorghum syrup business but gave it up when they found it to be uneconomic and too labor intensive. Following that they scoured the South for other syrups they could purchase. Then a UNICEF medical team, back from Biafra, came and examined everybody and found that while they were getting plenty of vitamins and minerals, they were not getting enough carbohydrates. When a carbohydrate deficiency exists, the body converts protein to carbohydrates so the protein, too, may become insufficient. After that the community members decided that white sugar was pure, clean energy, and that white flour and margarine were also fine in moderation. While nutritionally sophisticated people may criticize this stance, their per capita consumption of sugar is only about 25 pounds a year, 20 percent of the American average. Margarine was later dropped and oil is used instead.

The Farm has its own dentist, but he doesn't get a lot of business. The children who have grown up eating Farm food have required few fillings. The Farm uses fairly traditional health care practices. It maintains a well-equipped medical clinic and, when necessary, takes the more serious cases to the local hospital in its own ambulances. The Farm is well known for its midwives, who are among the most respected and important people in the community. For many years the Farm had been making this offer: "If you are thinking about getting an abortion, here is an alternative: we will deliver your baby by natural childbirth for free. If you decide to keep your baby, you can; or we will raise it for you. If you ever decide that you want the baby back, you can have it."

---

*Frances Moore Lappe, *Diet for a Small Planet* (New York: Ballentine, 1971).

Some 200 or more women took them up on the offer, but few ended up leaving without their babies. Either they took their babies home with them, or they stayed and became a part of the community. Now the midwives are charging $475 for a delivery plus $50 a week for room and board. However, they do have a small fund to help some needy cases.

After spending several years with each family doing its own wash, the members concluded that this heavy job, usually stuck on women, would be handled more efficiently if done communally. So they built a large laundry with heavy-duty equipment and its own staff. However, now that members must pay for laundry, many are again doing it at home and some even use a laundry in Summertown.

The Farm believes strongly in being responsible for educating its children and passing its values on to them. The schoolhouse is the best building on the Farm. It is built of cinder block, followed by four inches of foamboard insulation, followed by brick, with large windows in the roof to provide passive solar heating. It has six classrooms. It looks good and works well but inside, the cinder block has not yet been plastered or painted, and the ceilings have been spackled but not painted. These touches are not essential to its functioning; they will be done sometime when the construction crew has time back on the Farm; and meanwhile, it doesn't really matter.

What matters is what is taught. The pupil-teacher ratio is very low and students get a lot of help from parents. The curriculum is, on the whole, the same as that in public schools and students who have transferred out have done well. A closer and deeper relationship exists between students and teachers than elsewhere; they are more informal with each other and see a good deal of each other outside the classroom. Emphasis is placed on the moral and political values of the community and the history of the Farm.

Teachers are paid out of general revenues but parents pay for supplies and miscellaneous expenses. For the 1983–1984 school year this was expected to cost about $100 per student. To save money, the high school was closed down for this school year and its students were sent to the local public high schools. Members hope to be able to reopen it later.

In their spare time members pursue a variety of interests. During a recent celebration, performances ran for 12 hours and included a beginning girls' ballet, an over-35 ballet, belly and African dances, and several rock bands. The senior class recently staged a play based on an episode in the Chinese folk tale, "Monkey." A number of the women participate in an aerobic dance class. Some people are studying languages: Spanish, German, Russian, Chinese, Welsh, and a Mayan dialect. Some of these are in preparation for possible service abroad with Plenty. The Farm has no library yet (aside from the one in the school), but members hope to build one. Members do read a good deal, though. People who go outside often bring back books and these tend to get passed around.

An effort is made to strike a balance between the interests of the community and the people who constitute it. Individuals have an obligation to support the community since it takes care of them. On the other hand, members believe that no individual should ever be sacrificed for the sake of the community. Gaskin says:

The stuff we're learning as a community is an individual fulfillment too. You can't have it so your fulfillment comes only through your personal self. The Farm is a social *sadhana;* a path in itself. Our spiritual practice is the Farm—the entire trip, the whole thing. To save every little piece of string. To be as efficient as we can. To use junk if junk works good. To be as efficient as possible with the God-given resources of the world; to work without thought of reward. That's one of the hardest yogas, you know. That's a demanding yoga. Hoeing a row of corn can be a meditation; sawing a board can be a meditation.

None of the Farm's businesses is separately incorporated; all of them operate under the umbrella of the Foundation. Each keeps its own books (usually on its own computer), and interchanges among them are accounted for so that the profit or loss of each can be determined accurately. The Foundation has been audited twice by the Internal Revenue Service. Since the Foundation has nonprofit status under section 501 D of the Internal Revenue Code, the businesses pay license fees and sales tax, but no income tax. While profit-making businesses are required to pay tax under this section of the code, their level of income in relation to expenses is so low that it would have to increase several times over before they would become liable.

The Book Publishing Company was the first business begun after the failed sorghum syrup operation. It is now the largest. Gaskin's books had been distributed by Random House, but Farm leaders weren't happy with this arrangement and wanted to take publishing into their own hands. In 1973 one of the Farm members came into a $20,000 inheritance and it was decided that it should be spent to buy modern printing equipment. Paul Mandelstein, who had worked in his family's garment business, went to Nashville for a few months to learn how to operate printing equipment by working in printing plants. He now heads the company. One of the Farm buildings was extended with bits and pieces grafted onto its sides and top to make room for the equipment and offices. At first the Book Publishing Company published only Gaskin's books. But as others developed expertise in various fields, practical books began to appear. In its early years a number of members with ham radio and electronics experience convinced the Farm to use CB radio—and later shortwave radio—for its own communications. Following the Farm dictum that people can learn anything they really need and want to know, those who knew taught those that wanted to know.

Out of this came the Book Publishing Company's first nonideological book, *The Big Dummy's Guide to CB Radio* (1975), by Mark Long. It hit the market just as the wave of interest in CB was cresting, and became a best seller. To date more than 1.2 million copies have been sold. Another best seller is *Spiritual Midwifery* (1977), by Ina May Gaskin. And Margaret Nofziger, Stephen Gaskin's former wife, has written two books: *A Cooperative Method of Natural Birth Control* (1976), and *The Fertility Question* (1982). More recent books include *Tofu Cookery* (1982), by Louise Hagler, and *The World of Satellite Television* (1983), by Mark Long. The latter has already sold about 100,000 copies and the Farm hopes that it will do for the emerging wave of interest in satellite reception what the *Dummy's Guide* did for CB. The Book Publishing Company also publishes a quarterly magazine called *The Practicing Midwife* and it is considering starting a journal of political and philosophical opinion.

Except for the very large print runs of a few books and the full color photographic covers of *Tofu Cookery*, all of the steps involved in book production have been done at the Farm. The books sell because they are carefully researched, practical, and in many cases, make little effort to preach the Farm's ideology. They are sold mostly through distributors, though increasingly by direct sales to bookstores.

The second largest business, the Building Company, grew out of the Farm's own needs. At first few people even knew how to hit a nail properly. Construction was crude but, through trial and error and banged thumbs, they gradually learned. They went off the Farm to scavenge and tear down structures for hundreds of miles around, and out of the need to earn money they began taking on outside jobs. Today the Farm has a wide range of heavy equipment and 16 people who can do just about anything work on construction. They have built a 40-house subdivision, churches, even installed the carpets at the new Opryland in Nashville. In fact, they've been kept so busy on the outside that they haven't had time to attend to a lot of jobs that need doing on the Farm.

The third largest business is Farm Foods, producers of various soy products such as textured soy protein and Ice Bean. This soy dessert grew out of their own desire to find a nondairy substitute for ice cream. It was so popular with Farm members that they began to market it. For a while Farm Foods had its own plant in California but it found that arrangement unprofitable, so Ice Bean is now made on contract by an ice cream plant in Memphis. The soybeans are purchased outside but most of the honey comes from the Farm's own 230 hives. Sold for a number of years in health food stores around the country, it is now beginning to appear in supermarkets. Since it is kosher, pareve, low in calories, free of cholesterol—and even tastes good—its future commercial growth looks promising. It has even begun to engender competition. The challenge now for the Farm is to resist the temptation to spend the company's profits for other things and to reinvest them so that the company will grow quickly, thus preventing a food giant from taking over the market.

Solar Electronics manufactures a variety of high technology items: a Doppler fetoscope, which detects the fetal pulse, providing valuable clinical information to obstetricians; several kinds of small, relatively inexpensive radiation monitors; and the Skyscanner satellite television system. The radiation monitors are a useful tool for those who share the Farm's antinuclear stance since they can easily detect leakage, sometimes where authorities insist that none exists. In fact, they were taken into the Smithsonian Institution and the New York Museum of Natural History and revealed high enough levels of radiation from some of the exhibits that the museums changed them to protect the public. Five or six employees make a living selling and installing large parabolic satellite antennae around Tennessee and some have been sold internationally.

Solar Energy Works produces a solar hot water heater that was developed on the Farm. Selling for around $700, it consists of a black water tank inside a well-insulated solar collector on the roof, making a very simple yet effective system.

Tie Dye Tee Shirts is a cottage industry that four people run from their homes. The shirts, which are popular, are dyed brilliant colors that do not fade. Village Media Services includes a record company that has produced records of the Farm's band, called the Nuclear Regulatory Commission; the band itself; a recording studio that records the band and is available to outsiders for around $25 an hour; a tape company that produces educational tapes; and the TV crew that makes videotapes of Farm and Plenty activities, as well as instructional videotapes. The Truck Company consists of two 18-wheel tractor-trailer rigs that haul across the nation on contract.

A Farm restaurant in Nashville, called Everybody's Restaurant, came into being because one Farm member had experience in his family's restaurant and felt he could make his greatest contribution to the Farm by running a restaurant. His parents loaned him money to get it started. The restaurant has been successful and by 1983 the manager was able to repay the money he borrowed to start it. He and his family live with the rest of the people who work in the restaurant in a large group house that the Farm rents for them in Nashville. The house is much more attractive than Farm housing but the Farm members figure that's only fair since people make a big sacrifice when they agree to live away from the Farm.

Not every business has succeeded. In addition to the short-lived sorghum syrup business, the Farm opened and then closed a CB shop, a garage, and a produce market in the nearby town of Columbia. It also had a successful restaurant in California that was forced to close when it lost its lease.

Three generations ago a group of Amish bought a farm near Summertown and moved down from Lancaster, Pennsylvania. Because they were longhairs with strange religious beliefs, they initially encountered hostility from other residents. The local newspaper editor spoke up for them, urging his neighbors to give them the benefit of the doubt and make them feel welcome. In 1971 another group of longhairs bought another farm near Summertown. Residents expressed the same doubts and concerns and again the editor of the paper—now the grandson of the first one—went to bat for them. A local judge and a few other prominent people joined him. Their arrival proved to be a peaceful one.

The Farm members have always been aware of their impact in the county and understand how local residents could feel threatened by such a large collection of hippies moving in. They have tried therefore to be helpful to their neighbors so that they would feel the Farm is an asset rather than a liability. They have frequently made their ambulance and emergency medical services available to neighbors, at cost or even less. The ambulance is often used to transport elderly bedridden neighbors. Since many of their immediate neighbors are poorer than the people on the Farm, they have provided technical and practical assistance to them—such as building a new drain field or running an electric line.

At first the Farm decided to not vote in local district elections because it didn't want to overwhelm its neighbors at the polls. At its largest, its voting population constituted more than two-thirds of the voters in the district and 16 percent of the voters in the county. In 1982 it changed its position, deciding that its interests would be served best if it were represented at the county level. It told its neighbors that it would not participate in the local district election for constable, but would take two of the three seats the district was entitled to on the county board of commissioners, staying out of the vote on the third. Once members decide democratically what to do in local elections, they vote as a bloc, expecting each member to go along with the decision. Without overwhelming the neighbors, the Farm is now represented in the county by two out of 20 county commissioners.

By 1974, just three years after its inception, the Farm was ready to expand its definition of "neighborhood" from the county to the world. That was when it established Plenty as a charitable enterprise under section 501 C3 of the Internal Revenue Code. The name comes from the community's belief that there is plenty in the world to meet everyone's needs, but only if it is properly distributed and used. For example, cattle consume ten pounds of vegetable protein to yield one pound of beef. North America currently grows so many soybeans that they would fill most of the protein needs around the world if they were utilized as food, not feed.

At first the Farm's refrigerated truck took food to the hungry in Tennessee wherever they saw the need: Memphis, Nashville, Mount Pleasant, and a few rural areas. As they learned of more distant places that needed help they expanded their itineraries and drove as far as Los Angeles and the refugee communities in Miami. Construction crews went out in the Farm buses when they heard about flash floods in Colorado and tornadoes in Alabama.

Plenty made its leap into international activities when a massive earthquake struck the Guatemalan highlands in February 1976. A number of Farm carpenters went down to help the local Indians in the reconstruction of their homes. As soon as the emergency work was done, most of the international relief crews went home. But the Farm crew stayed because they had fallen in love with the Indians and thought they could help them with the kind of technology they used on the Farm. Somebody said, "The Canadians are doing something; why don't you talk to them?" So three hippie carpenters walked into the Canadian Embassy carrying their tool bags and managed to get in to see the ambassador. He told them, "We have a ship coming in to Guatemala right now with 7000 tons of building supplies, and we're not quite sure what we are going to do with them." One of the Farm crew grabbed a piece of paper and together they whipped out a design for a simple 12 foot by 24 foot prefabricated house using the Canadian wood. Everybody liked it so much that they later designed some simple school buildings. Another three-man crew was added, and together with some Canadian Franciscan monks and some local people, they went to work putting up these buildings in the small town of San Andreas de Chimultenango. In all, they built about 300 of the 1200 houses needed there, as well as two schools, and when they had finished they had trained the local people to continue the project.

But in the process of rebuilding houses and schools they had seen many other needs in the town and elsewhere. And as they went along, they kept in radio communication with the Farm so that the folks back home knew just what was going on and what the needs were. The local midwife needed a new clinic, so the Farm sent down a bus with a crew of skilled workers including some lab technicians. Medical supply houses and hospitals in Tennessee began donating thousands of dollars worth of supplies and equipment—often obsolete by their standards, but better than anyone in rural Guatemala had ever seen. Somebody donated a new Toyota Land Cruiser. The Farm converted it into an ambulance and sent it along. They had equipped it with a CB radio, which meant that they had to train the Indians in this technology too.

They followed this up with an FM radio transmitter for western Guatemala, FM radio kits, and a school bus. They brought several Guatemalans back to the Farm to learn various technologies. And because people at the Farm regard themselves as peasants, the Indians were able to relate to their teachers. The United States immigration authorities cooperated by giving 18-month training visas to the people the Farm brought in.

Over the next few years the Farm volunteers in Guatemala learned Spanish and some of the Indian languages, developed a primary health care program, set up an orphanage, and researched crop improvements. They spread interest in amaranth, which was a staple grain before the Spanish conquistadores banned it, and they introduced soybeans. With the cooperation of several other development agencies, 21 varieties of soybeans were grown at various altitudes and the best of them were accepted enthusiastically by the local farmers. Plenty volunteers showed the farmers' wives how to grind and cook soybeans with their existing utensils and how to integrate them into their diet. The final stage was to set up a soy dairy that produced tofu and Ice Bean. By 1980 the political situation in Guatemala had deteriorated so much that the Farm withdrew its technicians for their own safety. By this time, however, they had trained local workers and extension agents sufficiently that the soy dairy and many other health programs in the highlands are continuing.

Other Plenty foreign programs have included work on a clinic and orphanage and development of a solar-powered CB radio system in Bangladesh; work with Mother Theresa's people in Haiti; and reforestation, village development, and building another soy dairy in Lesotho. In 1982 Gaskin led a team on a boat trip around the Caribbean, exploring the possibilities for developing aid programs there. By early 1984 a few volunteers were working in St. Lucia, Dominica, and Jamaica on a variety of community development projects. Plenty was seeking funding for an expansion of this activity to include a half dozen more countries in the Caribbean basin.

In 1977 Farm members watching a television special on the South Bronx were appalled at the conditions there. Plenty sent some volunteers up to see how they could help, and they concluded that the most desperate need that they could fill was for a reliable free ambulance service. A group of emergency medical technicians went to the South Bronx with their families, rehabilitated a four-story brownstone and moved in, got jobs with a window installation company for income, and set up their ambulance service. Demand for it was strong, not only because it was free, but because it had an average response time of seven minutes compared with about a half hour for municipal ambulances. The Plenty volunteers established a program to train local residents as emergency medical technicians. More than 120 have been trained to date, and many went on to get good jobs with other ambulance services. *The Wall Street Journal* ran a front page story about the service in 1981,* and the project has received a number of private and public grants that have enabled it to buy better equipment. In a further effort to help the people of the South Bronx, Plenty began a summer program in 1982 to take children to their farm in the Catskills for a week or two of fresh air, swimming, hiking, weaving, and tie-dyeing.

Plenty is also the chief medium for carrying out the Farm's political concerns. Gaskin, however, doesn't call them political. "Doing stuff about whales and the Indians and the nukes and the poor folks isn't political," he said. "That's just stuff that's right or wrong that we should be doing right. It's not political to recognize right and wrong."

Plenty's group in Washington, D.C., runs an educational and health program for newly arrived political refugees, as well as coordinating actions with American Indian and environmental groups. Plenty radio technicians have gone out with Greenpeace expeditions to draw the world's attention to the clubbing of baby seals for their fur. Ambulance services have been provided at large social action gatherings. The Plenty Ethos Research Group studied chemical pollutants in the breast milk of the Farm's vegetarian women and found them significantly lower than in the general U.S. population. The group is now working on a health atlas of Tennessee that will relate mortality rates from various diseases to the locations of chemical plants there. The Plenty Natural Rights Center has filed briefs in a lawsuit to test the constitutionality of the Atomic Energy Act. The suit, filed on behalf of the American public, is based on the Nuclear Regulatory Commission's own estimates that routine operation of the nuclear power industry will result in 484 cancer deaths and 771 genetic defects during the rest of this century.

Altogether, more than 200 Farm members have participated as volunteers in one or more of the Plenty programs. Plenty is not just a sideline of the Farm; it is an integral part of the life of the Farm and its members. It is their way of expressing their belief in the essential unity of all mankind.

Gaskin summed it up at a 1981 meeting at the United Nations of financiers, press, and U.N. representatives:

The reason we exist at all, is that there is a lot of work to be done that nobody's doing. There are a few other groups like ours, but it's fallen to us because you guys with the neckties just aren't doing it.

There's a whole network out there of, well, I call them short-haired hippies, and they already understand what the issues are. Most of them came through the Vietnam years, and they're a trained peace group that we have waiting in the wings. But now they're ten years older and stronger and maybe trained in

---

*Michael Waldhulz, "In an Emergency, South Bronx Turns to Hippie Commune," *The Wall Street Journal*, April 15, 1981.

a profession, and this time they'll realize that they are not powerless. You've got to remember that democracy doesn't mean a thing on the page if people aren't out there participating. Don't get discouraged if you go to one meeting that doesn't work out. Go to another and say to yourself, "Hey, I'm one of the people who is going to close this nuclear plant, or save this village, or change this election." Just get out and participate.*

---

*Lillie Wilson, "The Plenty Project," *New Age* (July 1981), 26.

Part II

AUSTRALIA

Members of the Universal Brotherhood singing original inspirational songs.

CHAPTER 8

The Universal Brotherhood: Waiting for the UFOs

Perth, the capital city of Western Australia, calls itself the most isolated city in the world, separated as it is from the more populous eastern areas of Australia by thousands of miles of desert. Some 150 miles from Perth is the even more isolated town of Balingup—population about 200. Two miles from Balingup is the 317-acre community of the Universal Brotherhood. This is a group of people, mostly young, who (bucking counterculture ideology) strongly oppose nudity, drugs, and unmarried sex. Their apocalyptic view of the future includes a belief that extraterrestrial "elder brothers" in flying saucers are telepathically assisting humanity to expand its consciousness into a greater awareness of its responsibility to this planet, and the role of this planet within the universe. They say that when the earth is near destruction the elder brothers have the technology to evacuate instantly those persons who have demonstrated that they are worth saving through their practice of "the principles of Goodness, Truth and Beauty as exemplified in the life and teachings of Jesus of Nazareth, the sovereign ruler of this local universe and the commander of the UFO space fleet.*

It might seem that such an isolated spot is ideal for a group of people who share such beliefs. But on closer inspection they're not so isolated after all. They're only a three-hour drive from Perth and they have a forestry airstrip on the edge of the property that makes the distance seem even less. John Denver used their airstrip to fly down for a visit when he was performing in Perth. They have established friendly relations with their neighbors and local officials. And while many disagree with their beliefs, the fact is that they are the oldest and largest New Age community in Australia, with a central core of hardheaded, effective people.

Universal Brotherhood, Inc. and UFOs (Universal Brotherhood pamphlet, 1979), 5.

Stephen Carthew was born into an upper middle-class Australian family and grew up in Melbourne and Sydney, graduating from an exclusive private boys' school in the mid-1960s. He thereupon joined the Australian Commonwealth Film Unit and spent several years traveling around Australia and Asia making films. He experimented with drugs and yoga and health food, and wandered through India for a year, exploring the spiritual life. Eventually he set up a New Age information center in Sydney. This brought him into contact with Peter and Eileen Caddy of Findhorn, who advised him to get in touch with two other Australian harbingers of the New Age—Fred and Mary Robinson.

Fred Robinson, who died in 1983 at the age of 92, was one of Australia's most venerable and colorful characters. He was a sugar farmer who got wiped out by the Depression of the 1930s. After this, as he told it, he began his training in the field of New Age awareness under a teacher who had incarnated from another planet specifically to help lay a basis for the New Age to build on. Fred continued training under another teacher until the 1950s, when he began touring the east coast of Australia lecturing on the New Age and UFOs. Fred was a charismatic, loving man who inspired many people to move to intentional communities, not necessarily his own. Four times he started community living projects; four times he failed. In 1962 Fred met Mary, and in 1963 they started a New Age information center in the hills 20 miles south of Perth.

Rosemary Gilmore, Stephen's cousin, left her job in a Melbourne bank to do a year's teaching among the natives of New Guinea through the Australian Volunteers Abroad program. This was her first trip outside Australia, and the New Guinea native culture charmed her with its easiness and openness. She was distressed, however, by the racist white government of New Guinea, and decided to travel further to see how other people lived. She spent three and one-half years in Europe, studying macrobiotics and yoga in Germany and revolutionary theories of social anthropology in Sweden. She cut short her studies in Sweden when her father died, and returned to Australia to help close down his business. She saw her cousin Stephen during this time, and they found that they shared many opinions and ideals.

When Stephen met Fred, he found someone who not only had answers to his questions, but also someone that he enjoyed working with. They decided that they could accomplish much more together than separately. When Stephen introduced Rosemary to Fred, he told her that the time had come for her to consider working on a higher level. She could put her energies into either combating the old or building the new. Rosemary thought that the flying saucers sounded weird, but she decided to give his way a try. In 1971 she and Stephen went to

Perth to live with Fred and Mary and accompany them on national lecture tours.

Mary is 20 years younger than her late husband. And as she told us, the community started in her kitchen. "Fred brought people home and dumped them on me. Fred can't run a community—he can only tell people what is needed. I had no idea how to run a community either, but I knew that my kitchen was a mess so I began to tell people what to do. I found that they liked being given directions. I wasn't very good at it, but gradually I learned."

Soon the collection of people filled the house to overflowing. Mary's son had land at Carranya, about 150 miles north of Perth, and he offered to lease it to them for $1 a year. While Fred and Mary continued to live mainly in Perth, the younger people, led by Stephen, moved north to the hot, sandy land, and rapidly built a community. They built houses of rammed earth and adobe and also bought a number of narrow-gauge railroad cars, at $50 each, in which to live. Before long about 100 people lived in the community.

But all was not harmonious in their Garden of Eden. Mary's son married a woman who disliked her husband's interest in the community, and behaved hostilely toward them. As a result they decided that although they had no money, they must move. Rosemary suggested that they all move back to Perth and live in several low-rent communal houses. Each person who could do so would then take a job and turn over his or her paycheck to the community to build up a fund for the purchase of new land. A few people objected to this and dropped out, but the rest agreed to it and the plan was implemented. The fund grew at the rate of about $2000 a week. Fred and Mary sold their house for $30,000, and one member contributed $10,000. The leaders drove into the countryside looking for land. When they reached the farm near Balingup, with its 3700 square-foot old house and its fruit orchards, they knew at once that it was the right place. They bought it for $57,-000, paying cash. The community's period of exile in Perth had lasted only three months. The members moved the railroad cars and settled in on the farm they occupy today.

The second great crisis of the community took place in mid-1977. This was a crisis of ideas and standards, and it resulted in about half the community leaving.

The Universal Brotherhood regards itself as a light center, that is, a place where people try to live in accordance with God's will. A basic principle is that each should do what he or she knows to be right, and should not do what he or she knows to be wrong. Brotherhood members are mystical Christians, and each person is encouraged to listen to the voice of God within. But the Brotherhood says that in addition to hearing the voice of God (light), a person may hear the voice of Satan (darkness). How does a person know which is which? One way is by comparing the internal voice to those principles of right and wrong that have been handed down in the past, as for example, in the Ten Commandments. Another way is by "confirmation." Mary receives many messages in her dreams, which she always writes down; she does not act on these messages, however, until others have received similar messages or confirmation.

Although the crisis occurred in 1977, tensions had been building for some time, involving people who had been with the Brotherhood for as long as four years. One member, Matt Taylor, was a pop musician who was well known in Western Australia. As his song writing developed he reached into new areas; Stephen told him that his songs were not reflecting the consciousness of the Brotherhood. Matt felt he needed freedom to write as he chose, and so he left the community. This caused many other members to question the Brotherhood philosophy. They held several meetings to discuss their doubts about the authoritarian structure, and then asked Mary to allow them into the management committee. The management committee believed that the dark force was at work and reasserted its authority, reaffirming the original ideals, goals, and values of the Brotherhood.

As Mary expressed it, "The world is made up of chords. Our group represents a particular chord. Someone from a different chord will create a disharmony here. If people do not fit in here, they should leave and try to find a chord with which they are in harmony."

For several weeks the discussions raged. It was apparent that harmony did not exist. At a time when the community badly needed their energies, the leaders of the dissidents finally made their ultimate threat —unless policies were changed, they would leave en masse. The leaders of the community maintained their stand and the dissidents left.

While those who left had plans to start a new, more liberal community, this never happened. Many initially went to Perth, where they lived together in group houses for a few months until they could decide what to do. A number joined the Rajneesh ashram in India; a few eventually joined communities elsewhere. For most, however, it was the end of community life for them. They had put energy, enthusiasm, and several years into the Brotherhood, and they had denied themselves many pleasures; now they felt a great need to get as far as they could from that way of life. The pendulum swung to the other extreme. Many marriages broke up and the ordinary world recaptured most of them. They look back on their Brotherhood experience with sadness—sadness that they could not reconcile their youthful idealism for a better world with their human needs.

Those that stayed behind see it all quite differently. The Brotherhood went through its purge and the true believers remained. While they lost strength in numbers, they gained strength in unity and resolve. They believe that they were attacked by the force of darkness, who played on the weaknesses of the persons who opposed them. But the battle was won. The center held firm. The community, which today numbers about 30 adults and nearly 30 children, seems strong and harmonious and it slowly continues the process of regrowth.

The climate at Balingup is a gentle one, mild to warm, with an occasional light frost, and plenty of rain. The land is rolling hills of a rich, fertile loam that lends itself easily to organic agriculture. The community's farm is in a small valley, extending up the hillside to a forest reserve at the top. Only at the mouth of the valley does it impinge on the neighbors. The big house, which has been turned into Brotherhood headquarters with offices, sanctuary, meeting room, and guest rooms, sits halfway up the hill.

The property is managed with a view to the community becoming as self-sufficient as possible. Members grow crops of wheat, rye, oats, barley, vegetables, and herbs. The orchards consist of ten acres of apples, four of nectarines, and two of peaches. A small vineyard has been established and figs, plums, pears, quinces, oranges, loquats, bush lemons, and apricots are also grown. The community maintains bees, hens, goats, cows, and 200 sheep for wool. The wool and surplus agricultural produce—primarily from the orchards—is sold in Perth, bringing in about $4000 a year. The community plans to increase its agricultural production gradually, but to date most energy has gone into building construction.

A number of springs are located on the property, and these have been developed by constructing three dams above the level of the community buildings, impounding about 7 million gallons of water. Drinking water comes from rain water caught on roofs and stored in cisterns. All other water is piped down from the dams. The main living accommodations consist of five houses, eight chalets, and a few railroad cars and trailers. All have electricity but it is used sparingly because of the expense. One large, well-constructed bathroom building serves the trailer park. It contains separate toilet and washing facilities for men, women, and children, and the members intend to add a sauna (with men and women using it on different nights) when funds become available.

Most of the trailers were brought in by the members. If they leave they can take them along, sell them to new members, or donate them to the community. When houses are built, the cost of materials is paid for by the occupants and the community assists with the labor if and when it can. Such houses belong to the community and cannot be sold. All labor and contributions are considered to be dedicated to the cause for which the community has been created.

Only one new house has been built by the community thus far—a small brick cottage for Fred and Mary. Several other houses were dismantled elsewhere and then erected again in the community. Most of the houses are still fairly primitive, but gradually they are being finished to a reasonably high standard of comfort, with electricity and indoor plumbing. Ultimately, each family will have its own house.

The main source of income to the community comes from a weekly charge to each resident to cover board and participation. This has been increased gradually, and presently amounts to $20 a week per adult. No requirement that people donate their capital to the community exists, and all personal possessions are retained by them. The only thing they pool is their time and energy as they work together to carry out the daily maintenance and administration of the community.

Some people are able to pay the sum of $20 a week out of savings; others take temporary jobs in town or on neighboring farms to earn that amount. All need to have extra money for clothing and incidentals. Members of the community have a reputation as hard workers and are sometimes called on as a group, as when a nearby farmer must get the hay in quickly before an impending rain.

The Brotherhood hopes eventually to be able to fully support its members. At present, however, income from its operations amounts to about 5 or 6 percent of its total budget, and the balance is made up from these modest weekly charges. Some donations have been made, but the community is hesitant to accept any such money unless it is sure of the giver's motivations.

The legal organization and governing of the Brotherhood were not planned in advance, but worked out in day-to-day community life, and in fact are still being developed.

In 1974 a constitution was drawn up and the group was registered as the Universal Brotherhood, Inc. It is recognized by the government as a religious denomination. The idea of becoming a formal denomination evolved out of necessity, as a means of obtaining constitutional protection against harassment for its beliefs. The constitution says that the Brotherhood was formed to assist in the gathering together in communities of people of like mind adhering to the spiritual principles of universal brotherhood; to encourage persons to manifest the living principles of Christ within them; to create an environment in which people may live purely and in harmony with God and nature; to pursue a policy of nonviolence and obedience to the Ten Commandments; and to aim to bring about an ecological balance within its environment, including soil conservation, organic gardening, and recycling of all organic waste.

Within the Brotherhood is a hierarchy of authority: the members as a whole are at the bottom of this hierarchy; higher up are the policy makers, a group of 22 of the most stable and senior of the members; then comes the management committee, a group of 9 of the policy makers (which includes the 6 legal trustees of the Brotherhood); and finally, at the top, is the principal, Mary Robinson. Fred Robinson is considered the founder, but he never played any part in running the community while he was alive. He was often away visiting friends or lecturing. The trustees include Mary Robinson, principal; Stephen Carthew, vice-principal; Rosemary Gilmore, secretary; Sam Purves, treasurer; John Pasco, health officer; and John Berger, manager of community affairs. All have been in the Brotherhood for at least ten years. They appear to be a strong team with a high degree of unanimity among them.

Brotherhood members endeavor to base their decisions on divine guidance and principles. But if a suggestion comes through Mary or someone else as a channel, they judge it on its own merits, since they recognize that no channel is infallible. Issues are normally discussed and agreement reached at weekly meetings of the entire membership. Guests and visitors are welcome to attend these weekly meetings; their viewpoints, however, are regarded as only suggestions. If a proposal is to be implemented, all the members present at the meeting must agree with it. Even if only if one member feels strongly enough to reject a proposal, that is sufficient opposition to cause a review of the proposed course of action. Votes are not normally taken, as the objective is to reach a consensus. If agreement can't be reached, they adjourn the meeting and try again the next evening.

If it is necessary to make a decision but consensus cannot be reached, the next step is to begin again with the members of the policy makers. If consensus among them cannot be reached, the issue goes to the management committee. If they are unable to agree, the decision, in theory, is up to the principal. In practice, however, no issue has gone beyond the management committee or trustees.

The word *consensus* is defined by the community as "harmonious agreement." Members are discouraged from just going along with the majority, because an opposing opinion may be the correct one. They also believe that it is a mistake to base any society on a leader's charisma. They see the consensus process as a safeguard against the community being subject to the whims of any one member, while at the same time, giving due consideration to the viewpoint of each member.

Managers are appointed by the principal and chosen either because the person has begun spontaneously to carry out the responsibilities of a certain position, or because he or she has demonstrated the ability to fill that position. All managers are formally reviewed at each annual general meeting, but new appointments or changes in personnel may be made at any time.

Members call their system "fraternal democracy." Despite this, however, in implementing general policies, the management committee members hold themselves responsible to give direction when they feel it is needed. For example, many television shows are considered unsuitable even for adults, and the management committee, barred the children from seeing "Sesame Street" because the puppets bash each other.

Members are recruited through word of mouth, articles about the Brotherhood, and (in earlier days) Fred's talks. Frequently people come to visit for a weekend or a few days. If they like what they find, they move in for a period of at least six weeks. This is the trial period, and during this time newcomers participate in daily seminars on Brotherhood principles. Seminars cover such matters as morals, UFOs, and the principles of nutrition, and good health. After six weeks an applicant may write a letter to the policy makers asking for admittance. If it feels right to them, the applicant is accepted. Similarly, if the policy makers conclude that a member is no longer in harmony with the principles of the Brotherhood, he or she can be expelled.

Most members are between the ages of 25 and 35; one member is in his forties and Mary is in her seventies. Australians dominate the Brotherhood, but Yugoslavs, Dutch, English, Canadians, New Zealanders, and Americans are also represented. The majority had some university training; one was a consulting engineer. Few had any prior experience in intentional communities. Most of the members are married, with a total of nearly 30 children, the oldest of which is 13. Many of the marriages took place within the Brotherhood. While the Brotherhood does not condone premarital or extramarital sex, if a couple desiring to marry cannot do so because one cannot obtain a divorce, the Brotherhood makes an exception and allows them to live together.

Members of the Brotherhood are very involved in the education of their children, and plan to keep it within the group. In Australia parents have the right to educate their children, provided they can demonstrate to the authorities their ability to do so satisfactorily. At the time of our visit, four children were being taught by five teachers—perhaps the best student-teacher ratio in all Australia! The local authorities had checked them out and expressed complete satisfaction.

To the Brotherhood, character development is the most important aspect of education. As Mary says:

Each child is brought into the world to fulfill a specific role. All children are individuals. It is our responsibility to provide the training and character building so that they have the freedom to fulfill their own destinies. It's like growing a tree. If it has deep roots and a sturdy trunk it will succeed and grow well. The main thing that we educate our children to do is to get their own contact with God. If we've done our job right, we don't need to be worried that they won't be able to handle the "big bad world" when they go into it.

These are unprecedented times. The whole structure of society is changing. We cannot predict what it will be like when our children grow up. The best we can do is bring them up in a good environment.

Children are born at the local hospital; a doctor who uses the LeBoyer method ("birth without violence") and a lay midwife from the Brotherhood assist the birth. The father is in the delivery room and gives the baby its first bath. Three Brotherhood members, one an herbalist and yoga teacher, one a Touch for Health (Kinesiology) practitioner, and one an osteopath trainee, run a self-healing clinic. A next-door neighbor is a physician who is called on when the need arises.

In dealing with its neighbors, the Brotherhood's initial policy was to "stay in its own backyard" and deal with people at their level. "If you talk with a baker, you talk about bread." Gradually the group made friends. Now it is fairly active in regional affairs, often sending members to sing and dance at schools or meetings of groups such as the Kiwanis or Country Women's Association. A number of school classes have come to the community for a visit. The Brotherhood participated in a recent festival in Balingup to mark the 150-year anniversary of Western Australia, even writing a song for the occasion.

Some of the members get the daily newspapers or watch the news programs on television. Everybody votes, since it is required by law in Australia. While most support the Labour party, the community has no party line, and, in fact, the general feeling is that because the political parties represent vested interests they are not likely to have the true answers to Australia's problems.

The Brotherhood does speak out on moral issues. It recently took a strong stand against the Labour party's proposal to legalize marijuana. Members have also written letters to the newspapers opposing nuclear energy and public nudity, and refused to attend a large New Age gathering because public nudity had been permitted the previous year. While stands against marijuana and nudity do not win them friends among the counterculture, they do appeal to their conservative country neighbors.

Despite this, the Brotherhood has had problems with "anticult sentiments." It has received more press publicity of this nature than any other group in Australia. One parent threatened to hire a deprogrammer to free her child from the Brotherhood's influence. The group responded by soliciting letters of support from other parents.

The negative publicity impelled Mary to write an article in defense of the Brotherhood. After reviewing the ideals and practices of other groups, she concluded:

We have set a pattern here which meets the approval of the world Authorities and fulfills the requirements of the pervading New Age spirit of Peace and Goodwill. Our Policy is to "Do what we *know* is right and not do what we *know* is wrong." With this simple Policy—which is much easier to say than to do—when you think about it—we have made our way to this point in time with a clean and open sheet. Why then are we the Principal Target for these Anti-Cults?

If we are outworking the Spirit of Christ—which, of course, we are, could it be

that the Anti-Cults are an organized Anti-Christ movement? I can see no other
logic behind their actions. As the term Anti-Christ has many meanings for
many, many people, I will define it here as simply "That Spirit which is opposed
to the Spirit of Christ." It was that Spirit in man which crucified the Christ. . . .

To the parents I would say, I have reared a family of four, and each has gone
his separate way. The generation gap is a real thing—a gift from God—and not
a fad or a fancy fashion. We've had our opportunity to guide them, and mostly
we have failed. Love and bless them and pray the God within will guide them to
the light they seek. Each must find the place he fits. The harmony for which he
longs. The soul is seeking for its spiritual home. They will love you more than
you can comprehend if you trust them. My people do, that's how I know.*

So here is a community that has struggled against the problems of
loss of its original home, loss of half its members, and hostility from that
segment of the press and the public that sees only its "weird" beliefs and
not the love, harmony, and morality that are its hallmarks.

Where is the balance between, at one extreme, a group that denies
individuality and, at the other extreme, a group that allows a degree of
individual license that is antithetical to its own survival? All traditional
small communities impose restraints on the behavior and utterances—
perhaps even the thoughts of their members. And while many decry
the "brainwashing" in what they call cults, they generally accept without
question the "brainwashing" of those in Christian convents and monasteries.

Our own feelings on this subject are to be wary of groups with a
charismatic leader who can do no wrong, or who restrict their members
access to contrary ideas found in books or the outside world.

The Brotherhood has no charismatic leader who must be obeyed—
only the Ten Commandments. While other spiritual paths may be
judged harshly if they fail to live up to the moral standards of the
Brotherhood, the group has no objection to those paths being explored
or their literature read. Books are censored, but more for their moral
lapses than for their ideals. *The Lord of the Rings* was banned because the
management committee felt it placed an undue focus on the force of
darkness. Members are in contact with those in the outside world and
are free to go out into it when they wish. But they are also given affir-
mations to repeat when away from the Brotherhood to help them hold
onto their beliefs.

Where does the Brotherhood see itself headed? Members hope to
finish work on the buildings soon, so that they can place more emphasis
on agricultural production and become more self-sufficient. They are
nearly self-sufficient now in terms of energy. Most of their houses have
solar ovens, solar fruit dryers, and solar hot water systems, and mem-

---

*Mary Robinson, *The Anti-Cults Exposed* (monograph, Balingup, Australia: n.d.), 2–3.

bers are investigating solar cells to produce electricity. They would like to step up their educational efforts. They are considering formal week-end workshops to which people would come from Perth. They would like to publish a primer of their teachings and perhaps other books also. They feel that about 100 people is the maximum practical size for a community such as theirs. If they grow beyond that, they would like to start a new community.

Whether the Universal Brotherhood will achieve the growth and success it aims for is hard to say. Its moral standards are not that different from many ashrams and spiritual groups, and many people who have gone through unhappy experimentation with drugs and sex may find their way of life appealing. The UFO doctrine may be limiting, but most of the leadership is young and solid and seems capable of carrying the group forward for a long time to come.

We will watch its development with great interest.

Terrance in the herb garden at Homeland.

CHAPTER 9

Homeland: Is Attunement Enough?

Homeland is a product of three groups of people. Michael and Treenie Roads (both now 45 years old) come from English farming families. About 15 years ago they left England with their four children to settle on a large farm in Tasmania, an island off the southeast Australian coast. After a time they felt the call of what Michael terms the 'Findhorn spirit." They sold the farm, moved to the Australian continent, and set off in a camper to find or start a community that would exemplify and develop this spirit. The Roads had never been to Findhorn and knew little about it. Nonetheless they felt the call, and so began their quest.

One of their first stops was at Santosha, a small community on the border of the states of New South Wales and Victoria. The nucleus of Santosha was the Davis family—four sons and their parents. The inspiration for Santosha was Fred Robinson and the Universal Brotherhood community; they shared the same strict moral code and discipline. Bruce Davis, the oldest son and the guiding force, had given up a successful soccer career and a trainee position in the field of drafting to devote his energies to building a New Age center on the organic fruit farm that he had convinced his parents to begin. They had given up their comfortable middle-class existence in Melbourne to move to the arid countryside. The strictness of the discipline did not attract many others, so while it was called a community, Santosha was basically the Davis family farm.

Despite their differences in outlook and inspiration, the Davis and Roads families felt an immediate link. Nonetheless, the Roads family continued their quest, arriving five months later at the Universal Brotherhood in Western Australia. By chance, Mark Davis, the youngest son, arrived there the same day. They greeted each other joyously and the Roadses later decided to return to Santosha and build their community.

After they got back, however, they realized that Santosha was too hot and dry, too flat and barren. In addition, the elder Davises were tired of farming and wanted to sell the property and return to Melbourne.

While the Roads family traveled the highways in search of a dream and the Davis family lived and worked at Santosha, Terrance Plowright was building the New Awareness Center in Sydney. Plowright dropped out of school at 15, then worked for a while as a film editor with the Australian Broadcasting Company. At 21 he joined a psychic group. As he became more spiritually involved, he began to feel that his work was meaningless. He quit and moved to Tasmania where, with barely enough money for the down payment and virtually no farming experience, he bought 100 acres. Plowright had been told by a psychic that he would buy this land, that it would be a good investment, and that he would eventually link up with a group doing spiritual work in Scotland. All this came to pass—even though Terrance had not even heard of Findhorn when he was told this. He lived in Tasmania for a few years, then sold his land for a small profit, moved back to the mainland, and promptly ran into some people just back from Findhorn. They told him about the community and played some records of the New Troubadors, the Findhorn music group. It was enough. Plowright headed for Findhorn and stayed there nine months, becoming an important member of the community with close ties to Eileen Caddy, one of the founders.

One morning Plowright received what he believed was an inner directive to leave Findhorn and go to Australia to lay the foundation for a New Age center. While still in England he visited a center that incorporated a tea shop, bookstore, and classroom. He decided that this was the kind of center he would create in Australia. On his return he started the New Awareness Centre in Sydney with some friends, and through the center he met the Roads family and Bruce Davis, who by then were driving across Australia, looking for land on which to build one community. Intrigued, Plowright asked to be included in when they found their land.

Before they left Santosha on their trek, the Roads family and Davis had prayed a prayer of manifestation, asking for an area in southern Queensland with fertile soil, a center of spiritual power, an abundance of fresh water and trees, a house with outbuildings, hills and valleys surrounding the house, and the ocean close enough so they could benefit from its spiritual presence. Bruce Davis and Michael Roads drove thousands of miles and looked at an endless series of country properties —each time knowing that they had not yet found their home. And then their travels took them into the Bellinger Valley, 300 miles south of Brisbane.

Roads reported:

Here the vibration changed. Suddenly we both felt charged with a tremendous energy, a positive knowing that we were nearly there. The next day saw us on a tour of farms and land with an estate agent who was sensitive to our needs and had even heard of Findhorn. There it was, the perfect manifestation of our prayer. Hills and valleys on 345 acres of land. Mountains behind the magnificent Bellinger River with approximately 3 kilometers on the farm frontage. The homestead, the buildings, the trees—it was all there, put together in such a way that we were left spellbound.

Their mission completed, they hurried back to Sydney to tell Plowright and together formulate plans for the future. Now they needed $65,000 to pay for the land. The almost penniless group sincerely believed in the power of manifestation, and since they still had four months to gather the funds, they weren't worried. Ten days before the money was due, it still was not in sight. So the group held a seminar in Sydney—"Man, Nature and the New Age"—with song, talk, and communion. They raised $24,000 in interest-free loans and donations that night. Later that week the rest of the money was raised when friends cosigned on a high-interest commercial loan. By April 1, the due date, the land was bought.

Now the way was clear for the move to the community that soon became known as Homeland. About 25 more people dribbled in during April 1977. Of the new arrivals, 15 had come from the New Awareness Centre, and 9 were their children. Most had not seen the property before.

The people at Homeland speak of the spirit of attunement that they feel. As Anatole Kononewsky, one of the members, wrote:

At Homeland, life is providing the opportunity of creating a Centre of Light. This Centre of Light exists within each of us and yet, is more than just the individual. An interesting ingredient, here at Homeland, is that this creation is not by any one individual, rather the individual has to have the strength to move into and become vulnerable to a group process. This, in fact, takes far more courage, dedication, and a centredness than is necessary to simply do your own thing.

He went on to say:

Life will supply you with all you need, in unlimited abundance, to express the very thing you are. If you are expressing separative, negative, and selfish energies then life will quite naturally provide you with all the experiences and forms to express those energies. If on the other hand an individual or group of individuals are working from an unselfish approach to life, being positive, joyous, and loving in their actions, then once again, life will quite naturally provide all that is necessary to express the fundamental consciousness which the individual or group is at. Life is an incredible teacher, for inherent in its process is a principle which states: we attract to ourselves exactly what we are. Every person on this planet right now is using this principle. Everyone is totally responsible for the exact situation they find themselves in, whether they are conscious of it or not.*

The property of Homeland consists of about 200 acres of native bush and 150 acres of cleared land. Most of it is in an almost virgin state, and the Bellinger River is reputed to be one of the clearest and cleanest in Australia. It provides all the community's drinking water, as well as a wonderful swimming hole. The vegetation is lush, almost semitropical. A feeling of peace and oneness between nature and people is the basis of everyday existence there.

At its largest, in 1979, Homeland had 44 members, 10 of whom were children. Most were in their early thirties, not many were much younger, and a few were in their fifties and sixties. While Terrance Plowright and Michael Roads were both educational dropouts, over half the members of the community were former professionals. Members included psychologists, a biologist, an engineer, teachers, computer experts, researchers, and government bureaucrats. While the preponderance of members were Australian, Americans, Britons, Germans, and even one Burmese joined Homeland. They felt that they were living in a global village.

Those at Homeland see no difference between themselves and those who remain in the cities or on their own farms. Those who are at Homeland have simply chosen to be there. Treenie Roads told us that one part of her would like to be living her own life, not tied down to community routine, but that most of her wanted to be there. Terrance Plowright explained his presence at Homeland this way: "Living here is like taking steps in the dark. It requires total faith. I don't know where we are going, but it doesn't matter. I feel this group is my family. A big part of me moves into bewilderment as to why I'm here. It's the fulfillment and communion I receive that keep me here. But I could equally be called away." And in 1980 he did move on.

With the exception of the Santosha group, few of the members had extensive prior experience living in intentional communities before coming to Homeland. One couple had lived on an Israeli kibbutz and nearly 15 had visited Findhorn, several staying a few months.

Homeland is probably the best-known community in Australia, due in large part to the publicity it received from being the coordinators of Peter and Eileen Caddy's Findhorn tour in Australia. This was a commitment that Plowright had made prior to leaving Findhorn and an activity that consumed a great part of Homeland's energy in its first year. In conjunction with the Findhorn lectures, Plowright gave a series of talks and slide shows about Homeland.

---

*A. Kononewsky, "One Humanity," *Homecoming* 3 (January 1978): 1–2.

The requirements for membership have changed over time. For some months after the Findhorn tour, no new members were accepted. The group felt that consolidation was more important than growth, though paying guests have always been welcome. Guest fees, in fact, make up an important part of the community's income.

To become a member requires being a guest for three weeks (paying a $60 per week guest fee), then leaving the community for at least three weeks. After this, the potential member has a six-month probationary period, followed by a community decision as to whether the person is in harmony with the group. The community has never turned down someone who has stayed out the probationary period. If the harmony were not there, they say, it would have long since been felt and the individual would have left.

Probationary and full members pay $40 per week to stay at Homeland (with a lower charge for children). This means that some have to take outside jobs to raise the money. They also provide their own trailer to live in. It is insignificant whether people have simple or fancy trailers at Homeland, because material goods mean little to the residents. Members do not have to turn their private assets over to Homeland; a number do have significant private assets. Before arriving at Homeland, Michael Roads wrote two books (one on organic gardening and one on homesteading), which together have sold more than 30,000 copies. All of the income is his alone, though he has donated some of it to the community.

There is no notion that members must make a lifetime commitment to Homeland. Plowright talked with us about his desire to travel to the United States. Others spoke of a long-term commitment to the community, but the group's feeling was that people should stay only as long as they want. When they're ready to leave they leave with the community's blessing, and most retain a close relationship with Homeland.

Homeland is loosely organized. The Homeland Foundation is registered as a charitable trust, with nine trustees. Only one still lives in the community. The community has been approved as a trailer park by the local council. This means that more people can live on the property than would normally be permitted.

For the first six months of Homeland's existence, a core group, composed of Michael Roads, Treenie Roads, Terrance Plowright, Bruce Davis, and Yvonne Siems who was from the New Awareness Centre, dominated community life. The core group was dissolved after a three day meeting when the entire community gathered to discuss restructuring; members wanted to move away from the Findhorn model. At that meeting they developed the idea of "focalizers," who would be responsible for running departments. Departments were established for building, maintenance, finance (including general administration), homestead (cooking, cleaning, and so on), publications, audio, gardening, and guests.

During the next two years the governing of the community worked this way: any individual could suggest an innovation or change and share it at his or her department's daily meeting. When the department was satisfied with the suggestion and when it was pertinent to that department only, it was usually acted on then and there. When it was a decision that would affect the entire community, the focalizer would take it to the focalizers' Friday meeting. The focalizers could implement a minor decision, but any major decision would be discussed and relevant points referred back to all the departments and discussed at the Saturday department attunement meetings. At the attunement meetings, individual members gained an overview of what was happening in the community. The decision could be discussed again at the Monday meeting of the entire community. At this meeting major decisions could be made, rejected, or referred back to the department, thereby completing the cycle.

This elaborate structure became very cumbersome. The Saturday department attunement meetings lasted two hours or more, with discussions often continuing at the Monday community meeting. It got to the point of having meeting after meeting, hearing one opinion after another. It was good as therapy, but not a terribly efficient use of the community's time and energy.

Since 1979 the community has followed a new system in which the individual departments make their own decisions and present them to the community as a *fait accompli*—though the decisions can be disputed. Community members trust that each department is attuned to both its needs and those of the community at large, and the system works well. Often the focalizer alone makes decisions, feeling assured that through attunement he or she can speak for the department.

Attunement is an important element of life at Homeland. All department members have a period of attunement before they start work each work. Following breakfast a community sanctuary is also held each day for group meditation and attunement. The people at Homeland feel that by meditating together in this way, letting their energies come together in the same room while each seeks inner guidance for the tasks at hand, they will be in tune with each other regarding issues with which they have to deal.

As with so much of what happens at Homeland, there is no formal process for choosing a focalizer. Often someone starts a project and naturally becomes its focalizer. At other times the community chooses whomever it feels can best do the job. The focalizer might not even have had experience in his department. Terrance Plowright, for example, was focalizer for the Findhorn tour. When that was over, he was drafted by the community to head the building department, even though he knew next to nothing about construction. The two garden focalizers at that time, on the other hand, had extensive gardening experience. Many times focalizers choose to move to a new department, and others have to be chosen to replace them.

Homeland's original motivation was educational: Homeland was to be a center of light and truth similar to Findhorn. After a couple years of operation, however, the educational side began to be less emphasized. As Michael Roads said, expressing the community's views at the time of our visit: "This is a life center. We're not teaching anyone anything at all. We're all peeling away layers from ourselves; taking away the wrappers. Education is putting things in. Taking the layers off helps us to see more clearly."

In a sense then, it is not so much a group of people building a community as it is a community used as a vehicle for building a group of people. It is an opportunity for them to explore, through this medium, ways of reducing ego involvement and learning to attune to and trust others. Plowright said: "I am not building community, God is building it. If I feel that I am building it, there's an element of a lack of trust. To demonstrate this trust means freedom. Life is an orderly thing. If one tunes into the universe he will manifest order. We need as individuals to manifest the unknown in an orderly way; to approach civilization in a whole new way. The goal, if there is any, is to tune into God—and we define God as the cause or essence of all life.

In spite of this talk of God, no one in the community when we visited it would call himself or herself a follower of any religion. Some at Homeland had been Theosophists (an esoteric philosophy incorporating many Asian religious ideas). It is a popular spiritual path in Australia since two leading early Theosophists, C. W. Leadbeater and Geoffrey Hodson, had spent much of their lives there. Others had followed one or another Eastern philosophy, some had been Christians, while a few had previously had religious beliefs derived from Findhorn. But all felt that these beliefs have to be left behind if they are to truly grow together in awareness and attunement. Most didn't read books or newspapers. While members had some interest in world events, their involvement with Homeland was total, and the members' overriding feeling was that each person was at Homeland to fulfill some part of his or her destiny.

Right from the start Homeland has had a shaky economic base. When large amounts were needed, the members depended on the money manifesting itself. In the early days money to meet the weekly expenses came from tape and book distribution (mainly Findhorn material), *Homecoming Magazine* (about 250 paid subscriptions), donations, and membership fees. The first two businesses were begun at the

New Awareness Center and continued to be carried on at Homeland. In the first year $6000 came in from Homeland's percentage of the Findhorn tour receipts; Homeland members estimated this amounted to only 25¢ an hour for their labor.

Guests are a regular feature of life at Homeland and an important source of income. The maximum number accepted at any time is ten; the average is about seven. The guest roster is filled up months in advance for holiday and vacation periods. The guest program consists of a number of workshops and involvement in group work and community life. The charge of $10 a day, $60 a week, covers all meals, but guests must provide their own accommodations, either a trailer or a tent. Occasionally space in one of the community's trailers is available for an additional fee. Each morning the guests are told by their focalizer what the needs of the community are and they then choose what work they will do. The guests can attend all meetings and participate fully in the life at Homeland. One guest with whom we chatted explained that she thought of Homeland as her home away from home.

In addition to the money they bring in, the guests provide an additional source of labor. Work that requires many hands is often scheduled for when the largest number of guests will be in residence. Guests are not required to work, but it is hard to be a part of the community and not participate in the ongoing work.

During our visit we attended a community meeting at which Michael Roads presided. The topic was finances, and the purpose of the meeting was twofold: to explore Homeland's difficult financial situation and to tell the community about the finance committee's decision to tithe 10 percent of Homeland's already small income. Finances had been a major topic of discussion over the past few weeks, and Roads began by saying that a major part of Homeland's money problems was due to its "poverty consciousness," that is, feeling both that money is evil and that it will always be in short supply. He suggested a "consciousness of abundance," and explained his belief that money is just a symbolic system of measuring energy. To keep this energy moving, Roads said, Homeland must tithe. Accordingly, members of the finance committee had decided to tithe 10 percent of Homeland's income to the New Awareness Centre and they urged individuals to also tithe from their own income. The difference between Homeland's concept of tithing and that of groups such as the Mormon Church was that Homeland was giving away part of its very limited resources, not just collecting money from its members.

Roads explained:

Loss of fear leads to freedom. Once we put energy forward, it creates a vacuum and there is space for new energy to flow in. Once we put energy out, it will return. Others will tithe to us. The more that flows in, the more we can put back in. Tithing is an income tax, divinely assessed; a means of acknowledging God's law. To harvest wheat you have to sow wheat.

The reaction to Michael's proposal was one of acceptance, with a few expressions of gratitude. The justness of the decision was not questioned, nor was any feeling expressed that the entire community should have been consulted.

A number of other approaches to solving the community's financial problems were being explored also. One frequently discussed was the idea of members working outside Homeland and giving most of their earnings back to the community. A number of members had sought work and when they couldn't find any, they applied for unemployment compensation. Homeland members really wanted work, and they felt that this differentiated Homeland from the many hippie communes nearby that subsisted almost entirely on the dole with the members having no desire or intention of taking outside employment.

Community businesses were just getting started. Two experienced potters who had formerly had a successful business in the city had recently joined the community, and were in the process of setting up their studio. Surplus sprouts and tofu were already occasionally sold to health food stores in a neighboring town. The major consideration for any future business was that each should pay its own way.

Today, in 1984, Homeland has a full-fledged tofu industry and now supplies a much wider market. The business had to import equipment from Japan in order to make it in the larger quantities required. The company is inspected regularly by the Health Commission and the product is considered an excellent one. Selling sprouts is also a much larger business now, with the sprouts being sold to many more stores, including supermarkets. Many problems were encountered initially, including those caused by the hot, humid climate, but through trial and error these have been overcome. This business is now housed in its own building. The pottery business has changed hands, but is flourishing. Several other potteries are located in the valley, however, so Homeland does have competition. Another industry, this one still in its infancy, is bronzing. Homeland's first aboriginal member—a skilled sculptor—is learning to do bronzing at Homeland under the guidance of another member.

The family structure at Homeland is traditional. The majority of members are married, though some of these marriages are spiritual, rather than legal. Freedom is the key word in describing the community's way of life, and this extends to sexual matters. No strict moral code is imposed, though promiscuity is frowned on.

. The essence of interpersonal relations is consideration. An example is the community's attitude toward nudity. When we visited, two swimming areas were available—one for nude swimmers and one for swimmers wearing suits. The nude area was used by almost all the members of the community and was the more choice spot. But the other area was the larger one and people with suits could come to the nudist site if they wished. Nudity was discouraged outside of the swimming area because of the constant influx of guests, many of whom were more conservative.

Most of the homes are trailers, which are privately owned. Each person brings his or her own trailer or buys an existing one. The first permanent house was built in 1980 by a 17-year-old member who had been to technical college for one year studying carpentry and could not get work with a professional builder locally. So he built a handsome two-bedroom house for Yvonne Siems, the only one of the original members still living at Homeland. (Michael and Treenie Roads live nearby and are still trustees.) The amenities building with toilets, bathtubs and showers, laundry and sauna, was finished in 1982 and can serve 150 people; it uses solar heat for its hot water system, a heating method that Homeland would like to adopt, along with methane, in future buildings. The second permanent house was completed in 1983. As more buildings are erected, Homeland will become more of a community of permanent residents, and this will doubtless mean many changes for it.

The children of school age obtain their education outside the community; the parents feel that it is important that they do. "Moving away from the energy of Homeland creates balance in the kids," one parent said. In 1982 Homeland leased a beautiful section of its property, with river frontage and wonderful views, to a group of people who started a Waldorf school based on the educational principles of Rudolf Steiner. The school presently has three teachers and has prospects of further growth. In fact, some parents are moving into the area just to be near this school. While the school is completely autonomous, its spiritual approach is in harmony with the Homeland way of life.

Meals at Homeland are communal, though breakfast and lunch are buffet style and members often take the food back to their trailers to eat. Dinner is shared and people take turns waiting on the others. Other times of community sharing are during sanctuary, community meetings, occasional morning teas, and "light nights," when members entertain each other with skits and songs.

A strong ecological consciousness is in evidence at Homeland. Hundreds of trees are planted in the trailer park, each marked with a pole so it will not be trampled at night. Michael Roads created a spiral in the meadow composed of hundreds of trees, because he felt that the empty meadow looked unloved. Before long it will become an attractive park. It is hoped that the trees will bring back the birds, and many are now returning, including some colorful parrots.

The valley will soon become a wildlife refuge, a legal move that Homeland strongly supports. No pets are allowed to be brought in by members or guests, but one community cat and one community dog do live there. It is recognized that more dogs and cats would upset the ecological balance of the wildlife.

The community started out with a two-acre garden, but members found that this was too much to handle, so they later reduced it to a half-acre plot. They grow much of the community's food and use the organic method. They have one cow and several chickens. One of the newer members recently planted many fruit and nut trees, including tropical fruit trees and stone fruit trees. They will be a great asset in the future.

Relations with the outside world have been good. Not many of the original private farms are left in the Bellinger Valley. Craftspeople, sculptors, painters, and homesteaders are moving in. Large farms are being broken up and Homeland is surrounded by new people.

Members recognize the importance of having good relations with public officials. As Terrance Plowright said, "Dealing with the local council is like dealing with God—the council is God." He was aware that they felt differently and had different ideals. "But they are all holy; all manifestations of the divine. If you experience God within all people, then cooperation becomes easy because when you are cooperating with God you are cooperating with yourself."

It is now seven years since Homeland was begun. It has grown a lot during that time and has established itself for a solid future. It is still leaderless, which means everyone has to take responsibility for his or her own work and for the decisions that are made. Because of a continuing large turnover, Homeland suffers from a lack of continuity and it is difficult to get long-term projects started and working.

Members do express much love and caring for each other. "Attunement" and "harmony" are not merely words; they are the focus of the community. And yet no effort to mold people is made. Each person carries out his or her own particular project, and takes the responsibility that goes with it. Perhaps there is a sense of aimlessness at Homeland. But this, too, is a stage. As more people build homes and settle in, this doubtless will change.

Michael Roads once said:

Why I am here exemplifies my expectations for the future. I see man as an energy moving through evolution into time. Two streams of consciousness are separating—the selfish and the selfless. These streams have to diverge so that the New Age can be born and each of us has to choose whether to give or to take. I see Homeland as a bridge, helping to carry people to the new shore. Once there are enough of us, the old will destroy itself and the new world will be born.

Part III

FRANCE

Members of the Community of the Ark follow Gandhi's example in spinning their own wool to weave cloth for some of their clothing.

CHAPTER 10

The Community of the Ark: Gandhiism in the West

Fifty years ago, Lanza del Vasto, scion of a Sicilian noble family, was what we might now call a hippie, wandering through Europe taking odd jobs, living from hand to mouth, seeking God. With the Italian attack on Ethiopia and the likelihood of a general European war, Vasto made a pilgrimage to India and became a disciple of the man who had made nonviolence into an ideology and a movement—Mohandas K. Gandhi. In 1937 he arrived at Wardha, Gandhi's home village, where he joined many young Indians in a training program to go out to the villages and help them develop along Gandhian lines.

In addition to working for nonviolence and an end to the caste system, Gandhi espoused self-sufficiency and voluntary poverty:

No man is dispensed by nature from working with his hands. Even the man who devotes himself to the incomparably superior activities of the mind is not dispensed from hard work unless he gives up everything that has cost labour in this world below. If he dispenses himself from it and does not give up what costs labour, he is putting his burden on others and remains in their debt.

Desires should be reduced to needs. Manual labour will soon satisfy these; man will then find himself free. Good can only come from free men, and first and foremost from men free from debts and desires.

Let every man be self-sufficient, let every man think of himself and his own family first; that is charity well ordered. Provided he is content with what he produces himself. That is the principle of *Swadeshi* (self-reliance), the kernel and gauge of independence. Whenever a man cannot be self-sufficient, let his family be so; if his family cannot, let the village be so; if the village cannot, let the district and, lastly, the country be so.

Gandhi also preached the importance of meaningful work and decried the use of machines that demeaned the worker:

The truth is that man needs work even more than he needs a wage. Those who seek the welfare of the workers should be less anxious to obtain good pay, good holidays and good pensions for them than good work, which is the first of their goods. For the object of work is not so much to make objects as to make men. A man makes himself by making something. Work creates a direct contact with matter and ensures him a practical knowledge of it as well as direct contact and daily collaboration with other men; it imprints the form of man on matter and offers itself to him as a means of expression; it concentrates his attention and his abilities on one point or at least on a continuous line; it bridles the passions by strengthening the will.

But in order that work itself, and not just payment for it, shall profit a man, it must be human work, work in which the whole man is engaged: his body, his heart, his brain, his taste. The craftsman who fashions an object, polishes it, decorates it, sells it, and fits it for the requirements of the person he intends it for, is carrying out human work. The countryman who gives life to his fields and makes his flocks prosper by work attuned to the seasons is successfully accomplishing the task of a free man.

But the worker enslaved in serial production, who from one second to another repeats the same movement at speed dictated by the machine, fritters himself away in work which has no purpose for him, no end, no taste, no sense. The time he spends there is time lost, time sold: he is not selling his creation but his very lifetime. He is selling what a free man does not sell: his life. He is a slave.

If a machine is useful, then use it; if it becomes necessary, then it is your urgent duty to throw it away, for it will inevitably catch you up in its wheels and enslave you.*

Lanza del Vasto felt at home in India with Gandhi. This was to be his life. He asked Gandhi to give him a new name, and Gandhi renamed him Shantidas—"servant of peace." After three months at Wardha, Shantidas made the great pilgrimage to the source of the Ganges in the Himalayas—a pilgrimage that for the devout Hindu is like a trip to Mecca for a Muslim. It was a journey of adventure, hardship, and spiritual enlightenment. Barefoot, dressed in only a loincloth, often penniless, Shantidas was a European holy man—an object of wonderment and awe to the Indians. For Shantidas, making the holy pilgrimage did not mean giving up his Christianity. He believed that as a person ascends the path of enlightenment, from whatever his or her spiritual direction, the landscape becomes progressively more similar, until at the summit all paths meet. Shantidas found in India a depth and meaning to his Catholicism that had eluded him in Europe.

Something else happened on this pilgrimage. In a mountain village an inner voice told Shantidas that he was not to stay in India, that the place of Gandhi's Western disciple was in the West. His new goal became to found a community of people in the West, bound by solemn vows, who would live together according to the rules of *ahimsa* (nonviolence) and *swadeshi* (self-reliance). His ideal was to make this community

---

*Lanza del Vasto, *Return to the Source* (New York: Schocken Books, 1968).

thrive on poverty and hard bodily labor, and grow in independence, so that in time it would transform the life of Western people from within, eliminating bloodshed and revolution and the endless chain of wars.

A tall order! Shantidas returned to Wardha, gained Gandhi's blessing for his new task, and sailed home.

Eleven years passed before Shantidas was able to start his first community. With his new wife Chanterelle and one other couple, the Community of the Ark was founded in a wing of his wife's family's country home. Gradually it grew; twice it moved. In 1963 the present location was purchased: la Borie Noble (the noble borough)—1200 acres in southern France.

Driving northwest from Montpelier, through the fertile valley of Herault with its wineries and its orchards heavy with peaches, pears, and figs, one passes the ancient town of Lodeve and enters the mountains. The road narrows and winds upward, and the view becomes more spectacular while the cultivation becomes more sparse. Finally one drops into a little valley and discovers the pink tower of la Borie Noble. It is a beautiful setting in which to live, but not an easy one. Green and fecund in the summer, it is cold and rainy in the winter. Too high for fruit to grow, the land is poor and the farm—like many in the area—had been abandoned when the community bought it. They have restored the ruined houses, added a new wing and tower to the main building, and built new houses with care, love, and attention to detail.

We park our car in the visitor's parking lot, next to the large, well-maintained vegetable garden, and as we ascend the paved road to the main house, we sense an air of purposefulness and peacefulness. Arriving at the courtyard we find several women sitting in the sun before the great arches of the veranda, spinning wool. What could be more appropriate for a Gandhian community? We meet Jane Prentiss from Nebraska, the only American in this mostly French community. While living in San Francisco she heard Shantidas lecture and was moved by his message and his commitment. Eventually she made her way to France and la Borie Noble. Her goal now is to become a full member of the community, then return to the United States in a few years to help start a community there.

After a brief introduction Prentiss takes us around the grounds. La Borie Noble, with about 70 people, is the largest of the three residential communities on this land, all parts of the Community of the Ark. Each is self-governing, but la Borie Noble, as the first and largest, is the main headquarters of the organization and its bakery and primary school are also used by the others.

While the community aims at self-sufficiency, the goal is not an absolute one, since the members are equally concerned with their work in the world. As leaders in the nonviolence movement in France, they have been in the forefront of protests and fasts against military conscription, French torture in Algeria, and nuclear power. Much of their energy also goes into their outreach program. Each year they hold nine or ten one-week seminars for about 25 people and they also have a large two-month summer camp. This involves a great deal of organizing and correspondence.

The community members grow the bulk of their produce and much of their wheat. All of their bread is baked in the traditional way in a large wood-fired oven, with the excess heat used to heat water for baths. One member is a cheesemaker who produces about two and one-half kilos (five and one-half pounds) of hard cheese a day from the milk of their eight cows. While most of the vegetables are grown in their own organic gardens, which are gradually extended each year, we watched the women canning about a ton of purchased tomatoes. The community is vegetarian.

The women—and sometimes the men—spin wool and weave it into homespun (a coarse, loosely woven cloth) to make into clothes. But this activity is more symbolic than practical. The fleece is purchased from nearby farms, and the homespun clothes are worn primarily on Sundays and festival days. The long cotton skirts usually worn by the women, and the trousers usually worn by the men, are of factory-made blue denim.

While one of the vows of the community is poverty, it is a comfortable poverty and would be looked on as wealth in many parts of the world. True, individuals do not "own" anything. But as members of this extended family, they share in the use of all it possesses. The potter, his wife, and two small children have an apartment with three comfortable rooms: a sitting room and two bedrooms. A sink with running water is in the sitting room and next to it, a Jotul wood stove. Personal belongings include toys and a tricycle for the children, presents from their wedding five years ago, and a long shelf of books. Technically these all belong to the community. If they were to leave these would stay behind, unless they received permission to take some of them. But in practice they are theirs to care for and use. If another member wished to borrow a book, for example, he or she would be expected to ask permission.

Because the water flows freely from a spring on the hill above the community, running water is available without the necessity of a mechanical pump. Toilets are the French squat, water-sealed type that provide an insect barrier between the user and the hole below and are flushed with a bucket of water. Hot baths are taken once or twice a week by signing up for the use of the water heated either as a by-product of the daily bread baking or else in a wood-heated tank. The laundry consists of large tubs heated by wood, and it is usually shared by two people at a time so that they will have company in the long process of soaking, scrubbing, and rinsing the clothes and then hanging them up to dry. One house now has its water heated by methane gas obtained from the compost pile of a nearby farmhouse.

La Borie Noble is very much a community of families. Only a handful of the members are single. Breakfast is made and eaten at home. Lunch is taken communally in the main hall (which is also used for meetings and for yoga). Supper is prepared in the main kitchen but is usually eaten back in the individual quarters, *en famille*. While based on grains, the cuisine is basically French, with virtually no Indian or East Asian influence.

Children are everywhere. Although mothers often breastfeed their babies for many months, the children reach the age of independence early and receive less parental control than they would in a typical nuclear family. The parents are busy working and the children go where they want, when they want, without asking permission. This does not mean, however, that they run wild. At the age of three they start school in the community, attending two hours each day. After two years their classes last all day. The curriculum is not very different from the local schools—partly because French schools have become more progressive and practical in recent years. The school has been visited by the authorities and is respected by them. The children go to the village school for testing once a year. What is unique is that the children are expected to work to pay for their books and other necessities. They do this by producing a newspaper, greeting cards, and other small objects that are sold to visitors and friends outside the community. They also have a small garden where they grow their own produce and raise chickens. When they reach secondary school age they may go to live with family friends in town to attend their classes, returning to the community on weekends, or they make take classes by correspondence.

Perhaps it is the high proportion of families, as well as the age of the members, that has given the community a relatively high degree of stability. More adults in their thirties and forties than in their twenties are members. Of the children who have grown up in the community, all but two are now living in some community. The second generation prefers other communities, however, possibly because they find it difficult to make the transition from childhood to adulthood in the same extended family.

The other element of strength is the commitment that must be made over time in order to become a full member of the Order of the Ark. An order can be defined as a group of people bound together by vows and a common rule of behavior. Four stages are involved in becoming a full member. People begin by going to live in one of the communities, usually after attending a seminar or the summer camp. After a few months, if newcomers wish to enter the order, they become postulants. This usually lasts for two years, though it might be less if they have been with the community a long time. The next step is that of novice, and people remain in this position for one year. After taking the final vow, people become companions—full members of the order. There are only about 60 companions, most of them living on the property in southern France, but a few elsewhere, starting communities or engaged in nonviolent activities on behalf of the order. Possibly as many as 30 companions have left the order over the years for one reason or another, sometimes to enter more traditional religious communities. The seven vows are:

1. We vow to give ourselves up to the service of our brothers, which begins with the work of our hands, in order to at least burden no one, to work on ourselves and on behalf of the Order.

2. To obey the rules and disciplines of the Ark.

3. To assume responsibility for our acts, recognise our wrongs, and make amends for our faults, under the control of our Companions if the fault is known; in secret if we alone know it; and to make amends for the fault of our Companion if he refuses to do so himself.

4. To purify ourselves from all personal acrimony, from all spirit of gain or domination, from our attachments and our aversions and our prejudices.

5. To live in a simple, sober and proper fashion and to cherish poverty to the end of directing ourselves to detachment and perfect charity.

6. To serve truth.

7. To not harm any other human and, if possible, any other living creature, to defend justice, resolve conflicts and redress wrongs by non-violence.*

Reading the vows, one might think of the community as a religious order of a new kind. Looking at the members' practices, one might see the community as a conscious creation of a new form of traditional tribe. Both are fair analogies. The order is patriarchal, nonviolent, working, and ecumenical. Let us see what each of these means in practice.

The order is headed by a patriarch, Shantidas until his death in 1980, and now his successor, Pierre Parodi. It differs from the usual tribe in that kinship under the patriarch is based on vows and conscious intent, rather than blood. The patriarch is fed, lodged, and clothed the same as everyone else. He performs all kinds of work including, and especially, the most menial or lowly tasks, such as shoveling manure.

The patriarch is the guardian of the rule (the stated principles under which the members live and work) and the traditions. He may not order anything to be done that does not spring from the rule, or that is not

---

*Lanza del Vasto, *L'Arche Avait Pour Voilure Une Vigne* (Paris: Editions Denoel, 1978), 113–115.

dictated by the necessity of the moment. He blesses the bread and leads the common prayer. He grants dispensations or tightens the discipline. He also chooses his own successor, initiates him, and prepares him for his eventual position of leadership. One of the oldest of the companions, Pierre Parodi, a physician, was appointed successor many years before Shantidas died, and he filled the role of patriarch when Shantidas was away. Shantidas named him Mohandas after Gandhi's name. The role of patriarch embodies the essence of the order. As such, it is similar to the role of many traditional chiefs or kings, whose importance derived not from their personal powers, but from their embodiment of the spiritual power that directed the tribe.

All important decisions are made by the council composed of all the companions. Other members of the community may discuss the issues, in meetings or privately, but only companions take part in decision making. Decisions are made only through unanimous consent. This avoids schisms and helps to ensure agreement within the community. If talk and more talk does not lead to a unanimous decision, the next step is silence, prayer, and fasting. This may go on for a long time, and as people's minds and bodies are affected by the prolonged fast, so too are their opinions. Unanimity almost always results. If it does not, the issue is tabled for a while.

Admittance into the order also requires unanimity. Several years ago a couple sought admission, one of whom had previously been divorced. Most of the community favored their admittance, but some staunch Catholics opposed them as a matter of principle. Everybody fasted for a week to find a solution to the impasse. Although the members had fought during the meetings, they exhibited a great deal of love during the fast. The final decision was to admit the couple but not make any rule on the subject. Divorce among members of the community is another matter. One couple with nine children got divorced and had to leave the community. Birth control is a matter of personal choice. Abortion has never occurred, because it contradicts their ideas on respect for life. It would be practiced only under exceptional conditions: rape or the endangerment of a woman's health.

The administration of the rules is based on the principle that no free person has the right to punish another. Free people are those who know the law, recognize their faults, and punish themselves. Each night, after the prayers, the community assembles for the *culpa*. All members are expected to denounce in public their shortcomings or offenses against the rules and offer appropriate penance. If the offense was an inner or private one, the denunciation and penance can also be private. The second part of the vow of responsibility is coresponsibility. A member who sees another member doing wrong must tell him or her. If the wrongdoer refuses to repair the wrong or inflict self-punishment, the observer must repair the wrong or inflict punishment on himself or herself. This usually consists of fasting.

Government of the individual communities in the order is similar to government of the order. Each year a leader is chosen by consensus through a rotating system by which every male serves for one or more years. Though there is no rule against a woman holding this position, it hasn't happened and Shantidas felt that it is not a suitable role for a woman—they can exert influence through their husbands'. The leader is called the responsible. The job usually is not sought, but rather accepted. Weekly meetings are held at which problems are discussed and decisions reached unanimously. The responsible's role is to lead meetings and be a conciliator. He must try not to dominate the meetings, but rather seek to find the common position. A conscious effort is made by all members not to try to change other people's minds, but merely to state their own opinions and search for the common good. They recognize that others may be more right than themselves.

Most members of the community are Catholics; a few are Protestants. In principle the community is ecumenical, seeing one of its missions as religious reconciliation. It asks of each member fidelity to his or her own faith; devotion to and deepening of its traditional knowledge; passage from the so-called profane (secular) state to the religious or inner state. The day revolves around prayers. The first bell at 6:00 A.M. calls those who are interested to one-half hour of yoga in the meeting hall. This is followed by one-half hour of meditation. Morning prayer and breakfast is at 7:00. At 8:00 the work day begins. At 10:00 a break is held for common prayer; at 12:00 a break from work with singing is held, followed by lunch at 1:30. Work continues from 2:00 to 6:00, with a prayer break at 4:00. Supper is at 7:00, followed by prayer at 8:00.

Each day of the week is consecrated to a different faith: Monday—Hinduism; Tuesday—Islam; Wednesday—seekers of truth (no organized religion); Thursday—Buddhism; Friday—all Christian traditions; Saturday—Judaism; Sunday—Catholicism. In fact, no followers of non-Christian religions live in the community at present, although some are seekers of truth. One of them is the engineer responsible for rebuilding the mill. He has played an important role for a few years, but has not taken any vows yet, because of the order's emphasis on God—a concept with which he is not comfortable.

The community treats Sundays and four major Christian feast days, Christmas, Easter, St. John's Day (June 24), and Michaelmas (September 29), as especially holy. Of these, the Feast of St. John (the Baptist) is perhaps the most important; he is the patron saint of the Ark. Lesser feasts are the Epiphany (January 6) and the unofficial feasts for the men in March and the women in July. In these, one sex honors the other; the honored sex does no work that day.

Feasts are considered as important as work in the life of the community. The members all dress in white homespun and make of them great celebrations. They recognize that communal rituals are an important element in tying the community together. Other social activities throughout the year also create these ties. Folk dancing and group singing are both very popular. In fact, several records have been produced in France of Gregorian chants and other music sung by the group. Each community has one communal battery-operated record player, thus enabling the members to hear their own recordings. Aside from the social events, individual families have their own friends, although they tend to shift their primary friendships around to avoid becoming cliquish.

How do Gandhian principles affect the work life of the community? Gandhi's main thrust was a concern that machines not demean workers, an advocacy of the elimination of wage labor and exploitation of others, and an emphasis on meaningful work.

Everyone helps with the farming and the gardening in season. Certain other responsibilities are set for a whole year. A woman might, for example, be the cook every Thursday afternoon. If she were to fall ill it would be her responsibility to find a replacement. Other jobs are parceled out by agreement or through volunteering. If a person wishes to learn a new skill, he or she can go to the person performing it and ask to be taught. While most jobs follow traditional sex roles, this is not a policy. Men sometimes cook and women sometimes learn jobs usually held by men.

A basic principle is that each artisan should know and carry out his or her craft from beginning to end, making the whole object, from the raw material to the final decoration. Everybody is encouraged to learn several of the crafts and alternate them. These include spinning, weaving, sewing, baking bread, making cheese, woodworking, pottery, all kinds of construction, and farming.

On the issue of tools, members have backed away somewhat from the pure Gandhian ideology, and we suspect that in the future the concept of appropriate technology will take hold. The order is antitechnology on principle, because members see how society has misused it. At a more practical level, they try to keep things simple so that everyone can participate in many different activities. But when faced with the reality of all that they want to get done, they compromise. The order owns several motor vehicles, a telephone, and a few sewing machines, and some of the cooking is done by bottled gas. The only electricity line into the farm is used to run the mill that grinds the grain into flour. This is explained as a practical necessity, considering how much bread is baked. We would say, considering the number of people who eat the bread, it wouldn't be difficult to organize it so that each person could give a few cranks to a hand mill each day if avoiding the use of electricity were an absolute must.

The issue of electricity is now moot, however, because the community plans to generate its own. At one edge of the property is an abandoned water-powered mill. Several hundred years old, it had originally been a stone grist mill, but around the turn of the century was converted to a sawmill. It operated until the early 1950s, and some of the former workers still live in the neighborhood. Several years ago the community put a new tile roof on the sawmill and an adjoining stone barn to protect them from further deterioration. Then the question was raised, what do we do with them? The logical idea was to rebuild the sawmill so that the community would be able to cut and mill its own lumber. It would be nice, members thought, if the power could be used, through a series of pulleys and belts, to also drive the flour mill and some woodshop tools. But this didn't seem possible, because the RPM requirements and times of usage would vary so much. So that brought the thinking around to the idea of generating electricity with a simple turbine that they could maintain and repair themselves. Some said that this was going too far into the world of high technology. Others pointed out that the community already was using a little electricity from the French national utilities system, 2 percent of which was nuclear power. The decision, in which Shantidas concurred, was to generate their own electricity and use it only in the immediate area of the sawmill. When the construction is completed, the flour mill and carpentry shop will be moved to the sawmill and the connection with outside electricity at the main building will be cut.

Rebuilding the sawmill is a project that will require several years. The old machinery already has been removed, completely cleaned piece by piece, and rebuilt. A great deal of masonry and concrete work has been done on the sawmill buildings. A small group of people was sent to live in the buildings and were helped by outside volunteer labor during the summer. When we visited the site we saw a tractor and a gasoline-powered cement mixer standing by. Several men were working with hand tools, digging a three-foot trench about 500-feet long up to the dam, in which they were burying PVC pipe one foot in diameter to carry the water to the turbines. The cement mixer, the pipe—all represent compromises with the ideal of independence from the technological world. Each required some soul searching. In the end, each was accepted. The justification is that when the project is finished, the community will have a greater capacity for independence. It will be a technology simple enough that the community will be able to operate and maintain their machinery without outside help.

The community's independence is thus far more of an ideal than a reality. Cash income is received from the seminars it holds each month, from the camps, and from the few products (pottery, weaving, wood carving, furniture, books) that are sold outside. This is used to buy some of the food, cloth, and other necessities that are not produced by the group. It also allows the members the luxury of an annual vacation.

Each person can take two to three weeks off, and is given an amount of spending money that varies depending on the income of the community that year. The year we visited, the allowance was about $3 per person per day, with a maximum of about $100 per person. Not enough for high living, but members can visit their families, and members of the Friends of the Ark in various parts of Europe welcome them into their homes. During this period members can, if they wish, taste some of the frivolous pleasures that they gave up to live at the Ark.

Another aspect of the community's relationship with the money economy is taxes. Here, because of the nature of the French system, the community comes out ahead. Since the members have no individual incomes, they pay no income tax, but the French social security system pays a cash allowance to all parents to help support their children. And the community is full of children. So money comes in from the French taxation system, but members of the community do not feel it is morally justified to spend it on their families. Some of it pays the property taxes on the land. The remainder is used to help support Third World projects and even occasional campaigns of civil disobedience!

The relationship with the local government is one of keeping a bit of distance. The local government prefers to look the other way in most cases. But during the Algerian war two members of the community resisted military service as conscientious objectors and went to jail. Most members of the community vote in local elections; few in national ones. This is a matter of individual choice.

What of the future? Most members share a somewhat pessimistic view about the future of France and Europe, both economically and politically. They don't fear an extreme right government any more than an extreme left government. They sometimes feel that they should be more self-sufficient than they are. Meanwhile, they go on building, gradually improving their self-sufficiency. And they go on spreading the word, developing new friends and supporters, gaining new members who will seed the order more widely. Already a small group in Quebec is building on a piece of land they recently purchased to start a new community of the Ark; in Italy another group is looking for land for the organization of a local Community of the Ark. As more communities are created, the hope and expectation is that each will chart its own course, and that more variety will grow within the movement and the order.

The Community of the Ark is one of the most successful communities we have seen. It has created the ideology and mores that make for a strong and stable society. At the same time, it does not squelch individuality or try to cast everybody in the same mold. It should last a long time.

Le Maître and followers at sunrise service.

CHAPTER 11

Le Domaine du Bonfin: Living by the Light of the Sun

It is the dark before dawn. We are gently awakened by a soft mélange of violins, flutes, and guitars floating down from loudspeakers in the trees outside. We stir in our bunks and reflect on where we are. Yesterday we arrived at the Domaine du Bonfin (Estate of the Good Purpose), located in the countryside four miles from Fréjus, a popular tourist resort on the French Riviera. This is the largest center of the Fraternité Blanche Universelle (the Universal White Brotherhood), headed by a remarkable Bulgarian in his eighties, Maître Omraam Mikhaël Aïvanhov. He is usually called simply "Maître" (master) by his 4000 followers in France, Belgium, and Switzerland, 2000 followers in French Canada, and small numbers of followers elsewhere. Now it is August, and the 100 or so permanent residents of this community have been joined by about 600 more people who have arrived from all over France to pitch their tents or park their trailers. Some stay one week; some stay three months. It is a busy time at the Domaine.

Sleepily we put on our clothes, pick up pillows to sit on and blankets to shield us from the early morning chill, and go outside. We follow the stream of people walking through the community, heading through a gate, crossing the road, and then climbing the path that leads to the top of le Rocher, the great prayer rock on the east side of the community. We reach the top as the first glimmerings of light on the eastern horizon are seen, find ourselves a comfortable flat area of rock, sit on our pillows, and wait. The air is chilly, but sweet with the fragrance of wild thyme and marjoram. All is quiet, save the sound of footsteps on the gravel as more people make their way to the top. Around us many people are seated, some in positions of meditation: old people, young people, children. Some of the children are quietly drawing in notebooks. All of us are waiting expectantly for the magic moment when the sun will lift its face above the horizon, when night will turn to day, when the earth will spring to life once more.

Now we see the Maître himself arrive, a Moses figure with long white hair and a long white beard, dressed in white, carrying a walking stick, and wearing a fur hat. He takes his accustomed place at the top of the rock. As the day breaks and the blue of night gives way to the pink, orange, and tangerine of dawn, we each take up our position, seated cross-legged facing the sunrise, hands on our knees, palms up. And as some 300 people watch intently, the sun comes up and the new day begins.

Now the Maître stands up to give his first talk of the day:

Today I am going to give you a few illustrations to show you that the subject of personality and individuality is a whole world in itself. Personality is the role man must play during his existence. Man's personality changes but all the good qualities and wisdom he has acquired are handed down throughout his incarnations, forming his individuality.

To understand personality, take the earth as an example. The earth takes, absorbs, it gives nothing to the cosmos, contrary to the sun. Perhaps the earth can be seen by the other planets shining in space, but this is not the earth's own light. Earth is not able to produce its own light because it is still too self-centered. Nobody who is selfish and personal can project light; because light comes from within man, he must himself extract it out of the depths of his interior and project it. Then it is a manifestation of his love and goodness and generosity, and there is no more fear because there can be no fear where there is light.

The sun is the illustration of the spirit of giving, and the earth the illustration of the spirit of taking. This does not mean that the earth never gives anything at all; with what it receives it produces flowers, it produces fruit, but only for itself and its children, which is the same thing. Whereas the sun takes what it produces and projects it far out into infinite space for the benefit of all creatures.

So, my dear brothers and sisters, we all need to change our natures, our tendency to take and absorb and ingest everything into ourselves. When the sun rises before us, radiating, giving itself, streaming forth so generously, it is the sublime manifestation of individuality, of spirit, of God Himself. You stare and stare, but if no one has explained to you what is happening and how to interpret it, you can watch all your life and you will still take all you can take. If there is someone to tell you what is a sunrise, what it means, then you will be able to understand the power and grandeur and tremendousness of the act of giving. You will work on changing your inner self, and you will rejoice in the progress you make each day, little by little, until finally you resemble the sun yourself.*

When he has finished speaking, the Maître climbs down the rock and the people crowd close, with the children in front. He has a bag full of candies that he hands out one by one to the children; he salutes the crowd with his palm facing them and walks down the hill, back to the Domaine,

---

*Condensed from Omraam Mikhaël Aïvanhov, *To Take and to Give* (Fréjus, France: Prosveta, 1976), 1–6.

followed by the children and the crowd. Soon le Rocher has returned to its natural quiet and below, the day at the Domaine has begun.

Omraam Mikhaël Aïvanhov was born in 1900 in a village in Bulgarian Macedonia. As a boy he became interested in the spiritual life, and as a young teenager he read philosophy and experimented with Indian techniques of concentration, meditation, and breathing. At 16, in the middle of breathing exercises, he had an ecstatic experience that helped cast the direction of his future life.

At the age of 17, Aïvanhov met Peter Deunov, the founder of a spiritual movement that he led for more than 30 years until his death in 1944. Deunov's goal was to guide human activity towards an ideal of universal community: the Universal White Brotherhood. White here does not refer to skin. Just as white is the synthesis of all colors, it is used in this name to include men and women of all races, religions and nationalities.

Deunov's movement was a continuation of the long stream of Christian esotericism that started with St. John and continued through various heretical groups in the Middle Ages. One of these was the Bogomils, who were an important influence in Bulgaria for several centuries. And just as the Bogomils had been suppressed in the Middle Ages, causing many to flee to Western Europe, so it was with Peter Deunov. He was excommunicated from the Orthodox Church for his beliefs and teachings, and exiled from the Bulgarian capital, Sofia, to Varna, where Aïvanhov lived. Aïvanhov became Deunov's student, and continued his esoteric training while going to university and later becoming a schoolteacher and then headmaster.

As World War II approached, Deunov foresaw that his movement in Bulgaria—which by then had grown to 200,000 people—would probably be banned, and he chose Aïvanhov to save the teaching by carrying it to France. In 1937 he sent Aïvanhov to Paris with letters of recommendation to a small group of his followers there. In 1938 Aïvanhov began giving lectures to ever-increasing and varied audiences. In the same year he founded a small community with a group of steadfast disciples in Sèvres, a suburb of Paris. Gradually the teaching spread through families, friends, and friends of friends, to most of the cities of France and Switzerland, and to a lesser extent to other European countries, Canada, and French-speaking African countries. Usually 10 to 15 black Africans attend the summer gatherings at the Domaine.

The Maître calls his teaching "initiatic knowledge." He writes: "The knowledge of the Initiates will bring you neither money nor position, but it will transform you because it works upon your character. Armed with this knowledge, it is impossible for you to remain the same. As soon as you grasp a few of these truths, you are changed, and become capable of helping others."* He sometimes quotes from one of his many sources: the Bible, the Vedas, the Upanishads, the Tibetan Book of the Dead, the Tao Te Ching, the Qabala, the Talmud, or one of the other sacred books. But primarily he talks from his own spiritual experience, attempting to transpose onto the physical plane the experiences and realities of the spiritual world.

The philosophy starts with the concept that there are three worlds: the world of principles, the world of laws, and the world of occurrence and action. Or in other words, the divine world, the spiritual world, and the material world. Or the worlds of meaning, of content, and of form. The Maître uses the trilogy of light, love, and life to discuss his school. Light is the core of the organization. Love is its fruit. Life is the visible physical activity. "Let life flow and love will flow," says the Maître. Or as one of his disciples said: "He makes us go through the world of light so that we will see the source of life; the Sun! He makes us go through the world of warmth so that we will see each other, through the Sun. He makes us go through the material and economic world so that we will learn to let love flow as life flows, from the Sun."**

The Maître also points out that a human being is a trinity in the likeness of God: he or she thinks, feels, and acts. The correspondences are infinite. Under the heading of light come science, philosophy, knowledge, and learning. Under the heading of love come religion, ethics, and morality. Under the heading of life come movement, creation, and realization. Maître's message is that everything can be marvelous, and the Golden Age can come on earth once we understand where our interests lie, and that our function corresponds with the function of the sun: to give light, to give heat, to bring life.

Most people, he believes, emphasize self-gratification and earning a living—at whatever price—and their governments similarly focus on economics, finance, the military, and other concerns of the third category, with little attention to light and love. The Brotherhood was formed to provide an antidote to this. As a movement that constantly promotes light and love, it urges people to live together and look out for each other's interest, not just their own. As the Maître says:

Why is it that great Masters advocate collective living? Because it works a change in our consciousness. Instead of living in disorder and disharmony, man tries to be in tune with his fellow human beings, he is able to advance in his evolution because he is synchronized with the collectivity. The collectivity, in turn, attempts to be in harmony with the other collectivity, the cosmic collectivity.***

---

*Agnès Lejbowicz, *Maître Omraam Mikhaël Aïvanhov and the Teaching of the Fraternité Blanche Universelle* (Lyons, France: Prosveta, 1975) 10.

**Pierre C. Renard, *The Prophet* (Fréjus, France: Prosveta, 1979), 111.

***Omraam Mikhaël Aïvanhov, *The Great Universal White Brotherhood* (Fréjus, France: Prosveta, 1976), 74.

In line with this thought, the Maître also says that the nuclear family teaches narrowness and selfishness. He urges his followers to enlarge the idea of family, first to a community as a family, and then to a universal family of the whole world.

The first community of Sèvres was too small and too suburban. The Maître and his followers wanted to be close to nature so they could "learn from the book of nature." So several of them went looking for land in the south of France, where the sun shines much more strongly and more often than it does around Paris. Several years after the end of World War II they found it—about 65 acres outside Fréjus—and bought it very cheaply. Pierre Renard, an early member of the community described it when they bought it as "an isolated wooded area in the hills of Esterel, difficult to get to, with little water, no electricity, no conveniences, and no more than tumbledown ruins in which to set up our tents." Today it is bordered on one side by a military compound, and on the other by a large commercial zoo. Otherwise it is an area of small farms, punctuated by vacation homes.

For many years the property was used mainly in the summer as a place for community members and visitors to develop collective spiritual life. In the late 1960s some members moved to the property to enlarge and maintain the common facilities, grow more crops, and prepare for the summer gatherings. Thus they formed a small group of people living and working together on a year-round basis. They were joined in 1977 by more members who came to run the publishing and printing company.

After the pioneering years, funds became available to further develop the land and the facilities. Many members of the Brotherhood tithe, so there was a good flow of money for the projects, especially from some of the more well-to-do members in the cities. As an example, when the Great Hall was enlarged and the adjoining exercise field was built, they cost about $200,000. The need and budget were announced, people made contributions averaging $200 each, and the full amount was raised in nine months.

In addition to enlarging the buildings and making other physical improvements, the residents began growing vegetables and fruit on a fairly large scale and selling the surplus at a stand just outside the gate.

At the time of our visit in August 1981, residents numbered about 110 people year round. Most were unmarried, aged 18 to 25, but there were also about 10 retired members. Among the older, married members, the level of education was above average for France, but the younger group included quite a few from working-class backgrounds. Virtually all came from French-speaking backgrounds: France, Belgium, Switzerland, and French Canada. One Congolese worked in the print shop. Turnover was highest among the French Canadians, who often came with the intention of staying only a year. To stay in France for more than three months the government requires that they deposit about $2,000 and get a certificate from the community that food and lodging is being supplied to them.

Some 40 members live on the grounds, including a few of the retired who built their own chalets. They paid for the materials, the residents and the conference participants supplied most of the labor, and the chalets will become the property of the Brotherhood when their owners die. Others live outside the gates because of a shortage of space and facilities inside the main property. Six families live just down the road in a small group of trailers. This group consists of a dentist, a business school professor, two construction workers, and a nurse—all with their families—plus a retired woman who lives with her daughter, an interior decorator. Some of them work on the outside, but all are active in the community. Two of the families are Belgian, one Canadian, one half-Dutch, one half-American.

The Great Hall is the center of the Domaine. About 40 feet by 60 feet and capable of seating 800 people, it is used both as a lecture hall and a dining hall. Smaller buildings house a bakery, workshops, warehouses, a community store which serves as a social center, and children's corner. On one side is a large exercise field in which the Maître leads everyone in daily exercises for their spiritual development. Some of the roads and paths are paved, and trees and flowers are planted in profusion. The community has four acres of vineyards, from which it makes its own wine and grape juice, as well as fruit orchards and vegetable fields. Five acres are devoted to camp sites and trailer sites capable of handling up to 500 people in the summer, complete with communal bathrooms and laundry facilities. Regular housing consists of several buildings with a total of 21 small rooms, plus the private chalets. Plans have been drawn up to erect a collective lodging building on the grounds and a local government permit has been obtained, but at present the money is not available.

The works of the Maître, selected from his talks, are printed and published by a separate, Domaine-owned company called Prosveta, which means "teaching" in Bulgarian. The printing shop is located one mile closer to Fréjus in a large building rented by the company. The building has modern typesetting, printing, and binding equipment, as well as a warehouse and shipping department. Prosveta employs approximately ten people, all community members.

Year-round residence at the Domaine is limited to members. People usually first gain an interest by reading one of the dozens of books published by Prosveta or by learning through friends about a Brotherhood center near them. The next step is to purchase an auditor's card for $20 which lets them attend meetings at a local center for one year.

If they wish to attend conference sessions at the Domaine during Easter or summer vacations, they must belong to a local or national group. After a year as an auditor, they can ask to become a member. Membership costs $100 a year.

The Brotherhood in France exists as a public-benefit nonprofit corporation legally governed by a committee of 12, made up of people who meet and mostly live in Paris. The governing committee decides on new members, manages the association, and submits a moral and financial report that is voted on by the membership at the end of each year.

The organization of the Domaine is based on the tripartite concept we discussed earlier: the three parts are the authority, the power, and the economy. In this case the authority is the spiritual and moral authority represented by the Maître. The power devolves from the committee in Paris to an operating subcommittee at the Domaine. And the economy is represented by the individuals in charge of various activities.

The operating subcommittee, called the Bonfin managing council, includes the manager of the Domaine; a doctor, in charge of hygiene and health; an architect, in charge of construction and landscaping; a fiscal authority, in charge of accounting; a lady in charge of relationships with local authorities; and two representatives from Prosveta.

The Maître generally sticks to his teaching and does not get involved in the details of day-to-day management. His attitude is embodied in his expression, "Let life flow." Pierre Renard compares this philosophy with water: "Water (love), when it is allowed to flow, organizes everything, you can see it; water (with no schooling, no diplomas) knows exactly how to arrange things so they work properly. That is why the Master never bothers with organization; if the water flows, organization takes care of itself."

The former manager and his assistant encouraged the growth of crafts and planned the development of other commercial activities. They built a lovely gallery in the community with a wide variety of products—honey, jellies, pottery, weaving, macramé—for sale to people who came to stay at the Domaine during its big gatherings. Some of the artisans' equipment belonged to them; about half was supplied by the community. The people who worked at these crafts received room and board and the materials needed for their crafts, but no cash.

By 1980 the major part of the regular revenues came from the money paid for room and board by conference participants. Among the other revenues were the produce sales at the stand and the crafts sales. This economic mix had come about because of efforts on the part of the manager and his assistant, and the entrepreneurial talents of various individual members.

The trouble was that many of these initiatives were not submitted to

the national committee. Furthermore, several of the activities represented, to many people, a waste of physical and financial resources that
should have gone into spiritual work.

And so by mid-1981, a countermovement developed among many
Domaine residents to reemphasize spirituality, and therefore to limit
business activities to the minimum necessary for self-sufficiency. The
national committee confirmed this reorientation and appointed a subcommittee to organize a system of collective management of the Domaine. As a result, the manager and his assistant resigned and left the
Domaine at the end of the summer. This change in course and the
closing down or reduction of some activities caused a drop in the number of residents, which now stands at about 70 people. Most of the 40
members who left went back to their original Brotherhood groups and
centers in France, Switzerland, and Canada.

The people who live on the grounds of the Domaine eat morning and
noontime meals in silence in the large dining room. Small children eat
in a separate dining room, together with at least one of their parents.
Families usually have dinner together in their own quarters. Food is
vegetarian, though it does include eggs, cheese, and fish. The Maître
says that fish don't suffer from being killed the way other animals do, and
are not harmful to health. He recommends that people eat a lot of garlic,
onions, and almonds. He urges members to eat consciously and silently:
to chew food a long time and to think about it and to thank the forces
that created it. He says we have lost our links with the invisible world and
this is one of the ways to regain them. The food grown at the Domaine
is all organic.

Men and women are differentiated, polarized reflections of the same
cosmic spirit, according to the Maître's teachings, so they try hard to
find each other through love, tenderness, and affection. But the sexual
force can be all-consuming and lead to disillusionment if used only for
pleasure. The Maître discussed this one day:

You all know that in ancient time the savages lit their fires by taking two
branches and rubbing them together. The result was heat, because of the friction, the movement. If they continued rubbing their sticks together a flame
appeared: light, fire! Why is it that everyone, young and old, know when they
make love how to produce movement (friction) and heat (they must be hot since
they remove their clothing), but they don't know how to produce light? Something is escaping them: how to be enlightened and made divine by love, by the
way we love.*

Accordingly, the Maître teaches that sexual energy should be mastered
and, as much as possible, redirected toward spiritual aims.

The Maître also emphasizes the importance of a spiritual attitude in

---

*Pierre C. Renard, op. cit., 104–105.

conceiving a child, as well as during pregnancy. He says that the pregnant woman should practice *spiritual electroplating*, which is defined as having "thoughts of gold" rather than "thoughts of lead" to properly influence the physical and spiritual bodies of the child. Once the child is born, however, the Brotherhood, and thus the Domaine, do not place any undue emphasis on his or her development. Those of school age go to public school. A couple of teachers live at the Domaine, but so far they have no school of their own, one reason being that there are only seven children and they are of different ages.

The children do benefit from the communal ceremonies, such as watching the sunrises, and from the community's emphasis on nature. "If you have any problem," the Maître says to the children, "go to nature. Ask the trees, the flowers, the sun for help."

Since the previous manager left, and many of the business activities were closed down, the Domaine has given up most of the lands it rented to grow extra crops. Nonetheless the financial situation has improved considerably, because the new management encourages better use of resources.

In the future the leadership plans to continue to emphasize spirituality and the international growth of the Brotherhood. Books are now translated into eight different languages and distributed on all continents. Although the Maître is in his eighties, he and his followers believe that he will live another 20 years or more, so no heir apparent is being groomed. Some building will continue, including that of additional collective lodgings, and solar energy will be used to the extent feasible.

This is the third community we visited whose inspiration and teaching comes from an invisible universal brotherhood.* None of the three has any contact with the others, and each gets its inspiration in a different way. Each believes that some great cataclysm will occur by the end of the century, ushering in the Kingdom of God. Each urges its followers to make ready by striving for perfection and by living in love and harmony with others.

These are goals that few would question. But perhaps they try too hard, for each of these communities has had some kind of schism that has resulted in the walk-out of a substantial part of its membership—in two cases including part of its leadership. If the Kingdom of God is indeed at hand, it appears that it will be a small one.

---

*The others are Stelle, in Illinois, and the Universal Brotherhood, in Australia.

Part IV

GREAT BRITAIN

Dartington Hall manor.

CHAPTER 12

The Dartington Hall Trust: All That Money Can Buy?

The story of Dartington is no longer my personal story. It is the chronicle of a great common effort on the part of many others, fired by Leonard's imagination. At the start, it was an act of faith on our part to take over an old estate in a rural area, being at that time rapidly depopulated, and to believe that we could transform it into an active centre of life. For we never intended to make Dartington an economic experiment merely, concentrating mainly on farming and forestry and rural industry. From the beginning we envisaged something more—a place where education could be continuously carried on and where the arts could become an integral part of the life of the whole place. We believed that not only should we provide for the material wellbeing of our people here but for their cultural and social needs as well. And in our dream of the good life we counted on the human values of kindliness and friendship to bind the community together. We hoped that in this way a certain quality of life and human relationships would emerge, relatively free from fear and competition.

—DOROTHY WHITNEY STRAIGHT ELMHIRST

Dartington is unique among the communities we have surveyed. It is well known in England as a center for progressive education, the arts, music, and most recently, glass making. The idea of Dartington as an intentional community is not as well known. It is a community in the sense that it is located in a specific geographical area and a group of people are committed to, and inspired by, Dartington. It defies easy description, however, and has a history quite unlike any other community of which we know.

Dorothy Whitney Straight Elmhirst was born in 1887 in the United States. At the time her father, William Whitney, was secretary of the Navy in the administration of President Grover Cleveland. President and Mrs. Cleveland named the infant. They chose the name Dorothy for its meaning, "a gift of God." Although not born to wealth, William Whitney had married into it and soon created an even greater fortune in the period before the income tax was introduced.

Dorothy's mother died when she was 6 and her father died when she was 17, leaving her an estate of about $8 million. As an heiress with none to answer to except, on occasion, her elder brother and his wife, Gertrude (most noted for her creation of the Whitney Museum of Art in New York City), Dorothy was free to run her own life. She was a debutante and at times lived a frivolous life. But she was also a serious young woman who read widely and was involved in social work among the poor.

Dorothy married her first husband, international financier Willard Straight, in 1911 when she was 24. Over the years her interest in reform grew, and she gradually drew Willard into this sphere. Together they founded *The New Republic,* one of the foremost radical journals even today. They also founded *Asia Magazine.* Willard died in 1918, a victim of the world-wide influenza epidemic, and Dorothy was left—at 31—a widow with three children. She devoted even more time to liberal causes, and cherished Willard's memory.

It was this devotion to Willard that first brought her into contact with her next husband—and the cofounder of Dartington—Leonard Elmhirst. Leonard was an Englishman from Yorkshire who came from a line of parsons and vicars. He, too, was directed to the ministry. When he was eight, Leonard was sent to boarding school—a horrible experience for a sensitive boy, one that left its mark on him and helped to spark his life-long interest in progressive education. The ministry never quite fit and he gave up that dream after a stint in India as a missionary. While in India he had become involved in social work among the peasants as well as practical work showing them how to grow more food. After leaving India he went to the United States to study agricultural economics at Cornell University.

It was at Cornell—when Leonard was 27 and Dorothy 33—that the two met. He went to her on a fundraising mission for Cornell and convinced her to donate to Willard's alma mater in his memory. Around the same time Leonard met Rabindranath Tagore, a Nobel Laureate in literature who had great plans to revive rural Indian villages through a progressive school he had established there. He asked Leonard to help him work with the villages, diagnosing their troubles and giving them the tools and ideas with which to reestablish their economy, social balance, and arts.

Dorothy financed Leonard's work with Tagore and Tagore became a link between the two. They corresponded and met occasionally, and their letters were filled with talk about a school they hoped to start—a school that would be a social and educational experiment. They decided to conduct the experiment in England, and Leonard undertook his quest for the perfect site in Devon in southwestern England.

In 1925 he found his dream, the Dartington estate:

In we went and up and down some wonderful hills till we pulled up in a veritable fairy land—in winter too. What it would be like in spring or summer or autumn I dare not imagine. I wanted to kneel and worship the beauty of it all and every fresh vista only seemed the more to recommend the handiwork of nature joined with the reverent hand of generations of men ... unlimited farm buildings with roofs and windows and doors like a fairy land, and such farmer folk, and the gardens and trees you must see for yourself, the orchards, the river and the boathouse and all the nine-tenths that remained unexplored ... and the most ideal place for a children's growing ground I ever saw, with room to spread, and rooms to spare and be left empty if not wanted at the outset, and a thousand other delights.*

The estate dated back to the fourteenth century. The manor house had been built by the half-brother of King Richard II, John Holand, earl of Huntingdon and duke of Exeter. He was a jouster, and the sunken garden behind the house was probably a tiltyard where Holand practiced, watched by spectators sitting on the terraces. The estate was long abandoned and the hall was in ruins, with no roof, no glass in the windows, the kitchen fallen in, and the porch tower nearing collapse.

A week later Leonard left for New York and his wedding to Dorothy. After their honeymoon they went straight to Devon for her first look at the estate. Dorothy was equally enamored of it and the Dartington experiment began.

When the Elmhirsts bought Dartington, their first priority was to rehabilitate the estate. For an estate, they believed, was the basis of an entire integration of life. The run-down condition of this estate reflected the decline of the English countryside, a decline they sought to reverse.

At first they had few concrete ideas. They knew that they would restore Dartington Hall—the largest and most important medieval house in the west of England. They were influenced by Rabindranath Tagore's ideas of community development and by the gestating progressive education movement. And Leonard was interested in agricultural and forestry experimentation, and Dorothy in social arts and crafts experimentation.

The task was a formidable one. Some years later they described their initial aims as

no less than rehabilitation in the broadest sense: not only physical reconstruction and redevelopment of all the resources in contemporary terms, but also scope for a full life for everyone connected with the enterprise. Further, the multifarious experience arising from the Dartington experiment should, wherever possible, have a wider application to rural problems as a whole: and

---

*A *Dartington Anthology* (Totnes, Devon, England: Dartington Press, 1975), 12.

this experiment should, whatever the results, be made available to all those who had the future of the countryside at heart.*

In his biographical study, *The Elmhirsts of Dartington,* Michael Young —a current Dartington trustee and one of the original pupils—provides his own theories of the initial impulse of the Elmhirsts:

In practice they had utopian hopes without the rhetoric that often goes with them. . . . They derived their ideas not from the realm of what is but from the realm of what might be, and also went beyond what might be into what was probably unattainable, although still worth striving for. They were not so far from ordinary opinion to believe in the perfectability of man. But they did believe in his improvability, and about that they were perhaps more ambitious than most realists would say they had any right to be—even though they did not lay themselves open to one kind of challenge by being synthesizers in an intellectual sense like so many other founders of new communities. They were not so much fountains as channels or conduits through which travelled a constant flow of ideas to find outlets in Dartington, not so much innovators as enablers. The originality of the place rested in the combination and recombination of ideas gathered from many different sources.**

In taking over the estate, the Elmhirsts inherited an almost feudal system and they became the new lord and lady of the manor. They moved into a house adjoining the hall, complete with a butler and a team of maids. The Elmhirsts' goals in founding Dartington were broad. They believed that:

Mankind can be liberated through education.

A new flowering of the arts can transform a society impoverished by industrialization and secularization.

A society which combines the best of town and country combines the best of both worlds.

A pervasive concern for the individual human being and his right to self-determination can be combined with the efficient operation of agriculture and industry.***

In 1926 they started the most radical boarding school of its day in England. Virtually no book work was required: the children learned by working as apprentices in the farm, forest, and buildings of the estate. Believing that education was life, and not merely preparation for life, they set forth their four principles of education:

(1) Curriculum should flow from children's own interests.
(2) Children should learn by doing.

---

*Quoted in Mark Kidel, *Dartington* (Exeter, England: Webb & Bower, 1982).
**Michael Young, *The Elmhirsts of Dartington: The Creation of an Utopian Community* (London: Routledge, Kegan, Paul, 1982), 98–99.
***Ibid., 100.

(3) Adults should be friends, not authority figures.
(4) The school should be a self-governing commonwealth.

The notion of "deschooling" remains an ideal to this day at Darting-ton—but only an ideal. The idea of the estate-as-classroom was aban-doned in 1931 when Bill Curry became headmaster. He was a well-known educator who, more than anyone else, established the Darting-ton School's reputation as a progressive establishment and a fine school. It became a world unto itself, even relying on its own farm for its food. It also became a good deal more academic, though it remained ground-ed in the ideal of practical learning.

The school was one of many Dartington efforts to reform society. Michael Young writes:

The underlying hope was not that one or another of these ideals might be realised but that they all would be realised together in one place in an environ-ment of mutual support. New men would not be evolved except through the reform of education; they would not be able to fulfill themselves and express their feelings without the arts; they would not be whole without the beauty of nature near at hand to nourish them; and all would fail unless based securely on the foundation of a sound economy which did not sacrifice the individual to the machine or the organisation, and which was guided by science.*

The whole Dartington community—estate, industries, school—was seen as an agent of reintegration through which people could take col-lective responsibility for bringing together many different aspects of their lives. Management of the school, arts, workshop, farm, and forest would all be separately organized, within the matrix of a community that would also be, the Elmhirsts hoped, a fellowship of people of ideals and spirit.

From the beginning, authority at Dartington was not clearly defined. Its exercise has been described, at different times, as paternalistic, feu-dal, authoritarian, erratic, and chaotic. The Elmhirsts had many outside interests that took them around the world. Dartington was a central concern, but not an all-consuming one. Their need to be away from Dartington so often was one of the reasons they created the Dartington Hall Trust in 1931. This ensured the continuity of the enterprise and allowed it tax-exempt status. During their lifetimes the Elmhirsts were the authorities and the focus of loyalty to Dartington. With their deaths this focus no longer exists, and no person has stepped into that role.

The Elmhirsts favored the development of small industries that would use local raw materials, thus creating employment in rural areas. The first rural industry they established at Dartington was weaving. In the 1920s hand looms were worked in the hall courtyard. The wool

---

*Ibid., 101.

came from the estate's own sheep. In 1930, however, the looms were moved to a building off the estate and handweaving was abandoned in favor of mechanization. Economics won over tradition. Today the tweed mill is fully mechanized and processes wool from New Zealand through all stages of dyeing, carding, spinning, and weaving. However, the business is in serious trouble because of the decline of the British textile industry. It has been kept open only through the determined efforts and support of the Dartington Hall Trust. As Dartington's oldest industry, the tweeds are seen as a symbol of the viability of rural business and thus must be kept afloat.

Woodlands on the estate were developed along progressive and economic lines, eventually to achieve a sustained yield. Sawmills and a joinery were set up in the early 1930s to preocess the estate's own felled trees. Staverton Contractors evolved out of the reconstruction work on the hall. This firm eventually became one of the largest in southwest England and then merged with a large company in Bristol. The trust retains a share in the Bristol firm. The sawmill was sold. The Staverton Joinery manufactures furniture under contracts with the government and other large British and foreign customers. A subsidiary builds boats.

In the early years, a steady flow of experts and friends visited Dartington. During the 1930s, a formidable group of musicians and artists worked there. Among the best-known were Michael Chekhov, a pupil of Stanislavski and nephew of the playwright Anton Chekhov; Bernard Leach, the potter; and Mark Tobey, the abstract painter. This influx of talent made Dartington a lively place, but it also contributed to the compartmentalization on the estate, since many of the permanent residents felt that too much of Dartington's funds and energy went into the arts and not enough into the community itself. This conflict has continued to this day. Dartington's history—because of the broad interests and concerns of its founders—has hovered between the need for rootedness on the estate and a passion for the outside world.

It was only during the shortages of World War II that Dartington's businesses became truly profitable. At the same time, the artistic community dispersed. Dartington drew back on itself and strengthened its sense of identity. It was during this period that an estate committee was created as a medium of communication between employees and the Dartington trust. It remains the most important means of interchange. In the arts, Dartington began a collaboration with the Devon county council and with the precursor of the present-day arts council. The College of Arts and the Devon Centre for Further Education—both state-funded institutions located on the Dartington grounds—grew out of this.

The Dartington Hall Trust is now the hub of a relatively decentralized system. The College of Arts and the primary and secondary schools are separate entities within the estate—each sponsored by the trust, but managed by its own board of directors. The businesses on and off the estate—consisting today of textiles, glass, furniture, boat building, and financial institutions—are all part of Dartington Hall Corporation, a holding company wholly owned by the trust. The trustees are landlords, watchdogs, and initiators. They are the only ones able to view the whole, not limited by the narrow perspective of an individual department or business. All the present trustees live apart from the estate, often maintaining stronger links with the outside world than with Dartington. In addition to their inspirational role as guardians of Dartington's elusive spirit, they hold the purse strings, deciding which projects can be initiated, which funded, and which allowed to wither.

Many new projects have been undertaken since the era of the Elmhirsts. (Dorothy died in 1968; Leonard retired as chairman of the board of trustees in the early 1960s and died in 1974). Dartington's largest and most successful venture—the glassworks—was started in 1966. Located 50 miles north of the estate in a depressed rural area, it now employs 185 workers and is famous in England for its fine glass products. Dartington & Co. is an investment bank whose principal office is in Bristol, the largest metropolis in southwest England. It offers corporate finance services to small and medium-sized firms in the southwest— another way in which Dartington tries to improve the quality of life in the region. The range of interests of the trustees has continued to be wide under the direction of Maurice Ash, the Elmhirsts' son-in-law and chairman of the board of trustees. The Dartington trustees continue to be conscious of the need for rural regeneration and the creation of practical alternatives to the continuing centralization of Western society; this awareness is the key to many of the new enterprises launched by Dartington in the past 15 years.

It is this very social and philosophical consciousness, though, that has caused the most sustained conflicts among Dartington residents. Many of them are idealists, seeking to create and partake of a better world. They are interested in the transcendental rather than the practical. Often the two can exist harmoniously, but often there is conflict, and when the showdown comes the practical usually seems to win out at Dartington. But not always. The spirit of the Elmhirsts' initial inspiration does remain. This is reflected in the ties some of the members of the board of trustees have with spiritual and New Age groups, and in the openness to all faiths and traditions at Dartington. The estate has sponsored a number of New Age conferences and is a center for new social ideas. It has close ties with the Zen Center of San Francisco, some of whose residents have spent time at Dartington teaching Zen.

Several years ago some members of the board of trustees expressed an interest in starting a school for organic farming and appropriate technology. It was set up as an experimental program with an independent trust. Called the Yarner Trust, it operates two small farm schools, Beacon Farm and Welcombe Barton, one at Dartington and one in North Devon, which generally take students for a year, providing practical experience in soil management, plant and animal husbandry, and rural skills. It seeks to demonstrate that people can live in voluntary simplicity with limited material resources, producing a minimum of waste and pollution, and that living, work, and play can be integrated and balanced.

Dartington is a place of experimentation and learning, a loose community without creed or ideology, blueprints or leaders. Its history is one of successes, failures, and contradictions. Its survival into this decade—its sixth—has not been as a monument to bygone ideals or as a rich couple's plaything, but as a lively and continually changing social institution. Many utopian communities have failed to survive the death of their founders—if, indeed, they survived even that long. At Dartington, innovation is a constant factor. But this constant innovation has led, some believe, to lack of focus, and the concommitant lack of a strong leader has increased the problem.

One method used to strengthen the ties that hold Dartington together is the estate committee, mentioned earlier. It was founded by Dorothy in the 1940s and is a representative body designed to act as a channel of communication between employees and trustees. The committee has played an important role over the years in keeping alive the spirit of the founders. The estate committee, some say, stands for everything that is permanent at Dartington—in contrast to the trust, which has a commitment to experimentation.

A number of other groups at Dartington have their interests served through other arenas: a liaison committee for managers and trustees, land and design forums, managers' meetings. The interpretation office concerns itself both with public relations and also with helping residents realize the meaning of Dartington, with giving them a sense of Dartington as a whole rather than a sum of its parts. As Mark Kidel, Dartington's interpretation officer, wrote, "Dartington remains a community in search of itself."*

Trustee John Lane wrote in a paper for the trustees:

The real Dartington—the Dartington for which we devote our lives—is a state of mind. It is a state of mind which is continually regenerated by a changing body of people. But even these people are not the real Dartington because this is without physical form.

---

*Kidel, *Dartington*.

In addition there is another Dartington, the one in which we work. This has a legal entity and is called by the same name. It owns property, is capable of paying salaries and sending memos in triplicate. . . .

Confusion continually occurs in people who fail to see the difference, or more probably see the second Dartington, but who fail to see the first. The real Dartington exists elsewhere: it is a matter of the spirit and the heart.*

When Dartington was small it was a paternalistic environment, with the workers involved in the cultural side of the community. But the parents are no longer alive and the community has grown. It is now, as one resident, Michael Bower, said, "fissiparous." The bulk of the funds and many of the energies of the Dartington enterprises come from without—and therefore many in the enterprises tend to look to the outside. Only the trustees still continue to see the whole picture.

But the new Dartington is quite unlike the old. Many of the newest industries, as we have mentioned, are not located on the estate. In fact, the only new business to be set up on the estate in recent years is the Cider Press Centre, a lovely small shopping plaza at the foot of the estate that features a natural foods cafeteria and a variety of gift shops. The outside businesses have no connection with each other except that they are all part of Dartington. As time goes on, more people see only the second Dartington—Dartington the employer—and miss the first— the spirit and the heart.

The trust operates by consensus; trustees never take formal votes. Any proposal must be seconded before it can be considered. Each of the trustees has complete veto power and a lifetime term of office. Thus it is anything but a radical body. Yet many question what will happen when Maurice Ash retires—as he is expected to do shortly.

And when this change occurs, it is anyone's guess as to what the future of the community—if indeed it still can be called that—will be.

So Dartington is, in its way, an example to all those community residents who feel that if only they had unlimited financial resources they could create a new world. Dartington has a tremendous financial base with total assets of around 20 million pounds and a superb physical plant on a 1000-acre estate. But is it a community, or simply a large diversified business and educational institution with 600 employees and its own housing and cultural facilities? There are many on the outside and the inside who will argue either way.

If it is not a community, it is nevertheless an outstanding success. It is an inspiration to social planners the world over. The Elmhirsts succeeded in revitalizing a rural area, giving it new jobs and culture and some of the refinements of city life. The Totnes area of South Devon is unique in Britain because of Dartington. Its residents are an extraordi-

*A Dartington Anthology, 118.

nary pool of talent and ideas, and they have the opportunity to express them. And if many of the people in the area have only a slight connection with the formal institution called Dartington, does it really matter? Their lives have been enriched by this group, mostly immigrants, who dared to try many things to make their dreams come true.

The rear of the Firehouse with large mural.

CHAPTER 13

The London Buddhist Centre: Putting Right Livelihood Into Practice

If the nature of the work is properly appreciated and applied, it will stand in the same relation to the higher faculties as food is to the physical body. It nourishes and enlivens the higher man and urges him to produce the best he is capable of. It directs his free will along the proper course and disciplines the animal in him into progressive channels. It furnishes an excellent background for man to display his scale of values and develop his personality.

—J. C. KUMARAPPA as quoted
by E. F. Schumacher in *Good Work*

From the beginning of the Industrial Revolution in the eighteenth century, England has been a center for the promotion of new work ethics. Writers such as Charles Dickens inveighed against the prevailing conditions; nineteenth-century utopians and philosophers such as Karl Marx suggested new ways to integrate work with a satisfying life. Many saw English society as an ideal spawning ground for their pet ideas.

London today is the center for a small group—the Friends of the Western Buddhist Order—that is attempting to put many traditional Buddhist ideas into practice. A major theme is right livelihood, which members define broadly as a fundamental principle "that a man's work should not hinder his development but should be a part of his further growth as an individual." "Human growth," they stress, "takes place when the individual being refuses to accept that his environment has the final word in shaping him; when he begins to make himself."

In most cases, they say, this growth cannot take place in isolation. Many of us feel the desire, especially in our youth, to break free of the bonds of conditioning. But these bonds are strong, and for many the struggle is too great. To break free, most people require more than personal dedication. They need the support and encouragement of their peers, living arrangements that permit them to grow, and work that is right livelihood.

The founder of this eclectic Buddhist movement is the Venerable Sangharakshita, an Englishman (born Dennis Philip Edward Lingwood) who spent 20 years in India. While there he made contact with all the main traditional schools of Buddhism and also studied under several Tibetans. He was initiated into both the Theraveda and Mahayana traditions. On returning to the West to found a new order, his desire was to return to the original Buddhist teachings, but not concern himself with the form. He teaches that Buddhism expresses itself anew in each age and place, though its essence remains the same. He writes:

Buddhism, properly and deeply understood, and thoroughly and extensively applied, is revolutionary. It is revolutionary, that is to say, within the context of the established order. It is in this realization that our breakthrough consists: in the realization of the fact that Buddhism has to transform every aspect of our lives and be not just something that we theoretically understand, not just a little hobby with which we occupy ourselves once or twice a week, but the transforming agent—the catalyst, if you like—of our lives.*

In 1967 Sangharakshita founded the Friends of the Western Buddhist Order (FWBO). It is a movement whose purpose is "precisely to establish as widely as possible a new society within which as many people as possible are free to be individuals." FWBO has centers throughout Britain (they claim that one-third to one-half of the Buddhists in Britain are associated with them), as well as in Finland, Sweden, New Zealand, Australia, the United States, and India. The centers are typically made up of residential communities, business cooperatives, and teaching and practice areas.

We visited the largest center, the London Buddhist Centre in the Bethnal Green section of East London, to see how these ideas about work and community are carried out. The nucleus of the London Buddhist Centre is 50 people who live in small single-sex groupings of 4 to 20 people in housing provided by the Centre's Phoenix Housing Cooperative. They include full, ordained members of FWBO and *mitras,* persons who seek a close association with the intention of being ordained eventually. Another 60 "friends" of the order also live in the cooperative's housing. All live at the center itself or within a two mile radius. Headquarters of the London Buddhist Centre is a converted firehouse that contains offices, a teaching and practice center, a natural foods store, and accommodations for 20 people. The other community businesses are nearby.

Originally a number of small community residences were located in the area, as was a teaching and practice center. In 1974 the leadership

---

*Sangharakshita, *Peace Is a Fire* (London: Windhorse Press, 1979), 37.

heard that the Greater London Council (the governing board of the city) sought someone to take on the rehabilitation of the derelict Victorian firehouse that had been abandoned after suffering a fire itself.

The East London area in which the firehouse is located is a typical English working-class area, filled with low buildings of no architectural distinction, providing a mix of small shops, lower-income housing, and public housing. It is not a neighborhood in which one would expect to find residents with a deep interest in Buddhism or in alternative living and working situations. But it does provide inexpensive housing, and so FWBO selected it as a base. A subway station is nearby; members and supporters can travel easily to their jobs or homes in other parts of the city.

Two FWBO leaders met with representatives of the Greater London Council and put forth their case for the old firehouse. Several other groups were competing for the building. Though the FWBO representatives obviously were naive (for example, they estimated that rehabilitation would take £5000—it took almost 40 times that amount), something of the sincerity and energy of the group must have come through, for they were offered a long-term lease on the property. And this despite a local press campaign that warned against letting "bald Easterners in nighties" into the neighborhood—not an apt description anyway, since members of FWBO have normal hair and wear Western clothes.

The London group raised about £25,000 through donations to rehabilitate the building. Immediately 6 people moved into the building to live and begin renovation. The number of workers (and participating members) grew to 25 over the next year until funds ran out and the project halted for about a year. Finally, in 1977, the center obtained a £160,000 grant to repair the property, supplied under the British Mankind Services Act. The basis of the grant was the socially beneficial nature of the project and the employment it provided. The funds covered both wages and materials, and proved to be enough money to complete the project. The rent on the space, after completion, was set at £3500 per year—though now the Greater London Council is threatening to raise it to £10,000 because the improvements increased the property value.

In late 1978 the center opened, public use began, and the number of people who wished to live nearby and actively participate grew to 30. At the same time, with the termination of the grant, came a big financial hole that needed filling—businesses needed to be started to bring in revenue to support the center and provide employment for members and friends of the order.

The first business to open up was Friends Food, a natural foods store. It is located in the front of the old firehouse building, and it actually began operations before the center was completed. The shop was a natural outgrowth of the need of members for natural food and fresh produce. The Friends Building Service continued the construction focus that was begun with the remodeling of the firehouse. It employs electricians, plumbers, carpenters, and designers. A third business, Windhorse Photosetters, does typesetting. It and the Windhorse Associates Design Studio have many outside clients (including like-minded groups, such as Friends of the Earth) as well as performing the role of in-house agencies. Windhorse Press was, until recently, also located in Bethnal Green (it is now in Glasgow). The two newest businesses are Cherry Orchard, a vegetarian restaurant in an adjoining building, and Jambala, a small retail shop selling secondhand clothes, books, and other goods, and new jewelry and cards.

Each business runs on its own, buys its own equipment and stock or supplies, hires and fires, and has its own bank account. Each is a member of an umbrella organization, the Pure Land Cooperative Ltd. The businesses are run by FWBO members and friends, though the leadership we talked with said that they hoped in the future that the businesses would become part of the FWBO outreach program, involving outsiders as well. A number of the employees are not members of FWBO, but most are at least loosely associated. Two weeks before our visit, however, the restaurant had just hired three women who had no knowledge of, or particular interest in, FWBO. Sangharakshita suggests a formula of four committed to one uncommitted. Any fewer committed, he feels, would dilute the effort.

The businesses have developed organically as the need has arisen. A number of positions involve little or no special training, so workers can easily move into these positions, or move from job to job. There has been, in fact, an inordinate amount of job switching, due perhaps to the mundane nature of the tasks involved. More specialized businesses have been suggested lately, such as a computer software firm. This is a probable future path, as the members with technical skills commit themselves further to FWBO. In each case the merits of the business and also the stability, personality, and devotion of the individuals will be looked at.

The managers of the various businesses tend to emerge from the participants. FWBO and its governing council take into account experience dealing with others as well as experience in business in making their management selections. Good interpersonal abilities are seen as a fundamental basis of success in business management. As in many other communities, positions of responsibility are not particularly sought after, but rather accepted.

A weekly meeting of managers of all the businesses is held to make general policy decisions. Each separate business also holds its own weekly meetings. The discussion in these meetings is about topics specific to the business and includes questions of staffing and vacations. In each case, as in all FWBO meetings, consensus is sought. No voting takes place, although the bylaws allow it, should it become necessary. If consensus cannot be reached, the matter is not dropped, but the discussion continues at a later date until the truth can be identified. Each worker is paid £29 a week for whatever job he or she performs.

The FWBO approach to businesses and work is summed up by E. F. Schumacher in *Small Is Beautiful:* "The Buddhist point of view takes work to be at least threefold: to give a man a chance to utilize and develop his faculties; to enable him to overcome his ego-centeredness by joining with other people in a common task; and to bring forth the goods and services needed for a becoming existence."*

The third of these is the easiest to understand. This is the most basic function of work, but not every product is needed for a "becoming existence." Work that actually produces what society needs—be it baking, building, or brain surgery—is looked on by the FWBO as more satisfying than work such as butchery, usury, or dealing in or making arms or poisons. Such work is specifically discouraged by the Buddha. And FWBO extends this discouragement to include any occupation based on violence to the workers, other people, or the environment, or any work that exploits others, or encourages greed or stupidity.

The first role of work—to give a person "a chance to utilize and develop his faculties"—is also emphasized by FWBO. Work is seen as a means of self-creation, helping an individual learn how he or she can become both productive and creative.

And work is also viewed as a means of overcoming ego-centeredness and selfishness—a very human problem and one that is a central focus of Buddhism.

In an FWBO newsletter, two members spoke of right livelihood:

Work is an activity which humankind is obliged to do, work keeps the human race alive, and every civilization is built on the foundation of work. As individuals, work has an enormous influence on us, and because of this it is an invaluable tool. Work can be one of the most effective supports for our attempts to make ourselves. It makes the Buddha's achievement all the more remarkable; the Buddha, as Sangharakshita points out, never did an honest day's work in his life.**

Work, of course, is only one aspect of an individual's or a community's life. Living arrangements and relationships between people are also quite important. The very form of its living relationships is the most unique feature of the FWBO communities. Members and "mitras" (those who have made a provisional commitment to FWBO) live together in single-sex communities that range in size from four to twenty,

---

*E. F. Schumacher, *Small Is Beautiful* (New York: Harper & Row, 1973), 51.
**Atula and Dhammarati, "Work," *FWBO Newsletter*, 53 (1982):12.

the largest being a group of men who live on the top floors of the old firehouse.

Why single-sex communities? They explained that initially—before there were communities of FWBO members and "mitras" living together—it was discovered that retreats went more smoothly and better results were obtained if only one sex was in attendance. There was less distraction and game playing, and more concentration on the practice of Buddhism. As the communities developed, this single-sex concept was carried on, since it had been shown to stimulate spiritual growth, and also permit an individual to develop qualities that otherwise might not come out. The principle extends to the businesses, all of which are single-sex also.

As in all other aspects of personal conduct in FWBO, no hard and fast rules are handed down from above. The only real guidelines are those of the Buddhist Eightfold Path: right views, right intentions, right speech, right conduct, right livelihood, right effort, right thought or mindfulness, and the right state of a peaceful mind. No authority figure or group tells members to live in single-sex communities. Some experiments with family communities have been tried in other FWBO centers.

Members acknowledge that a prejudice against families exists in FWBO, partly because of the youthfulness of the FWBO population. Not many are currently married, and a number of the married couples are content to live apart.

Women seem to be the ones concerned with the family. In the families living apart who have children, the mother has the children to support and care for, while the father lives with other men. The woman usually lives in a nuclear unit with the children, serving as both father and mother. To some this may seem selfish on the part of the man, and unfair to the children who lose a father—but it is an accepted part of FWBO.

When we were at the center we saw a number of notices on the bulletin board put up by women with children who were interested in forming group houses. This, perhaps, is the wave of the future, allowing companionship for both the children and the mothers.

The question of sex does not seem as important at the London Buddhist Centre as it does in other communities. No restrictions are laid down except avoidance of exploitations. The rule on whether a particular living center will be open or closed to visits from members of the opposite sex is established when the living center itself is established. It can be changed at any time by the general consensus of those living together, though usually it is not. Members move a fair amount from one location to another as their needs—sexual and otherwise—change. Sometimes they might be involved in a relationship and want a housing center where their mate can spend the night. Or they might feel that it is healthier to live without the emotional turbulence and complications that so often accompany relationships. It is rare for two individuals to live together as a couple, though it does happen.

The emphasis at the center is on maintaining deep and honest relationships. If a person has problems, more experienced or clearer members are always ready to help out. Each of the individual housing centers holds a weekly meeting to discuss general problems and financial matters. Sometimes the meetings are just social, allowing for an unstructured interchange.

Up to now people have lived in what FWBO calls "deprived living situations." Financially deprived, that is. This was especially true in the early days, when the workers in the firehouse lived in rubble, with no plumbing or electricity. Now there is a move toward creating a more comfortable way of life, with people usually having their own room. But housing remains a problem. One of the current ideas is to set up a hostel for some of the more transient members and friends, but no money is available yet for this.

The Phoenix Housing Cooperative oversees all of the local individual housing arrangements, and helps friends and new members find adequate housing in the area. It deals with landlords and the city housing authority, and all payments are funneled through it.

Out of the £29 workers get each week, they pay a housing fee of £10. This will probably increase, because it is not covering costs. Lunch is free if it is eaten in the center, but members pay for the other meals. Food is bought in bulk by each living center and meals are cooked and eaten communally. Members pay about £4 for their meals each week, leaving £15 for clothes and recreation. Increasing the pay, either by paying the British minimum wage or by supplementing wages in cases of special need, is being considered.

Those who need extra money approach the treasurer of their business to make their case. If for some reason the treasurer cannot evaluate the merits of the request, it is discussed at the weekly business meeting and the workers come to a consensus—though this situation is rare.

Vacations are thought of as necessary breaks from the routine of daily life, permitting members to travel or go on retreats and deepen their meditative experience. Vacation time usually amounts to six weeks and is usually taken in blocks of one or two weeks. The vacations are paid for by the worker's business, and the worker also receives his or her £29 for the week, as the rent must still be paid.

In many ways FWBO has the least authoritarian structure of any community we have visited. Sangharakshita's role is a spiritual one, not an administrative one. He spends his time studying, practicing, reading, and teaching. He is a spiritual inspiration to the whole order, maintaining an extensive correspondence and often seeing people individually in his house in Norfolk, in his retreats and seminars, and on his trips to London. He is the only one who can induct a new member into the order. The order consists of about 200 members worldwide, 75 percent of whom are men and 25 percent of whom are women. It is growing at the rate of 20 to 30 new members a year. There is little attrition since members look on ordination as a lifelong commitment.

The London Buddhist Centre is just one of 17 centers or branches of FWBO. With about 40 members (30 men, 10 women), plus *mitras* and friends, it consists of three interconnected organizations: the FWBO, the Pure Land Cooperative, and the Phoenix Housing Cooperative. Each has its own chair elected by its own members. The FWBO Council consists of 20 members, elected by the 40 local members of FWBO. It has three officers: chairman, secretary and treasurer, each elected for a one-year term. The first two have served for many years; the treasurer changes frequently. The officers play a strong role in both administrative and spiritual matters, and their selection is based on their spiritual vision as well as their administrative ability.

The FWBO council meets every two weeks, alternating between administrative and policy agendas. Many members also participate in meetings of the national order each month and meetings of the international order twice a year. All decisions at all levels are based on consensus. The unity reflects in part a similarity of outlook and in part a well-functioning hierarchy and deep inner commitment.

Individuality is stressed in the teachings and in the living, work, and practice situations. While there is a common vocabulary, members consciously avoid the use of jargon which can help to isolate a group. Still, isolation is a danger because many members feel that FWBO is the true exponent of Buddhist teachings, with a much more authentic, albeit eclectic, approach than that of groups who focus solely on one way of teaching, such as Zen or the Tibetan tantric tradition. As a result, FWBO members don't mingle much with members of other spiritual groups. Members of the London Buddhist Centre are also isolated in their own neighborhood. Their working-class neighbors have little time for, or interest in, a strange foreign practice. They might shop in the stores or eat in the restaurant because they are convenient and cheap, but they don't come to the center's events.

The members' main friendships are within the group. When they travel or go out it is generally with other members of the community. Nonetheless, the atmosphere is not stifling. Most people read and pursue their individual interests in sports and recreation. Sangharakshita is very well-read and he encourages this in others. In addition to books on Buddhism, many members have a strong interest in literature, philosophy, and the arts.

No vow of poverty is taken and FWBO members are free to retain whatever goods and property they have. If they work on the outside and earn a good salary, it is theirs to keep—though a subtle pressure to donate some of it is often exerted because of the group's constant financial problems, and some funding has been obtained through donations and loans from more affluent members.

A strong outreach effort is made by FWBO. The group often invites schools to visit, and members set up tables at fairs and other public events. A weekend course designed to give schoolteachers a basic grounding in Buddhism is also offered. One of the major outreach vehicles is a quarterly newsletter with a circulation of 3000. Of this number, about half are given away to members and friends around the world; the rest are sold for 65 pence per issue.

Ecological considerations are not an important part of the FWBO ideology, although members try to avoid abuse of the environment. Some members do have an interest in issues such as the antinuclear movement and appropriate technology, but it is a sympathetic, not active, interest.

During our visit Nagabodhi, the editor of the newsletter, summed up in one word what he saw as the major problem facing FWBO: complacency. He said that as the group becomes more settled it faces the possibility of losing its outward drive and becoming simply a pleasant place for people to live and work. But this is not enough, according to Buddhist teachings. A constant reassessment of the group's spiritual commitment is necessary, as well as a monitoring of its expansion to make sure that it grows slowly, putting down firm roots.

The experiment is still in its infancy. Time will tell how FWBO will deal with the problems to come as the organization and membership grow, the businesses expand, the capital is provided for future expansion, and the young members pair up and produce children.

One of the gardens at Findhorn.

CHAPTER 14

Findhorn: Between Community and University

Findhorn is perhaps the best-known intentional community in the world and has a strong influence on many others. It advocates a spiritual approach to solving the world's problems through what it calls a "network of light"—a growing network of spiritually attuned people. While Findhorn is very much a community, its major focus and source of income is as an educational center, which draws 3000 to 6000 people each year from all over the world. As a result the community itself is an international one, more ethnically diverse than perhaps any other intentional community.

The story of Findhorn dates back to the 1960s. From 1957 to 1962 Peter and Eileen Caddy, both English, and Dorothy MacLean, a Canadian, ran the 150-bed Cluny Hill Hotel, 26 miles east of Inverness in the far north of Scotland. In 1962 they suddenly lost their jobs. For years Eileen had received guidance during meditations on how to run the hotel. Now her guidance told her that they would be going back to Cluny Hill "quite soon," but in the meantime they were to live in their small trailer at a nearby commercial trailer park in the village of Findhorn, near the beach of the Moray Firth. Their trailer was situated a little away from the others, near a rubbish dump. Their first task, they were advised, was to clean up the area, "putting light into everything we did to ground positive energies into the place," as Peter explained. They were told to cultivate a garden, and eat as much homegrown food as possible to raise their "vibrational level." They were also told to tune into the *devas*—the archetypal life force of each species of plant. The *deva* messages contained specific instructions about the treatment the different plants preferred. They carried out these instructions and the results were remarkable, despite very poor beach soil. To the amazement of soil and garden experts who visited from all over Britain, the plants grew fantastically. The most notable success of these three was the raising of 40-pound cabbages.

As word of these horticultural miracles spread, others joined the three and formed a small community. One of the new members, R. Ogilvie Crombie, began to communicate with the elemental forces of nature, which he perceived as elves, fairies, and gnomes. The *devas* and nature spirits sent many messages through Eileen Caddy and R. Ogilvie Crombie about the necessity and opportunities for cooperation between humans and nature. As the consciousness of the group grew, its numbers also grew; members believed this was the process of manifestation at work. This manifestation required absolute faith that God would provide for their needs as long as they were doing his work. As they needed money to expand accommodations, build a sanctuary, or build a communal kitchen, it flowed in from other sources. The manifestation of their needs also came in the form of just the right people to do a particular job or the opportunity to acquire what was needed just when it was needed.

In 1970, when 20 members were in the community, David Spangler, an American arrived. During his three years at Findhorn he received transmissions from a source he knew as Limitless Love and Truth; he talks about this in his book, *Revelation: The Birth of a New Age.** This book discusses, more than any other, the philosophical basis of Findhorn. David became a codirector of Findhorn, along with Peter, and started the community's educational program, which later became the Findhorn Foundation.

For nine years the community operated largely on Eileen's guidance, Peter's intuition, and Dorothy's interpretations. In 1972 Eileen was told in meditation that she should stop giving guidance, so that members would learn to become attuned with God's will themselves. By this time Findhorn was at the beginning of an explosive growth that brought it to 80 members that year, 150 in 1974, and 300 in 1978. The growth was fueled by the 1975 publication of Paul Hawken's book, *The Magic of Findhorn,*** followed by the community's own book, *The Findhorn Garden.**** Starting with a mimeograph machine, which was used to print and distribute Eileen's guidance and Dorothy's interpretations, the community gradually acquired increasingly complex equipment for printing and binding. It now operates modern presses and does most of its own production, publishing a variety of books as well as a magazine, various pamphlets, and brochures.

In 1973 the community was given one and one-half acres adjoining the trailer park. A house on the land was remodeled to provide a li-

*David Spangler, *Revelation: The Birth of a New Age* (San Francisco: Rainbow Bridge, 1976).

**Paul Hawken, *The Magic of Findhorn* (New York: Bantam Books, 1975).

***Findhorn Community, *The Findhorn Garden* (New York: Harper & Row, 1975).

brary, offices, meeting rooms, and small sanctuary. In July 1974, ground was broken on this same land for the building of Universal Hall, a pentagonal building designed to seat 300 people for cultural events and conferences. It was a big undertaking for the community and was not completed until 1983, after the expenditure of nearly £300,000 and untold human energy. However, it makes it possible for Findhorn to serve as a conference center for outside organizations. The first such conference was the 3rd World Wilderness Congress in October 1983.

A more significant milestone was the purchase in 1975 of the by then run-down Cluny Hill Hotel for £60,000, fulfilling the guidance that they would return there. "Quite soon" turned out to be 13 years to the day since the original three were forced to leave. This vast building on six acres was renamed Cluny Hill College and became the center for the guest and workshop programs, in addition to providing housing for some 20 members.

In 1978 the community bought Cullerne House, a large stone farmhouse on eight acres near the edge of the trailer park. Now the site of the successful Garden School, the purchase was something of an accident and also a lesson in how not to go about expanding. The owner of the trailer park put it on the market at £80,000, Eileen's guidance said "buy," and members of the board of trustees got very excited about its potential. An Australian couple was visiting Findhorn at the time, and when a member told them about the opportunity they offered a loan of £8000. They talked about it at some length, and every time the Australians said £8000, the member heard £80,000. The wonderful offer of £80,000 was reported to the board of trustees and the house was quickly purchased. When the truth became known, Findhorn realized that it was obligated to raise a great deal of money without any idea how to do it. The process by which the purchase was made was roundly criticized within the community and much energy was spent in the next year coping with the ramifications of that decision. Eileen's guidance said "sell" to reduce the tensions in the community, so the board of trustees concurred and put Cullerne House on the market again. Then two things happened to save Cullerne House. One was that no ready buyer came forth. The other was that the members living in the house assumed the responsibility of raising the money to pay it off. Other members and friends on the outside also rallied to help meet the obligation. The board of trustees set various deadlines and financial goals and although they were seldom met in full, enough progress was made to keep going. The effort was eventually successful. In 1980 the Garden School was started at Cullerne House, and it is one of the most interesting programs at Findhorn.

A mansion, Drumduan House, was given to the community in 1978. The cost of repairing it was great, since it had been vandalized and was in a terrible state. Nevertheless the community set to repairing it with energy and enthusiasm, and it now houses seven people, an art gallery open to the public on Sundays and for special events, conference rooms, and Findhorn's communication department.

Also in 1978, the Dutch owners of Erraid Island, near Iona off the west coast of Scotland, offered the community the use of the island for eleven months each year, retaining its use for one month for their own vacation. Erraid Island had been uninhabited since 1952, when the lighthouse keepers and their families left their 100-year-old houses for the attractions of the mainland. The island's houses and other facilities had fallen into ruin. Now a community of nine adults and five children live on the island, growing food, fishing, caring for animals, rehabilitating the facilities, and welcoming weekly parties of guests. When they took over, the nine houses suffered from both wet rot and dry rot. In the first several years the houses were repaired; water pipes, showers, baths, sinks, and wood-burning stoves were installed; and outhouses were dug. Five walled gardens were planted, and small animals were brought in.

The aim was to develop self-sufficiency. At first the island dwellers received financial and personal help from the main Findhorn community, and offered, in turn, a setting in which its principles could be applied in a down-to-earth way. By 1981 the island dwellers were able to dispense with direct financial support from the main community because they generated enough from their farming, fishing, and guest programs to cover their expenses.

Another former hotel, which is near Cluny Hill College, Newbold House, had been leased by Findhorn for a short period and then was offered for sale by its owners. Harley and Margaret Miller, one couple who lived there, wanted to buy it and negotiated a very reasonable price of £80,000. After the chastening experience with Cullerne House, the community as a whole had no heart for the task of financing another large building. So Harley and Margaret, along with six other members who lived there, decided to take on the responsibility themselves. They formed a separate trust, raised the money for the down-payment, and in two years raised nearly the entire purchase price in donations and loans. They offer a number of educational courses of their own, as well as running a bed and breakfast establishment for up to 30 people at a time. Their New Creation Workshop is a two-week program for people in transition—often newly unemployed, divorced, or facing a crisis. They make no fixed charge for anything they do, practicing the principle of manifestation and inviting their guests to pay whatever they feel is appropriate. They have managed in this way to cover their £40,000 a year costs as well as make a monthly donation to Findhorn.

In addition to the above properties, the community today occupies much of the trailer park; about two dozen members have bought their own trailers. Several people are housed in the old railway station house in Findhorn village, which the community purchased with low-interest loans from friends. In addition, members also live in two smaller houses in Findhorn village, on a small farm outside the neighboring town of Forres, and at a spiritual retreat on the sacred island of Iona. One member lives in a cottage at the foot of Cluny Hill. It is a scattered community, yet it is united in spirit. Findhorn operates a free bus service to connect its various parts, since people often have to commute five miles or more from home to work.

Despite the growth of facilities, the size of the community has fallen by nearly half since it reached its peak of about 300 people in 1978. One of the most significant features of Findhorn is the way in which it has managed to keep going and operate efficiently despite a high rate of turnover. Virtually no one thinks of Findhorn as a permanent home. It is a place people live for a while to contribute to its effort to bring light to the world and also to develop their own spiritual life and practical knowledge so they can make their life count somewhere else. When they feel that they've learned as much as they can, they move on. Fortunately for Findhorn, the average stay has been gradually getting longer. In the mid-1970s the average stay was about six months. Now it is three and one-half years. This reflects, in part, the maturing of the community and its participants (the average age has risen from the early twenties to the mid-thirties); it also reflects the recently enacted Findhorn policy to not accept anyone as a member who does not have the intention of staying at least two years. Thus the decline in membership is a function in part of a lower rate of turnover, weeding out those who would wish to stay a short while; in part of a return to normalcy after a period of overexpansion because of the publicity it received in the mid-1970s; and in part, perhaps, to some lessening of outside interest as the novelty of Findhorn wears off and other similar communities are created elsewhere. The maturing of the community and the longer stays have also caused members to want better housing. So the fewer than 200 people now at Findhorn occupy space that once accommodated 300. The changing standards mean that space is still at a premium, however, deterring the acceptance of new members, especially families, unless they can supply their own housing.

At the beginning of 1984 membership stood at 167. Of these, 108 were adults in the work force without children; 26 were parents, half of whom were in the work force; 7 were elderly, working half-time or less; and 26 were children. Of the total, 87 were from Great Britain, 43 were from the United States, 7 were from Canada, 5 were from Holland, 4 each were from France, Germany, and Sweden, 3 were from Australia and Switzerland, and one each were from Italy, New Zealand, South Africa, Yugoslavia, and Zimbabwe. All were white; most had at least one year of college.

The process of becoming a member is monitored by the personnel department, which also matches members with jobs and provides job counseling when necessary. The first step is to attend a Findhorn Experience Week, which runs throughout the year and costs £110. This is the basic program at Findhorn for all first-time visitors. It provides an introduction to the spiritual principles on which the community is based. It involves discussion, meditation, sacred dance, audiovisuals, and member's sharings, and includes half-days of work in the various Findhorn departments. For many people the loving acceptance is a euphoric high, and it is easy for them to think they would like to join the community. If they are so inclined, the next step is for them to stay on for at least another week as a guest, working in one department. The cost of this is £85 a week. During this period they talk over their interest in joining with two personnel department members, and they in turn talk with other members who have worked with them. If all agree that they would fit in, they are asked to return home until the time of the next orientation program for new members. This gives them a chance to evaluate their experience and decide if they really want to move to Findhorn.

Virginia Lloyd Davis, for example, had a successful career in public relations and wanted to join Findhorn so that she could use her skills on its behalf. She was asked if she would still want to come if she were assigned to the kitchen. "Oh, that would be lovely," she said. "I adore working in the kitchen." She was accepted and before long she was assigned to do the public relations.

Orientation programs are usually held two or three times a year. The program lasts about six weeks, involving the newcomer in all aspects of the community and providing a further opportunity for conversations between personnel department members and other members regarding the suitability of the choice. At the end of that period the applicant becomes a member if all concerned agree that this is appropriate.

If Findhorn members feel that the applicant won't fit in, this is conveyed in such a way that the person himself or herself arrives at the same conclusion. The personnel department staff usually say that the time is not ripe for the move. Similarly, the exit process tends to be expressed on both sides in terms of the cycle of one's life making it time to depart. Usually if the community feels that someone should depart, that person feels it too and there is little problem. Sometimes this feeling needs to be expressed in stronger terms. One woman who had been at Findhorn for ten years seemed to be stagnating. As time went on, she began to experience difficulty working with people and was hypersensitive and disruptive in meetings, but was terrified by the thought of leaving. After sufficient encouragement she made the break and eventually found that life outside wasn't as difficult as she had imagined.

There are only two rules at Findhorn: no smoking in public places, and no illegal drugs. Several years ago three members were picked up

by the police for smoking marijuana in another town. They were un-
ceremoniously expelled from Findhorn. Six months later, two of them
applied for, and were granted, readmittance.

Some people leave Findhorn to travel or work at other jobs, then
eventually return. The community expects to see more of this pattern
in the future.

As previously mentioned, new members are asked to make a commitment of at least two years. They are expected to contribute £125 a
month during the first year for their room and board, and to provide
their own pocket money for the second year. After that they can become
staff members and receive the regular Findhorn allowance of £7 a week
plus room and board. Many variations on these financial arrangements
cover people with their own accommodations, outside jobs, or other
special requirements. These are worked out by agreement between the
member and the personnel department. Findhorn does not expect
people to turn over all their resources to the community. Some members
have private cars, others own cars jointly. Some who have outside funds
lend money to Findhorn at low interest or no interest; others respond to
appeals for contributions.

Living conditions are by now fairly comfortable. Most individuals and
couples have a trailer with its own kitchen and toilet facilities, or else a
private room in one of the buildings. Meals are eaten together in the
various dining rooms, though individuals may obtain food from one of
the two Findhorn shops and cook it themselves. Members don't have to
pay for this food, but a record is kept of the value of what they take to
reduce waste.

At the same time the workload has increased, since a work force of
about 125 persons now has to do the work that once employed nearly
twice that number. As one person said,

I love the work I'm doing. I put a lot into it and get a lot of fulfillment from
doing it and doing it well. But there's too much of it and feeling that I *have* to
do it makes it seem like a trap. I have to grit my teeth and make myself carry on
with it and put in a lot of extra time, because it has to be done and there's no
one else available to do it. I sometimes wonder if there's life outside work!

The theoretical work week is 33 hours, plus a 2- to 3-hour depart-
mental attunement each week. (This is a time for meditation and discussion, allowing members of the department to develop a common
feeling about the jobs to be done and the role each will play.) But to
meet their responsibilities, many work longer than this. Then there are
the rotating tasks, such as kitchen cleanup, guest tours, and Sunday
cooking. Also, people in the trailer park now have responsibility for
care of the gardens around their trailers—chores that used to be done
by the Findhorn garden and maintenance departments.

At one of Findhorn's annual three-day conferences on spirituality, this problem was the major focus. The question was how to bring more inspiration and creativity back into members' lives. The core group retired to Erraid Island for a week to discuss this issue after the conference ended. They came back with proposals that community members eagerly approved. One is that everyone stop work at 4:00 during the winter season, to allow time for study and relaxation. Those who can't stop then should take some other time. A main meditation time is set for 12:15, in addition to the short sanctuary periods in the morning and evening. Members are asked to ban business conversations at lunchtime. These changes are all part of a process that leads many at Findhorn to believe that the community is moving into a more spiritual phase after spending several years getting its material house in order.

The growing number of families has also brought about changes at Findhorn. Findhorn has always strongly supported the nuclear family and believes that children should attend the state schools so that they will not be alienated from the world outside, and will have choices about how they want to direct their lives, just as their parents did. Young adults who have lived at Findhorn as children must ask to become members and go through orientation, just like an outsider.

Nevertheless, the question of how to raise children in the New Age continues to occupy a great deal of attention. A morning school with two teachers trained in Rudolf Steiner's Waldorf methods is available for five-year-olds and six-year-olds (the latter is the age at which regular schooling becomes compulsory in Scotland) and a play group is held in the afternoon for younger children. Many of these activities take place in the family house. Mothers are expected to put parenting first, and they are not counted as part of the work force. The fathers may alternate or share in this. While there is some talk of full-time child care that would permit both parents to join the work force, this hasn't happened yet.

While most couples are married, this is not universal, and Findhorn has no rules about people's sexual behavior except to expect that they will act responsibly. There are some gay men and women, and this is regarded as their own business. The community would object, however, if they attempted to make it a platform for propagating their political ideas, just as it would object to any other group doing the same. It debated at length its stand on nuclear disarmament and finally adopted the following statement:

We see our own contribution as a Foundation as an educational and spiritual one rather than in the area of direct social action. Our focus is on the development of a greater alignment with the spiritual values of unity, relatedness and interconnectedness, and on the creation of forms that are more reflective of these values. We support the numerous moves towards peace coming forth from many governments, churches, organizations and individuals; we support those who in different fields are working to embody a more holistic consciousness; and we encourage our individual members to take part in whatever activities spring from their own hearts' commitment to peace and the vision of a holistic world, with the understanding that their involvement be as individuals and not as representatives of the Findhorn Foundation.*

This avoidance of endorsement was occasioned in part by Findhorn's large international contingent and its consequent concern to keep the immigration authorities happy. Most intentional communities have few members of foreign nationality because of the difficulties raised by immigration officials. But its international composition is part of Findhorn's *raison d'être,* and it has therefore engaged in lengthy negotiations with the British Home Office to permit it to keep its foreign students and members for extended periods of time. It has been helped in this by the fact that it brings a good deal of foreign exchange into Great Britain; not only does it attract 3000 students (most of whom are foreign) to its programs each year, it is also one of the largest tourist attractions in the north of Scotland. On the other hand, just what Findhorn is has puzzled officials at times. The Findhorn Foundation in 1982 finally prepared a formal application to the Home Office for recognition as a "bona fide private residential religious/educational institution."

The application pointed out that the foundation members have committed themselves to the study and practice of universal religious and spiritual truths and their translation into everyday life, and that Findhorn sees itself simultaneously as a community, monastery, college, and "University of Light," because no one of these terms is sufficient to describe its devotion to the "One Light and One Life which manifests in all Creation." The document went on to say:

Our intent has been both to facilitate the growth and development of this centre in its entirety as a living demonstration and educational model of the practical spiritual life, and, in the process, to train members in the dynamics and demands of world service, a commitment they are expected to continue in related activities and centres around the planet.

The essential conviction which lies at the heart of our life and our educational philosophy at Findhorn is that true spirituality consists less of what we believe than of the qualities we exemplify in the course of our life and work, qualities of aspiration, commitment, courage, discipline, joy, peace, love, creativity, clarity and cooperation that we associate with our inherent, if potential, divinity.

The Home Office was impressed with the presentation and with Findhorn itself and it has usually granted annual renewals of the visas of those classified as students or staff at Findhorn. A recent arrangement offers visas for up to seven years for staff members.

Findhorn Newsletter (July 1982):11.

Findhorn's method of government has evolved over the years. In the beginning it was pretty much an autocracy, with Peter Caddy directing everybody with the crisp efficiency he had used as a hotel manager and before that as a Royal Air Force officer. At the same time, Findhorn was saved the problem of having a guru, since leadership responsibilities were divided among its original triumvirate. When David Spangler arrived, Peter shared some of his responsibilities with him and he gradually learned to delegate and to listen to others. If he didn't, he sometimes found that no one listened to him. For example, Peter chose an interior decorator for Cluny Hill that no one else wanted. When the decorator saw that he was getting no cooperation from the community, he left.

Fortunately, Peter understood that the community needed to become self-governing, so over a period of several years in the late 1970s he gradually withdrew his authoritarian hold over the community and let go. This doubtless reflected both his awareness of the community's needs and those of his own. Peter had a strongly developed mind and will, but a poorly developed heart. Eileen was just the opposite. Thus they balanced each other very well while raising a family and getting Findhorn off the ground, but the time came for Peter, as it does for many men in middle age, when he felt that the other side of his personality needed a lot more attention. He finally passed the job of community focalizer to François Duquesne, a 33-year-old member who was generally regarded as the strongest person for such a role. And in 1980 Peter left Eileen and Findhorn to live first in Hawaii and then in California with a new wife and child.

Eileen went through a difficult time, but with the help of counseling and love from the community, she came to accept what was, and went on to further develop her own strength. She went out on the lecture circuit as Peter had done previously, and now plays a more active role in the community. And Peter continues to spread the light of Findhorn wherever he goes, coming back from time to time to attend meetings or conferences.

Peter's departure brought about the conditions under which Findhorn could explore a variety of new forms of governance which were rooted in the concept of attunement, with each person taking full responsibility for his or her own actions.

The Findhorn Foundation is legally governed by a board of trustees. This is a self-perpetuating board of ten members that meets quarterly, five of whom currently live at Findhorn. The tendency of the board of trustees is to devolve power to lower levels or to act in response to the expressed will of the community. The key word at Findhorn is "focalizer"—one who focuses the energy of the group, rather than directs it.

The top group within the community is the core group, which presently consists of ten people, headed by François Duquesne as core group focalizer. The core group has spiritual, executive, and political functions. About half of the group consists of focalizers of the key departments, and the rest is open to general membership. The latter may be invited to serve or they may ask to be invited. Core group meetings are generally open and other community members can drop in. Those who want to be members of the core group are asked to sit in for a month or two first to see if they work well with the group.

Under the core group are the various houses and departments, each with its own focalizer, and the executive committee, which has the main administrative responsibility for Findhorn.

There is also a village council; a representative body with membership drawn from different groups and living areas in the community. It serves mainly as a sounding board, responding to proposals from the various groups and exploring their implications. Since frequent community meetings are held, as well as much informal consultation at all levels, some see the village council as a useless appendage; at the present time it is inactive.

Findhorn is not a democracy in the sense of voting for anything. Decisions are made through attunement and consensus. The nearest members came to taking a vote was in 1980, when two members circulated a questionnaire asking other members' opinions regarding a proposal to set up a recording studio to make and market records of people such as John Denver and Paul Horn, who are not Findhorn members. About 60 percent favored the idea, but the opposition was sufficient to kill it. The two members who had proposed it left the community soon after.

Someone once described Findhorn as a "divine anarchy." The belief at Findhorn is that if people take full responsibility for their lives and develop a kind of 360° perspective, they don't need someone on top to control them. Floyd Tift described his experience on the executive committee: "People did their homework, checked the laws, studied the economics, considered all the parameters. Each would argue his or her position on the subject. Then someone would say, 'Let's all meditate for awhile and see what feels right.' This would usually lead to a consensus. If not, the group would listen to the various positions again and try again for consensus."

Leadership selection is a mixture of self-selection and invitations to fill certain roles. Often a person has to release an attachment to a particular job before the community will give it to him or her. An interesting example of self-selection occurred when 7 people were needed to go to London for a particular mission. The focalizer, who was American, asked for volunteers in an open meeting and 7 people, all American, raised their hands. Knowing that Americans tend to be more forward in such matters, the focalizer probed further and finally found 13 people who wanted to go. She suggested that they go off in a group and find out which 6 would like to give the gift of not going. The process they then went through so pleased the 13 that for several weeks thereafter they met together just to enjoy each others' company.

The Findhorn Foundation, which owns the facilities and employs most of the members, is the major, but not the only, part of the Findhorn community. The community also includes private businesses, as well as independent members who have spent at least a year in the community and who are self-supporting and not part of the regular workforce. This includes the members of Newbold House, who run a bed and breakfast and workshops.

Approximately 52 percent of the foundation's net income comes from its various educational programs, 10 percent comes from donations and members fees, and the remaining 38 percent comes from business operations such as the trailer park, publications, and the shop. During 1983, total income was over £1 million. Because the various programs are so interdependent, it is difficult to assign profit or loss to any of them.

The Findhorn courses begin with the Findhorn Experience week, described earlier. Findhorn offers these in French, German, and Dutch as well as English, and also offers one tailored for persons older than 60. A two-month Essence of Findhorn program is available for those who seek a deeper understanding of the community. Special courses have included: Sacred Dance Instructor Training, Wilderness Workshop, The Artist Within, The Creative Challenge of Dance, Living Lightly on the Earth, New Games, Authority, Power and Inner Knowing, and Esoteric Philosophy. One interesting week-long workshop at Findhorn is The Game of Life. It is a board game that recreates the drama of a soul's journey through transformation. Everybody wins in this game; if you finish first you go back to help others along the path. From challenges encountered and insights gained, players increase their awareness and their capabilities for wise and loving service. The game has been conducted in Europe and the United States by the members who developed it, and opportunities to participate in it are expanding.

The Garden School at Cullerne House, offering week-long workshops as well as three-month to one-year apprenticeships, is just now beginning to pay its own way. With 12 students and a staff of 7, it focalizes all of Findhorn's work with nature, including the various other gardens. Findhorn grows only about 10 percent of the food it consumes, although when one considers the thousands of people who pass through each year, this is a sizable amount of vegetables. Findhorn is predominantly vegetarian, though fish is served once every couple weeks, and recently chicken has been introduced as well. The Garden

School keeps about 500 chickens and normally supplies all of Findhorn's chicken and eggs. Staff and students have constructed a number
of greenhouses and experimented with a variety of modified plant envi-
ronments. The largest of these is a polyethylene tunnel that includes
drip irrigation and solar-assisted under-soil heating. It is part of a cooperative experimental project with the Arcosanti community in Arizona.
Staff and students operate a tree nursery to supply all of the Findhorn
grounds and to establish species best suited to the area as sources of
shelter, food, and fuel. They also run a growing developmental program in appropriate technology called ATEC—Appropriate Technology Exchange between Communities. Findhorn's research has included
the growing experiments previously mentioned, a Russian masonry
fireplace that holds heat a long time, solar-assisted hot water facilities,
and greenhouse solar collectors. They are planning a series of seminars
and gatherings with other organizations in the ATEC network.

The publications department at one time employed 22 people but
now has about 12. It has a list of several dozen titles, including a number of books published by the Thule Press, a Scottish publishing firm
that went bankrupt and was taken over by Findhorn. Findhorn sells
directly wholesale and retail, and also distributes through a number of
independent book distributors in Great Britain, the United States, Australia, New Zealand, and South Africa. Most of the production, including printing and binding, is done in-house. Findhorn also produces a
bimonthly magazine called *One Earth,* which has about 2500 subscribers
and a print run of 4000. The publications department makes a profit,
but its workers are paid only £120 a month. If they were paid regular
salaries, it probably would not be a profitable department.

Findhorn operates two shops—one at Cluny Hill and one in the trailer park—that sell books, handcrafted items, health food, and toiletries.
At one time Findhorn had craft studios devoted to weaving, pottery,
candle making, and other crafts. These were hard to keep staffed and
in 1981 all but the weaving studio were closed down. That continues
under Kate Martin, a long-term member with two children. All the
work there is adjusted to her time schedule as a mother.

Another artist at Findhorn, Alice Rigan, was interested in Celtic designs and did a number of modern renderings of them. She and some
friends wanted to start a business making greeting cards of these designs, but the community wasn't interested. So in 1978 they took on the
responsibility themselves and established a profit-making business
called Daybreak Designs. This was the first profit-making business associated with the nonprofit Findhorn Foundation, and many people in
the community had difficulty seeing how the two could fit together.
The business was fairly successful. The owners printed 5000 each of ten
designs and sold them at fairs, at the Findhorn shops, and through mail
order. The Scottish Arts Foundation gave the business its stamp of ap-

proval. The Findhorn Press published a coloring book of Alice's designs, and Harper & Row published an American edition. When Alice left the community, Daybreak Designs was reintegrated into the foundation, and then later was taken over by an independent member as a private economic venture.

Another private business in the community is Weatherwise Homes, started in 1979. It employs eight to ten people, mostly community members but sometimes outsiders when needed. The main business of Weatherwise Homes is insulating houses with a highly efficient pellet made of recycled paper. Its biggest contract was insulating a large number of houses for the regional police force. In 1982 employees developed an improved solar panel and commenced design and parts assembly for a 65-square-yard system on the roof of Cluny Hill College, which they estimated would save enough in the costs of heating hot water to pay for itself in five years. Weatherwise Homes pays Findhorn for the time used by its member-employees that would otherwise be available for Findhorn work.

Findhorn has outreach all over the world, largely through the communications department, which employs two full-time people and maintains what is probably the most complete file in the world on spiritual communities. In 1981 the communications department staff attempted to put their files onto a computer but they dropped the project when they ran into computer problems. In addition to maintaining reciprocal mailings with many other groups, the communications department invites every guest at Findhorn to fill out a card expressing various interests, and to become part of the outreach network. The principal nexus of the network is about 150 resource people scattered around the world. They receive at least two general mailings a year, and there are personal communications and meetings where feasible. Resource people represent Findhorn, and help to focalize "light energy" (that is spiritually influenced energy) in their own communities. In this respect Findhorn views itself as just a vehicle to promote planetary citizenship—"to establish the Divine Plan on Earth."

Findhorn has special connections with certain communities. Several years ago an American put up the money to develop a project for cooperation among Findhorn, Arcosanti in Arizona, and Auroville in India. The project involved erecting the Hexiad House at Findhorn as a headquarters and arranging exchanges of members and an annual joint meeting. After a couple years the American's financial support came to an end, but the project has continued in a small way on its own momentum. Another exchange of members has been with the Esalen Institute in Big Sur, California. Esalen was set up primarily as an educational center, but in time its staff wanted it to develop as more of a community. Members of the communities have learned much through spending time with each other.

On the whole, the Findhorn community has amicable relations with the local community though there are still those who do not understand it and who find it somewhat threatening to their Scottish conservatism. Findhorn has a full-time publicity and public relations person and an important part of her duties is to maintain good relations with the local press and influential people. Annual programs and open houses are held for Findhorn's neighbors.

In 1982 Findhorn members drew up a plan to build Findhorn into an ecologically sound planetary village. As one of the members said to us, "Findhorn is an ecological disaster." She was referring particularly to the poorly insulated trailers, which are heated by oil and electricity. And so in the summer of 1982 François Duquesne made a lengthy trip to the United States to raise funds for this undertaking, and the fall international conference at Findhorn that year was devoted to the subject.

In perfect timing with the community's desire to control the use of the land they live on, came an opportunity to purchase the trailer park. During the 1982 fall conference the members agreed by consensus to ask friends around the world for help in buying the property.

During 1983, more than half of the £380,000 required was raised by cash gifts and pledges from over a thousand well wishers around the world. The purchase was completed in November, 1983, with the sellers taking a note for the balance. This, and completion of the Universal Hall, raised Findhorn's debt from the level of around £330,000 where it had hovered for the past five years, to nearly £500,000. However, the assets of the trailer park include £100,000 worth of trailers for rental to summer vacationers. The community feels confident that within a few years the annual profit from this business will clear their long indebtedness. So a new and very substantial means of growth for Findhorn has manifested itself.

Kay and Floyd Tift are two Americans who, after retiring in their late fifties, moved to Findhorn in 1977. Their skills were needed and they soon found themselves working harder than ever before, in positions of responsibility. But as they moved into their sixties, Kay and Floyd said they were getting just as much from Findhorn as they were putting into it.

"I came to Findhorn to work on my heart chakra," Kay told us. "This is the best place I know where in a group setting we can help each person to contribute positively to the energy flow moving in the same direction. We are learning to become group beings without losing our own individuality. And love is what makes it all work."

Part V

ISRAEL

Some of the offices and communal areas at Yodfat.

CHAPTER 15

Yodfat: A Spiritual Cooperative

Israel today has a communal movement that is unique in the world. Its roots go back to the second wave of immigrants to Palestine, those who came after the failure of the 1905 Russian Revolution. These immigrants were largely young Jewish socialists—educated young men and women from middle-class families, whose mission in life was to return to the Promised Land and reconstruct Jewish society. By choosing to become agriculturists they sought to establish a close connection with the land and to create a better balance in the Jewish social structure, which traditionally had devalued manual labor.

These new immigrants did not fit into the existing settlements in Palestine, so they built their own. They wanted to create an entirely new society, based on brotherhood, equality, and mutual aid. The "kibbutz" (in-gathering) movement developed out of their early experience. A rudimentary World Zionist Organization already existed in Palestine, dedicated to helping those immigrants who had no means of their own to build settlements.

In 1907 land was purchased by the World Zionist Organization in the Jordan Valley where the Sea of Galilee flows into the Jordan River. It assigned a settlement group to prepare the soil for cultivation. The land was little better than a swamp, but the workers persisted and eventually turned it into a fertile area. Soon after, they were invited to settle on the land permanently. These ten men and two women were offered 750 acres on the east bank of the river under an automatically renewable long-term lease at a nominal rental fee. They called their new community *Deganiah*, which means "God's wheat." The average age of the group was 20. They were an extended family, taking their meals together in a communal dining hall. The first *sabra* (native-born Israeli) born to this group of settlers was Moshe Dayan.

This commune was the genesis of the kibbutz movement. Deganiah and similar settlements that quickly sprang up became the vanguard of the new state of Israel and the first kibbutzniks were among Israel's founders and early heroes.

The first group at Deganiah had few concrete ideas about the kind of society they wanted. They had brought with them some abstract theories about abolishing money and hired labor, and living in mutual cooperation. They had a dream of a new society based on human kinship, with no place for exploiters, far from the wicked city. They translated these principles into practice as they went along—and thus the kibbutz was born.

The utopian vision of the founders of the kibbutz movement was directed toward the creation of a new type of human. To uncover the underlying love and kindness and sense of kinship that they believed made up human nature, they wanted to create a social system based on manual labor and a love of nature, in which cooperation would be stressed.

The settlers decided against following the pattern of the older Jewish settlements, which relied on Arab labor and raised specialized crops for sale. Instead, they raised their own food to satisfy their own needs. What their communal table didn't need, they sold locally. Deganiah members lived as one family, sharing income, expenses, and possessions. Problems that arose were discussed by the entire membership after supper in the wooden shack that served as the first communal dining room. Decisions reached at those meetings became the fundamental principles of the kibbutz movement.

The birth of the first children at Deganiah raised some new questions. Where did the children fit in? A series of seemingly endless discussions were held; the conclusion was that the children belonged to their parents, but the responsibility for them must be shared by all. The kibbutz accordingly set aside a house for a nursery and selected a woman to look after the babies. This arrangement freed the mothers to do other work. In the evenings and on weekends, the parents visited their children.

The basic Deganiah principles were adopted by the entire kibbutz movement, but most of the newer settlements were still more extreme. They maintained separate sleeping quarters for their children, and parents visited them only briefly. The education and upbringing of the children were therefore out of the parents' hands. All decisions regarding the children were made communally, based on what was best for the entire group rather than for each individual child or parent.

Lately the trend has been to return to the original practice of having children sleep in their parents' home, and the parents now take a more active role in their upbringing. This may be in part due to criticisms of the kibbutz system, most notably by Bruno Bettelheim, reporting an inordinate amount of bed-wetting, thumb sucking, and night fears in kibbutz nurseries, which they attribute to lack of parental care.

Other social practices have also been modified. Originally the concept of marriage was a loose one. A couple who decided to announce their attachment officially usually did not take a formal religious vow. (Under Israeli law marriage requires a religious rather than a civil ceremony and most of the kibbutzniks are secular.) They would request a joint room, which sometimes had to be shared with another couple. Generally they referred to each other as "friends" rather than husband and wife, even after they had children. This practice led to a high separation rate among the couples. Gradually the traditional formalities of marriage became accepted in the kibbutzim and with this return to tradition came a dramatic drop in the separation rate.

Originally women's work was little different from men's work. They labored side by side in the fields and in the factories. Now women have, in large measure, gravitated back to domestic roles or work in the service sector, although most still work outside the household. With the acceptance of responsibility for the rearing of children, they have returned to what some pioneer *kibbutz* women distainfully describe as the role of the Jewish mother or housewife.

More than 255 kibbutzim have been founded since Deganiah was founded; the combined population is more than 110,000 members. The early kibbutzim now include second- and third-generation members. The movement has been successful not only by virtue of sheer survival, but by other criteria as well. Although they make up only 3 percent of the total Israeli population, the kibbutzniks produce more than 12 percent of the gross national product, including 6 percent of the country's industrial output. From their ranks have come a disproportionately large percentage of the officers and pilots of the Israeli armed forces, many athletes, members of the Knesset, and cabinet ministers. Many believe that the kibbutz schools are the best in the country, and the kibbutzim claim an unusually high percentage of the country's novelists, poets, painters, and sculptors—as well as an incredibly low percentage of its criminals. According to a number of sources, one murder and one embezzlement are the total recorded crimes committed by kibbutznicks in the history of the movement.

The Israeli kibbutzim constitute perhaps the only large-scale free society in the world where individual property, by personal agreement, is invested in the community—thus creating an order where all members are economically equal. Each of the kibbutzim has its own individuality as regards the personalities, background, political views, and religious views of its membership. Some have prospered and some are struggling. But all follow the general principles devised more than seven decades ago.

In tandem with the development of the kibbutz movement has been the lesser known *moshav* movement. Like the kibbutz, the *moshav* is an idealistic society. It is not as radical, however, in its social and economic approach. Altogether 400 *moshavim*, with a total population of about 144,000, exist in Israel. A *moshav* is a cooperative that leases national land (usually for 49 years), makes joint sales and purchases, and prohibits hired labor if possible. Its members share farm machinery.

There are two types of *moshavim: ovdim* and *shitufi.* The *ovdim* are dominant and are the fastest-growing communal movement in Israel. In a *moshav ovdim* each family has its own plot of land or business and each is economically independent. Each lives in its own house and is free to make almost any economic decision concerning the family. The interchange among the members of a *moshav ovdim* is mainly on the social level, though the underlying idealism is an important source of communal cohesiveness.

The *moshav shitufi,* on the other hand, socially resembles a *moshav ovdim,* and economically resembles a kibbutz. About 35 such *moshavim* with a combined population of about 8000 exist in Israel. Each family, including the children, lives in its own house and receives a salary. This salary is not dependent on the specific work performed, but rather on the size of the family.

There is no distinct line separating the *moshav* and the kibbutz. Many of the successful, less traditional kibbutzim have taken on aspects of the *moshavim,* and some of the *moshavim shitufim* would be hard to tell from a kibbutz. Each type of settlement receives a significant subsidy from public funds. The government provides roads, electricity, and technical assistance to all citizens. The Jewish Agency helps new settlements with loans. The Jewish National Fund undertakes land reclamation and reforestation. Together the kibbutzim and *moshavim* perform pioneer work in underdeveloped and border areas and contribute to the national ability to absorb new immigrants.

Moshav Shitufi Yodfat is located in the hilly Galilee surrounded by twelve Arab villages and several Bedouin tribes. The area is full of rocks and wild underbrush, though it was once a very fertile area known as the "breadbasket of Palestine." For centuries, though, the Turks and native population cut down almost all the trees and used them as fuel and building material. Grazing herds of goats and sheep kept the few left from propagating. It is a hard land for a community to make a living from—especially if it bases its economy on agriculture, as Yodfat does. But this is no ordinary community, and the members of Yodfat have created a very special space, flowering both outwardly and inwardly.

The roots of Yodfat go back to the early 1950s and to a group of high school students in Haifa. Their teacher, Dr. Joseph Schecter, discussed the problems of modern humanity, posing many questions. They studied Hasidism, Tolstoy, Kierkegaard, Buber, Gurdjieff, Ouspensky, Jung, A. D. Gordon, and the traditions of the Far East.

The group, then numbering about 20, decided to form a community, and they tried to obtain land and sponsorship from the Israeli government. But the government did not want to help them—they were too small, too atypical, and did not belong to any settlement movement. Most kibbutzim and *moshavim* in Israel belong to settlement movements, which wield some political power. The government felt that only those with strong ties to a movement could successfully work together and build a strong *moshav*.

Schecter's students agreed with Buber's critique of the kibbutz. Buber believed that contemporary spirituality could be thought of as a throwback to eighteenth-century Hasidism. At its best it could serve as a healing center in an age of alienation that has shaken the three vital human relationships—those between God and humans, humans and humans, and humans and nature. These relationships can be restored only by humans again meeting the being who stands over them on all three levels—the divine, the human, and the natural. Buber's criticism of the *kibbutz* was that generally members disregarded the relationship between humans and God, doubting or denying the existence of a divine counterpart. In the interpersonal area, they fulfilled God's commandment to build a just community while denying the divine origin of the imperative.

Schecter's students believed that a divine imperative existed, and believed in the importance of establishing a community where they could harmonize inner and outer work. Many of them had been together in the *Nachal*, a special military force that combines military and agricultural training and also establishes new border settlements. They were convinced that the combination of their spiritual ideals and hard work would build a strong community. But they were unable to convince the bureaucrats.

For more than four years the group, now called *Yuvalim* (which means "streams"—a word with special significance in this arid land) moved from one kibbutz to another. This is a long time for a group to remain cohesive but it did, even though some of the original members had left the group and been replaced by younger members. They all continued their spiritual work and their studies with Schecter and other teachers. Some of them studied bodywork, others studied meditation, and some, of course, studied Judaism. They tried to incorporate all of these into their everyday life. Again and again they refused to join existing settlements, convinced that their inclinations were not in harmony with any of the existing communities. They believed that socialism is not a complete outlook on life; that fraternity and participation are more important than equality; that family and community life must be properly balanced, and that no external way of organization can really change one's life. It was not only their spiritual beliefs and awareness of the importance of the inner person that set them apart; they were also interested in organic farming, an approach unheard of in Israel in the late 1950s and early 1960s.

Finally, in 1960, about 20 of the group were hired to work in a reforestation station in the area of Yodfat. At first the government gave them a small amount of land of their own on a yearly lease. They worked for the Jewish National Fund in the reforestation projects. After eight long years they were recognized as a *moshav* and given public aid in the form of water, electricity, roads, technical assistance, and loans. Now they have about 900 acres.

When Yodfat was incorporated as a *moshav,* only one other Jewish settlement existed in the area. In recent years, more than 20 new settlements have appeared on the hills around it. Yodfat can accommodate 80 families; by 1983, 40 families with 100 children lived there.

Yodfat follows some of the typical *moshav shitufi* arrangements—all property except what is inside each house belongs to the community. Children live at home and the community's obligations to them includes paying for schooling and a range of extra activities, such as music lessons (recorder and piano); trips to different areas of Israel; arts and crafts lessons in a large, well-stocked room; and an animal park. The animal park—a project started by one of the members and now managed almost completely by the children—has many animals living together in harmony in a large fenced-in area.

The children remain at Yodfat until they reach age six. After that they travel daily to a nearby regional school. The children are encouraged to have natural, open relationships, and are given responsibilities at an early age. Visitors often remark on the fact that older and younger children play together quite happily at Yodfat.

Although the site of Yodfat is a rocky mountaintop, the members have succeeded in landscaping it, using mostly native trees and shrubs. Every year large compost piles are made from the earth that is brought up with the flower bulbs—one of Yodfat's agricultural products. By spreading it around the houses, soil has been created deep enough for fruit trees and flower and vegetable gardens to flourish in. Many of the families also keep a small chicken coop and goats.

For years there was no monthly budget; everyone simply withdrew money as needed. But as the group grew, this became impractical. Finally, after intense, community-wide discussions, a basic budget was agreed on. Half of each member's salary is automatically deposited in his or her family's bank account at the end of each month, while the other half is used to pay for taxes, education, and the medical and pension funds. The half available to a family with two children is about $360 a month, a bit less than the average worker's salary in Israel. It is difficult to make ends meet with this allotment, but the members do live fairly comfortably and have many modern conveniences. The allotment does not cover basic furniture and electrical appliances; these are provided to families according to its size and the number of years of membership. For example, with the first child Yodfat provides the family with a refrigerator; with the second it provides a washing machine. The community also gives financial assistance and labor to help add additional rooms when needed.

Yodfat has a long-term lease on its land. It is self-supporting, but still depends on substantial public loans for development. The early years were a struggle and only now are things becoming somewhat easier. It is difficult to subsist only on agriculture, however, because of the depressed world market. One of its members opened up a small carpentry shop and does specialized contract work. The community is currently looking for other profitable undertakings.

In recent years several members have begun to work outside the community. One is a lawyer who has a practice in the region, another a doctor who works in a nearby Haifa hospital and also in local clinics, a third is the treasurer of the new regional council of settlements. All their salaries go directly to Yodfat.

Yodfat is governed in much the same way as any other *moshav* or *kibbutz*. An elected secretariat consisting of seven members is selected yearly by a democratic vote of each community member. A general manager is chosen for a three-year to four-year term. The job is rotated among the most responsible senior people. So far it has always been assigned to a man—women have been asked, but they have turned it down—though some women are members of the secretariat. According to the importance of the issue, the secretariat decides whether to bring a discussion to a general meeting of all Yodfat members. About six or seven general meetings are held each year, scheduled only as needed.

The general meetings and meetings of the secretariat are open to Yodfat members only. Other meetings, held to discuss philosophical issues, are usually open to all residents of the community. For decision making, they try to decide by consensus rather than by voting. When a consensus cannot be reached at a secretariat meeting or general meeting, the decision is usually postponed, and further discussion eventually yields a consensus. When a small group of people feels strongly about an issue, it can usually sway the others.

Two thirds of the Yodfat members are *sabras*, while the rest are from the United States, Canada, and England. The *moshav* accepts a number of single people, and prefers that its prospective members be young (up to age 28), but this is not an inflexible rule. The oldest member is in his forties and the youngest in his early twenties. The median age of adults is 30. One of the conditions for becoming a member is Israeli citizenship. A major source of new members is the *Nachal;* some young troops in the *Nachal* spend part of their three-year service living and working at Yodfat.

People who express an interest in joining Yodfat meet with a member of the absorption committee, who considers their motivation, balance, and ability to live and work in harmony with the other members. This meeting takes place outside Yodfat, usually in a nearby city. Yodfat members feel that prospective candidates should not be unduly influenced by the physical beauty of the place or by the amenities that come with membership. If an initial visit goes well, candidates are invited back to the community for a longer visit. During this time they stay in a room on the *moshav* and participate in the daily work. They may then become candidates for membership if the secretariat agrees. After a year of candidacy, a vote is taken at a general meeting. Two thirds of the members must vote yes in order for applicants to be accepted as new members.

At this time, houses are offered to families and small apartments to single people. New members sign a form agreeing that no improvements to the property belong to them if they and their family leave Yodfat. If a family leaves after making extensive improvements, however, under certain conditions some compensation would be made. This has not been a problem at Yodfat, since few members have left over the years.

It is not easy to become a member of Yodfat. The individual or family must be highly motivated. Life in this pioneer community is not an easy one and since the spiritual life is so important to community members, a true harmony must be felt or the applicant will be rejected.

A new community center was recently built, but most entertainment and socializing takes place in private homes. Single people eat with each other, live in their own area, and socialize together. The entire community eats together every Friday evening and on holidays. Films are shown a couple times a month. Musical evenings are held occasionally. Yodfat has several professional folk music troupes including Black Velvet, an Irish folk group, and Galilee Grass, a bluegrass group. Many other pastimes are pursued during leisure hours, including making ceramics and sewing Yemenite embroidery, folk dancing, singing in the Yodfat choir, and pursuing a subject such as Jewish literature, Arabic, French, or English in one of a host of study groups.

The focus on spiritual work is one of the major differences that set Yodfat apart from other Israeli collectives. Gurdjieff and the Hasidic and Sufi teaching stories all emphasize being "awake" and aware of this world. At Yodfat these teachings are well known and practiced by many. The spirituality of Yodfat is not otherworldly; it is a down-to-earth practice centered on work—work on oneself, work with others, and work in the everyday world. This focus illuminates all aspects of Yodfat. The relations between the members are different than in many of the other *moshavim*—more care and more understanding of the spiritual search of each individual is exhibited. This search may involve different paths for different people. There is no one community path; the idea that one's search may be different from another's is respected.

Yodfat practices a form of Judaism even though most of the members are not religious in the usual sense of the word. The communal dining room is kosher, a synagogue has been erected, a simple ceremony to usher in the Sabbath is held each Friday evening, and the Jewish holidays are celebrated. Dr. Schecter, now in his eighties, still visits Yodfat and his influence is still strongly felt.

Yodfat's economy is based almost entirely on agriculture. The community has 450 acres of cotton, 200 acres of various grains, 50 acres of flower bulbs, a 100-acre avocado orchard, a 25-acre apricot orchard, and 400 head of sheep. The moshav organic agriculture practices are unusual in Israel. The first organic crop planted at Yodfat was apricots. They are dried and exported to Europe, where they are sold in health food stores. These were followed by organic tomatoes, chickpeas, peanuts, onions, and corn. Later the organic avocado orchard was added. But at one point Yodfat decided that in order to make ends meet a more profitable agricultural product was needed, so the members began to grow cotton, albeit with great reluctance. The reluctance was due to the necessity of using strong poisonous sprays when growing cotton commercially. Today Yodfat's cotton yields are among the best in Israel. The flower bulbs, mainly iris and narcissus, began on one-quarter acre; their income per acre is four times that of cotton. As mentioned earlier, in the past several years agriculture has not been profitable, so Yodfat is looking for alternatives to it.

In trying to build a better world, Yodfat is particularly eager to achieve friendly relations with its Arab neighbors. Relations have been good with most of the Arab population because Yodfat respects their way of life, culture, and heritage. When the Yodfat pioneers first came to the area the Bedouins were extremely cooperative and taught them much about Arab life. Yodfat and the Bedouins today are quite friendly —they take part in each other's funerals, weddings, and other celebrations, and visit regularly. Most Yodfat members speak Arabic. Relations with other Arab villagers are not as easy. Some of them opposed the building of the settlement for nationalistic reasons and they remain aloof, reflecting the general political mood of the Israeli Arabs. No serious incidents between the two groups have occurred, however; only everyday problems, such as the Arabs' goats wandering into Yodfat's fields. Some cooperation takes place: hitchhiking, loans, and hired workers, and the Yodfat doctor and lawyer both have clientele in the nearby Arab villages.

The members of Yodfat wish for peace—as do all Israelis—though some believe that peace might bring its own hazards. As long as war and external challenges exist, many internal political and social problems receive less attention than they deserve. Peace could lead to more and more reliance on Arabs to do hard manual work at low wages, which was the situation before the first *kibbutz* was built. On the other hand, if the energy that now goes to support the war effort were to go in a positive direction, the results could be stupendous. Only time will tell. In the meantime, Yodfat members serve as reservists in the Israeli Defense Forces, and participate in the regional organization of settlements. Yodfat is now linked with one of the three national kibbutz movements, however, it retains its political independence and its right to be the sole decider of its own way of organization and operation.

Yodfat's successful integration of the inner and outer is probably unique in Israel; at the same time it is probably only in Israel that it could exist. It relies heavily on public support and on the idealism of a true pioneer society. It is a community that works well and is a fulfilling place in which to live.

Druse women weaving tapestries at the Mambush's atelier in Ein Hod.

CHAPTER 16

Ein Hod: The Artists' Village

Winding up a steep hill in the Carmel range, about 15 miles from Haifa, is the uniquely picturesque village of Ein Hod—"the source of beauty." It occupies a site that is useless for agriculture but breathtakingly beautiful, with many views of the deep blue Mediterranean, just 3 miles away. Of what value is a village whose only natural resource is its beauty? It's a perfect home for artists.

The story of Ein Hod begins in 1950. Marcel Janco, a well-known painter of the Dada school, was sent by the Government Planning Authority of Israel to explore the mountains of Israel and make recommendations for a national park. Clambering through the Carmel hills he came upon a stone village, abandoned several years earlier by Arabs fleeing during Israel's war of independence. He was staggered by the beauty of the setting and impressed by the special character of the stone buildings. Back in Haifa he learned that the government had decided that the village had no economic value and it would therefore be demolished.

Janco felt there was something special about this place that called for its preservation. He considered a variety of alternatives: make it a monument within a national park, establish an agricultural village of new immigrants, keep it as a tourist attraction. One by one he discarded these schemes until finally it became clear: the site must be used to create an artists' village. It would entail a great deal of work because many of the buildings were falling down and there was no electricity.

Government officials were dubious, but Janco was persistent. He volunteered to gather together the people who could rebuild the village and oversee the project himself. He gained the support of the mayor of Haifa who was both intrigued by the romance of the scheme and practical enough to know that it would be an asset to his city. So Janco got the go-ahead. He contacted a young friend, Malka Schlesinger, secretary of the Painters and Sculptors Association in Israel, and asked her to help recruit a group of artists who would accept the challenge. A group of 20 was found, some from Haifa, most from Tel Aviv. Most were in their twenties or early thirties; Janco was fifty-two.

On May 1, 1953, they gathered together. They took sleeping bags, blankets, and hand tools. It was a long climb in the hot sun and they had to cut paths before they could even approach the houses. The place was overgrown with weeds and overrun with flies, mosquitoes, scorpions, and snakes. The buildings were in ruins. But youthful idealism was undaunted. Individuals and couples picked out their future houses —this one for the view, that one for a beautiful arch—and the work began. This was not a group who moved to the country to make a new life. This was a group of city people, with jobs and homes back there, who were willing to devote their weekends and holidays to see what they could make of this ruin. Malka and Shmuel Schlesinger, for example, lived in Haifa and worked over a period of seven years to build their house from the one room they found standing. One early addition to their new home was a refrigerator, laboriously dragged up the hill and ceremoniously installed in their kitchen. No electricity would be available for years to come, but the presence of the machine gave them a psychological lift and a promise for the future.

So the artists repaired their own houses and they cooperated in planting trees and creating common facilities. They made a deal with the city of Haifa. They gave their paintings to the city and the city supplied laborers to build the roads. The rubble was dumped in a natural amphitheater and soon became the basis for a stone amphitheater suitable for plays and concerts.

With Marcel Janco elected its first mayor, Ein Hod began to take shape. Some people came to live there full-time. Early on they decided that they needed a cooperative art gallery and a restaurant. The gallery was built and gradually enlarged until today it has four large rooms at various levels and attracts people from all over the world to buy residents' work. The artists receive two thirds of the sale price; the village the rest. The gallery is managed by a paid staff. The restaurant attracts tourists and Haifa residents who drive out for the evening to mingle with the artists. For many years, the restaurant was a problem for the community, because none of the artists could cook or manage it. So they gave the concession to a series of outsiders to run on a one-year lease, constantly looking for just the right person to run it. As one artist said, "If the man is nice, the food is lousy; if the food is good, the man is lousy." In 1982, one of the sculptors took over the restaurant and proved to be a wonderful chef, making the restaurant a masterpiece in its own right.

For a long time little growth in the size of the community took place, but the members gradually realized that they were all growing older and new blood was needed. So around 1965 they began to seek new members; about 100 families are now in residence, including painters, sculptors, photographers, dancers, writers, ceramicists, philosophers, an architect, and even a doctor who is married to a weaver. Residents have considered opening the community to nonartists, so as to give it more balance and include those with skills that would be immediately useful. But the majority continue to feel that to do so would jeopardize the uniqueness that makes Ein Hod what it is and helps artists to succeed at their profession.

Once a year a general assembly of the community is held, at which problems are discussed and voted on and committees are elected to administer the community for the coming year. The major committees are administration, finance, membership, gallery, artistic, and quarreling (which attempts to settle disputes between members). Ein Hod no longer has a mayor, but the chair of the administration committee serves as village head. The chairing of each committee rotates once a month among its members. Thus many people have an opportunity— or obligation—to serve in this capacity. In general, committee membership is not sought after by budding politicians, but rather urged on people who the community feels are best able to serve.

To become a member of the community, the first requirement (which is somewhat liberally interpreted) is to be an artist or be married to an artist. Prospective members apply to the membership committee for permission to stay in Ein Hod as a visiting artist. They rent a space to live, or at least to work, during this period. After a year, the five-person central committee of the community votes on whether to accept them as members. Two thirds must vote yes for prospective members to be allowed in. Following a yes vote they are permitted to buy a 64-year lease on a plot of land from the government on which to build a house and studio. For those who can't afford to build a studio, communal studios for ceramics, sculpture, and lithography are available; these are owned by the community and available to any community member who wishes to use them.

The house design must be approved by the building committee to assure that it fits in with the character of the village. Originally all new houses had to be built of stone, to assure homogeneity. In recent years the price of stonework has skyrocketed, so greater variety is now allowed. In fact, however, the newer members are generally building houses that are bigger and fancier than the older houses—a reflection of the rising standard of living in Israel.

Demand to get into Ein Hod exceeds the capacity of the village to absorb new members. Because of a low turnover few existing houses are available, and so to some extent the opportunity to join is limited to those who have sufficient financial means to buy land and build a house. Since members are selected on their artistic excellence as well as their personalities, it follows that many applicants are established artists with some earning capacity. One new couple are Russian expatriates who have been settled with a government grant. Unlike the kibbutzim, which generally admit only Jews, Ein Hod is liberal about factors other than artistic ability. It is a cosmopolitan community with members from all over the world; several non-Jews who are married to Jews live there, as does one Druse painter who worked in the village as a gardener when he was a boy. Indeed, most artists would have a hard time in a kibbutz because they are such individualists. Each kibbutz belongs to a particular political party and its members have a unity of purpose. The people at Ein Hod belong to all parties, including those of the extreme right and the extreme left. All respect the individuality of others in regard to politics as well as way of life.

More than 40 children live in the community. Those at the elementary school level attend school on a nearby *moshav*. The older children go to regular public high schools. The issue of education is a personal one for each parent. As is true in many small communities we have visited, the children are very free and unafraid. Their world is small and friendly enough that they can master it.

The major source of income for the community is the commission earned by the gallery. Taxes are paid to the government for water and electricity. Smaller amounts are received from the restaurant concession and from performances at the amphitheater and various festivals. At Purim (a religious festival during February or March) a big bazaar and carnival is held and thousands come to visit. Many put up tents and camp out in the village.

Another important enterprise is an art school that provides employment to a number of resident artists as teachers. The school offers a two-year course in arts and crafts, using an apprentice system to train serious artists, not beginners. A number of kibbutzim send students to the school, and a hostel is available for those who live too far away to commute. The student fees go to the village. The teachers receive regular monthly salaries from the village, based on the number of hours they teach, regardless of whether they have 5 or 15 pupils. As class sizes are small, the school is presently running a deficit. A series of ten-day seminars for kindergarten and public school teachers is held regularly to help them better understand art. The seminars are subsidized by the Ministry of Education and Culture, and persons attending are selected by the Department of Education. Several international symposia on art and a summer theater workshop have also been held. In 1983 the three-story Marcel Janco Museum was opened. It features a large collection of his work and that of other Dadaists, and includes a gallery for exhibitions by artists from Ein Hod and elsewhere.

Ein Hod is much less communal than most communities we have visited. A wide range of incomes exists, depending on the success of the individual artists. One fairly large private business has been established —the tapestry studio of Itzhak and Aviva Mambush. Both grew up in Israel, then went to Paris to study art. When they returned they jumped at the chance to help create Ein Hod. For the first decade they were primarily painters, like most of the community founders. But then they decided to start a tapestry workshop so that their own and other artists' paintings could be expressed in another medium. They began by hiring a master weaver from the famous workshops at Aubusson, France. Gradually they trained local women—both Jews and Druses—to do this work. Each tapestry begins with a cartoon drawn or painted by an artist, which is then copied by the weaver. It is exacting work that requires the skills of an artisan, but not the creativity of an artist. Thus the 15 to 20 people who work for the Mambushes are workers, not artists. They live in other towns and commute to Ein Hod.

Ein Hod plays a major role in the artistic life of Israel. In this respect also it differs from most intentional communities, which tend to locate in out-of-the-way places and live a life separate from the larger society. Ein Hod is very much a part of that larger society.

As Ein Hod has given, so has it received. Like so many groups in Israel, Ein Hod has been the beneficiary of foreign philanthropy. Several of the communal studios and the students' hostel were built and equipped with funds from donors in the United States, in particular the B'nai Zion Lodge. The Haifa municipality has also been generous with assistance.

So here is an intentional community whose members don't follow any particular leader or ideology, but who share a passion for art. This passion gives the group its cohesiveness. And since their art must be displayed and sold to the outside world, so must the community be involved with the outside world. The problems it faces are similar to the problems faced by any other village in Israel. It seeks further government support for its educational programs. It is considering whether to build a small hotel for visitors. It worries about how to keep the public areas cleaner. It debates whether to strive for a more balanced population.

Ein Hod is a very pleasant community. It has all the virtues of an intentional community, along with a comfortable, middle-class way of life that tolerates, even encourages, individualism. Strange that no one has tried to duplicate it elsewhere!

Part VI

JAPAN

The pagoda symbolizes the meeting of all religions at Yamatoyama. In the background is the administration building.

CHAPTER 17

Yamatoyama: Man, Nature, and the Spirit of the Mountain

The population of Japan is slightly over 100 million. Of these, Shinto claims 98 million and Buddhism claims 87 million—clearly, religion in Japan is not exclusive. One can follow many paths. Most Japanese, in fact, are not particularly observant of either religion. Japan has been a largely secular society for 300 years. Traditional religions form a backdrop to life, a part of the culture that exists but is rarely given special attention.

Shinto is the original folk religion of Japan. Before Buddhism was brought to Japan in the sixth century, the Japanese practiced an animistic religion that focused on the spiritual essence in nature and in all animate and inanimate objects. The Japanese word for spiritual essence is *kami* (also written *okami*, the letter *o* being an honorific), which is sometimes translated as "deity." But we should not confuse these *kami* with the monotheistic God of Christianity, Judaism, or Islam—a figure who is omnipotent and infinite. The Shinto religion is a form of nature worship in which humanity is seen as an integral part of nature, not as superior beings standing above nature and possessing the right to bend it to their will. The *kami* (which can include ancestors along with the sun, mountains, trees, and the fertility process) are worshiped through offerings, prayers, and festivals held at countless shrines throughout the country.

During most of the premodern period, Shinto was regarded as the local Japanese adjunct to the more universal Buddhism. Buddhism provided the moral values and broader cosmology; Shintoism expressed the Japanese love for nature. And Confucianism, too, had its place in the rules governing family, social, and government relationships. After the Meiji Restoration in 1868, the government downplayed Buddhism and encouraged Shintoism as an element of Japanese patriotism. A form of state Shinto was promoted that involved emperor worship and was not so much a religion as a state propaganda apparatus. It reached its full fruition in the 1930s and 1940s when the militaristic regime used deification of the emperor to buttress its efforts at conquest. In the post–World War II reforms the propaganda apparatus was dismantled and church and state were separated.

Since then, a general lack of interest in religion has been evident in Japan. As a result, those people feeling a need for religious participation have tended to look away from the traditional religions (including Christianity, which has about one million followers in Japan). This has given rise to what are called the New Religions, of which there are perhaps 250, with a total membership in the tens of millions. These have developed largely in this century, particularly since World War II, and their number and scope are a phenomenon unique to Japan.

Several generalizations can be made about the New Religions. They have tended to concentrate their initial proselytizing among farmers and working-class people, later moving to the middle-class. They tend to combine or reconcile different belief systems, including Shinto, Buddhist, and sometimes Western philosophies, though their doctrine and philosophy are often not strongly developed. Most are basically Shinto in their leanings. The New Religions usually stress success in this life, rather than concern for an afterlife, emphasizing health, prosperity, self-improvement, and happiness through faith or through miraculous cures. Some were founded by individuals who believed they were possessed by deities. In 60 or more of the New Religions the leaders claim divine inspiration or revelation. Leadership in these religions is frequently hereditary and their organization tends to be hierarchical. Most are tolerant of other religious creeds. They are easy to understand and easy to join. They have their own holy land in Japan. They offer highly emotional rituals. Their followers are taught to believe in their own personal dignity and importance and are provided with a tightly organized and protective social community—something very important in the Japanese culture.

With this brief background, let us examine three intentional communities in Japan, each of which is a part of the New Religions phenomenon.

We take the train from Tokyo on a 440-mile trip to Aomori prefecture (district) at the far north of Honshu, Japan's largest island. As we leave behind the gray industrial suburbs of the world's largest city, the landscape gradually becomes more green and agricultural, finally changing to mile after mile of rice fields that become terraced as we move north into more hilly country. A land of great natural beauty, northern Japan has retained many of its traditional ways. It is an appropriate location for Yamatoyama, a small community that is the headquarters for a New Religion of about 60,000 Japanese nature worshipers.

We are met at Kominato station by Norihisa Kadowaki; he is the English teacher in the community's high school, and will serve as translator during our stay. It is a 20-minute drive up to the narrow valley in the mountains where the community is located. Yamatoyama comprises 5000 acres, making it in area possibly the largest intentional community in the world. The name is a combination of *Yamato,* an old name for Japan meaning "land of great harmony," and *yama,* meaning "mountain."

At the center of the community is a large four-story building that houses the administrative offices, dining hall, sundries shop, and a number of guest rooms. It connects with an adjoining worship hall, about 5500 square feet in area. In front of the main building is a beautiful Japanese garden with a pond and a white *tori* gate, the unique Japanese archway seen at all Shinto shrines. Along the main road in front of the headquarters are a number of substantial two-story dwellings of masonry or wood that provide housing for the 45 families and 30 single persons who live in the community. The original wood hut of the founder, in which he was living when he was inspired to start the religion, is preserved in a larger wood-and-glass structure. Close to the housing is the bathhouse, with a separate communal pool for each sex. Beyond it is the play area for the nursery school, which cares for the 25 preschool children in the community; children of elementary and junior high school age commute in buses to public schools outside the community.

Up the hill to one side are four or five large greenhouses in which thousands of bonsai plants are grown before being shipped out for sale all over Japan. Nearby are several large traditional buildings that serve as dormitories for believers from elsewhere in Japan when they come for the two-day meetings that are held five or six times a year. Beyond these buildings is a small five-storied pagoda, a symbol of the belief that all religions meet together in this place. Near it is a small black stone temple that is a mausoleum for the cremated bones of believers.

Farther down the road is the high school, a large long wood building that accommodates 160 students and 20 teachers. The building, which is two stories high and 375 feet long, had been a government school located one-half mile away. It was abandoned some time ago and the community bought it for the very reasonable sum of $1200, dismantled it, transported it by truck to Yamatoyama, then reerected it with a new roof. Around it are three dormitories (two for boys, one for girls), a large gymnasium, and a music building. Still farther down the road and outside the main entrance to the community, are the agricultural fields, two buildings that house the woodworking shops, and several buildings that house the organic fertilizer factory. The agricultural area consists of 15 acres of rice and 11 acres of vegetables, all of which are used to feed the community. All in all, Yamatoyama is a large and impressive establishment.

The story of Yamatoyama begins with the story of its founder, Sei-shirō Tazawa. Born in 1884, he was the only son of a well-to-do merchant in the city of Aomori. Although nominally Buddhists, Tazawa's family was not religious. His early adult life was spent working in his father's business. At the age of 35 he set up an office in the mountains 25 miles away. He soon began to have profound spiritual experiences, and shortly after his move he built a small mountain shrine for himself. In August 1919 he experienced what he believed was a divine revelation and determined to dedicate the rest of his life to the spirit that communicated with him. He did not know the name of this deity, so he just called him, "a deity of the mountain."

A little farther up the valley was a beautiful waterfall, about 25 feet high. Tazawa regularly stood under it, participating in the ancient Shinto custom of purification by water. He gradually acquired a reputation for his ability to cure the sick, often using this water. In 1922 his father died. He had come to realize his son's sincere devotion to his religious mission, and so bequeathed his estate to him with permission for him to lead whatever way of life he wished and to spend the wealth for the sake of people in need if he so desired. Accordingly, Tazawa sold the business and began to devote himself fully to his mission, as did his wife and three children.

Then a most mysterious incident occurred. To Tazawa's great surprise, his 13-year-old daughter, Tomiko, began to dictate letters of revelation. One of these indicated that the invisible deity should thereafter be called Yamatoyama Okami—"the deity of Yamatoyama." The revelations said further that rather than distinguishing numerous deities from one another, the myriads of them as a whole should be called "the only one deity." They also contained predictions of world events, criticisms of the times, suggestions on living daily life, and advice on forming an organization to be called Shoroku Shinto Yamatoyama. Shŏ means "pine" roku means "green," and shinto means "the way of the deity." The implication was that the organization would be full of blessings and be the way of the deity that is as everlasting as the green of the pines.

For 12 years Tazawa led an ascetic life, but had no disciples and gave no sermons. He spent all of his father's wealth and he and his family were reduced to living in poverty. In 1931 he went down from the mountain and launched a full-fledged missionary effort. In his appeals he deplored the formality of religions, criticized the degradation of traditional religions, and urged the awakening of the mind. He taught that religions should contribute to the wellbeing of humanity by their members respecting and cooperating with each other.

"No teachers, but self-enlightenment," was one of his basic principles. Another was the idea that religious exaltation is best attained through uniting with others, thus returning to the state of original unity with god. Everything can be obtained through one's own effort, he said, as long as it is made in cooperation with others. This concept provides a religious basis for people living together as a community, stressing mutual prosperity as opposed to competition and conflict.

While Tazawa's message may seem eminently reasonable to us today, it did not seem reasonable to the militarily dominated government of Japan in the 1930s, and government officials harassed him. Consequently he withdrew again to the mountains in 1937 and stayed there through the war years, receiving frequent visits from the followers he had gained.

The beginning of Yamatoyama as a community dates from 1946 when Seishirō Tazawa's son, Yasusaburo Tazawa—now leader of the community—returned from Tokyo. Yasusaburo Tazawa had graduated from Tokyo Imperial University in 1938 with a degree in the history of religion. Until 1946 he worked there as an assistant in the department of religion. In that year he returned to Aomori to help his father form a Shintoist religious community. He continued as his father's principal assistant until 1966 when the elder Tazawa died and Yasusaburo Tazawa became leader.

Originally they leased a small area around the hut where the elder Tazawa had his revelation. Although Seishirō Tazawa had started to attract followers in 1931, few people came to join him there, and only a few wood structures offered shelter prior to World War II. A number of charcoal burners' and foresters' villages were scattered throughout the nearby mountains. The local people were mostly employed by absentee landlords who owned the forests. Especially after the war, the great demand for wood, coupled with the mechanization of forestry work, accelerated reckless deforestation. The denudation of the tree cover destroyed the ecological balance, causing floods in 1959 and 1966. In 1959 Yamatoyama petitioned the governor of the prefecture for help for the villagers throughout the area, and soon afterward the Department of Forestry Conservation established erosion control facilities as a public works. After the 1966 flood, the department stepped up its efforts.

By the time most of the adjacent land came into the hands of Yamatoyama in 1969, most of the forest cover had been destroyed, and the task of the community was to rebuild it, paralleling the government's efforts on public lands. This was undertaken as a priority project for ecological, spiritual, and economic reasons. From the economic standpoint, the efficient management of 5000 acres of forest on a sustained-yield basis will eventually provide sufficient income to support the community. Accordingly, all the members of the community and visiting believers devote some time to planting trees. To date, more than 700 acres have been reforested.

But we are getting ahead of our story. After his return from Tokyo,

Yasusaburo Tazawa recruited a group of believers as Yamatoyama settlers. Shortly afterward, he began a building and real estate company called *Kokudosha,* which means "contributing to the development of Japan." The company built many of the buildings at Yamatoyama, as well as houses and other construction works on the outside. Today it is located in the nearby town of Kominato and employs about 130 workers, most of whom are believers but only 7 of whom live in the community.

In 1955 Yasusaburo Tazawa established a small private school as a center of religious education. This was later expanded into the senior high school that today is one of the major activities of Yamatoyama. Attracting students from all over Japan, it now educates about 96 boys and 64 girls, all of whom live in dormitories. Much of the curriculum is standard, mandated by the Ministry of Education, but much is unique. The students rise at 5:30 (during most of the year it is already daylight) and go out for a one-and-one-half mile run. At 6:30 they attend religious services with the adults in the main building. Then they return to their own cafeteria for breakfast. Classes start at 8:30. One hour a week is devoted to religion (much of it comparative religion) and four or five hours are spent on English. All of the students study *ken-do* (Japanese fencing), and the mandolin, learning to play mostly Italian classical pieces. All of the students participate in the school symphony orchestra. Each year the orchestra tours either Taiwan or Korea. Tuition is $32 a month and, in addition, parents pay $110 a month for room and board. The foreign travel is an additional cost. The school makes a small profit, which helps to support the community. Most of the students start jobs when they finish high school, but 18 to 20 continue on to university each year.

The largest business in the community is the organic fertilizer plant. This plant, which occupies several buildings at the foot of the valley, produces 600 tons of fertilizer each year from minerals mined on the property. It consists of 36 ingredients, including ammonium sulfate, urea, sulfur, guano, and phosphoric acid. It is bagged in the plant and sold all over Japan. Since Japanese agriculture is dominated by chemical methods, Yamatoyama is able to make another contribution to the ecology of the country in this way, as well as fulfill its own religious beliefs. The fertilizer plant was started about ten years ago, and now employes about 20 community members.

The bonsai business employs one person. Two community members, a married couple, own a small restaurant in Kominato, which they have run for 20 years. The Yamatoyama Publishing Company produces religious texts and other materials. Its editorial and administrative activities are located at Yamatoyama and the printing and distribution is done by contract with firms in the city of Aomori.

These companies are operated according to sound business principles. Each accumulates its own capital for expansion, and does not contribute directly to the community. But the individuals who work in them do. The community also receives support from about 60,000 believers around Japan, each of whom contributes $8 a year.

For many years Yamatoyama members received no pay, but were given room and board and a small allowance. Recently, however, the Japanese government passed a law requiring that all workers receive at least the official minimum wage. Accordingly, most members now receive from $280 to $720 a month, plus room and board. A few who live outside the community get much more, since they have to provide their own food, housing, and transportation.

Though no prohibition against them exists, no community member owns a private car. A community bus, which is free to members, goes twice daily to Kominato. In addition, if a member needs to borrow a community car for any worthwhile purpose, he or she will be granted permission to do so. The community has its own gasoline pump, and even gasoline is provided free of charge. Members need not give up personal possessions or private financial resources, though few have much in the way of outside resources. About a quarter of the present members are university graduates. Most of the rest have a junior high school training at best and come from relatively poor families.

Turnover is low. Each year 10 to 20 new members arrive and an equal number leave. The leadership is satisfied with the present size of the community and plans no significant further growth. People usually leave because of marriage to an outsider or because of obtaining a better job elsewhere, not because of dissatisfaction with community life or a loss of belief. It must be remembered that Japan has a very stable society in which most people aspire to work for only one employer until retirement. The big companies are paternalistic, providing for virtually all the needs of their employees.

Yamatoyama is not run as a democracy. In theory, the community is like a very large family. The leader is the father, and he makes all the family decisions. As befits an organization of this size, the reality is a bit more complex than that. As the headquarters for a religion that is about 60,000 strong, Yamatoyama plays an integral role in the affairs of the religion. The religion is organized into about 280 groups around the country, and each of them elects a member of the general board, which meets every April. The general board makes policy decisions for the religion, including planning the daily religious activities of the members and the overall goals for the coming year.

These are implemented at Yamatoyama by Yasusaburo Tazawa with the help of a small staff of key people who are organized into four divisions: financial, personnel, teaching, and religious affairs. His two principal assistants are his adopted sons-in-law. (It is a common Japanese custom for a man with no sons to adopt a son-in-law to carry on his name and line). These sons-in-law are also named Tazawa, and it is likely that one of them will eventually succeed him.

A meeting of community members is held each month to work out the details of the following month's schedule. At these meetings individuals can raise problems for discussion, but the final decisions are made by Yasusaburo Tazawa.

Yamatoyama, reflecting the views of its leader, is very much concerned with world problems and world peace. Yasusaburo Tazawa attended the World Conference on Religion and Peace in Kyoto, Japan, in 1970, in Louvain, Belgium, in 1974, and in Princeton, New Jersey, in 1979. He met many other religious leaders, which created the opportunity for a variety of ecumenical activities. As a result of the first conference, Yamatoyama was asked in 1971 to provide a month's training in organic apple and rice cultivation and the communal way of life for eight Koreans. Yasusaburo Tazawa shared his life with these trainees for a month, eating, working, and bathing with them. The next year he visited them in Korea to see how Yamatoyama could best cooperate in the development of that nation. Its contribution was to donate seeds, young apple trees, and a special ferment that is used to make a compost for organic farming. In 1973 a second team of Korean trainees came to Yamatoyama, staying three months.

In 1974, following the conference in Louvain, Yasusaburo Tazawa proposed to his followers that they refrain from eating breakfast one day a month, or make some other small sacrifice, and that the money they saved in this way be donated to a world peace organization. Others in Japan also participated, with the result that between $75,000 and $100,000 has been collected each year and donated to the Japanese branch of the World Congress on Religion and Peace. The money has been used to support leprosy hospitals in Korea and Taiwan and to help Vietnamese boat people.

Yamatoyama's associated body of believers is about 60,000 strong and growing at a rate of about 3000 a year. Together they constitute a small but potent force for loving and protecting the planet, for living in a thoughtful and reasonable way, and for cooperating with other religions in the interest of world peace. What are their plans for the future?

Although the leadership of the religion does not wish the population of the community to grow, they do seek growth among the believers around the country. Three major development projects for the community are planned that will bring about greater interchange between the community and the outside world. A much larger meeting hall and associated facilities for religious services will be built so that larger groups of believers can visit Yamatoyama. A school will be started to train full-time priests for the religion. (At present most group leaders fulfill this role in their spare time, supporting themselves by other means.) Also, a medical clinic will be built near a natural spring on the property; the clinic will use the spring water, which is supposed to have curative powers. The spring has come to be called the "Lourdes of the Orient." Scientific analysis of these waters has revealed a chemical similarity, as both have a high concentration of germanium.

Yamatoyama has been quite active in publicity. Yamatoyama Publishing Company has published a series of large, beautifully printed and illustrated, full-color histories of the community called the *Yamatoyama Graphic Magazine*. They have also produced a number of lovely films on community life, incorporating exquisite nature close-ups in the most delicate Japanese style. One film received a Ministry of Education prize. Another prize-winning film portrays the process of apple growing in Aomori prefecture.

We close this account of Yamatoyama with the words of its leader, Yasusaburo Tazawa:

Abuse and destruction of nature, it is often said, may be ascribed to the teaching that a human being is a special kind of creation, which has the image of God and so they are entitled to utilize the rest of nature for their purposes. A new thinking is now developing, however, according to which human beings and nature are interdependent and bound by "life together." There has been an awareness that a system which allows the abundance of the rich on the one hand and poverty and discrimination against poor people on the other has to be criticized. A new concept of equality and justice has been explored so that uncritical seeking after riches is to be curbed and the exploitation to be terminated according to the standard of equity. Does freedom mean to be set free from restraints, or as Chinese characters signifying it imply, to be self-reliant and self-determining? In the place of the simple way of thinking that the earth, the resources on it, or human capacity have no limitation, our religious anthropology has to assume a role to point out that everything is limited and it is a task of religion to explain the meaning of this limitation. There is an awakening of religious spirit on the part of many people today, who are contented with a simple life and honest poverty rather than the fulfillment of worldly desires and who are adopting an inner asceticism as a new moral orientation, so that they may enjoy an everlasting life. It will show the people how to live a life to seek and serve others.*

---

*Yasusaburo Tazawa, *My Response to the Challenge of Peace* (Aomori, Japan: Yamatoyama Publishing Co., 1980), 37–38.

Entrance gate to Ittoen.

CHAPTER 18

Ittoen: Thirty Years of Selfless Service

Ittoen, which means "garden of the one Light," is located in the suburbs of the old imperial city of Kyoto. Physicially it is the most beautiful and highly developed community that we have seen anywhere in the world. It was started in 1905 by one of Japan's leading spiritual teachers of the twentieth century; a man who advocated homelessness, nonpossession, and unpaid service to others. While the beauty and stability of the present community may seem to be a contradiction to this philosophy, they are not; the approximately 270 people in this community are devoted to this way of life.

The story begins with Tenko Nishida, who was born into a well-to-do merchant family in 1872. At the age of 20, after receiving only a primary school education, he chose, as an alternative to military conscription, to go to the undeveloped northern island of Hokkaido to help cultivate the land. With the encouragement of the governor of his district, he persuaded 100 families to join him and rented 2000 acres. After some years, a clash of interests developed between the peasants with whom he was working and the businessmen who were providing his funds. He could not justify to himself taking either side against the other. He agonized over the problem, read various inspirational books (including Tolstoy's *My Religion*), and finally decided to give up everything, to die in his old life and be reborn into a new one.

This meant leaving his wife and children, as the Buddha had done. His wife had come from a wealthy family so they had a means of support. He hoped that they would join him; his children eventually did, but his wife did not. He was 32 years old when he left family and home behind. He spent the next several days meditating in a small Buddhist temple. A revelation came to him that if he had nothing, and only tried to serve others in the lowliest of ways, he would be taken care of. He decided to undertake a life of *Roto*, that is, the state of a homeless beggar. *Roto* is now defined by Ittoen as the spiritual state of one not attached to knowledge, pride, or worldly love, and not resentful of physical or mental suffering. This nonattachment is seen as true spiritual freedom, just as homelessness is seen as true physical freedom.

For several years Tenko Nishida, who became known as Tenko San (San is an honorific, somewhat like Mr.) followed this way of life, working in menial positions and accepting food and shelter when he felt it was offered with a clear heart. He constantly tried to follow Light (his term for God), and soon attracted followers. In this way, while he had started out merely searching on his own, he soon found himself a leader, helping others in handling their problems.

In 1905 he was given a small house in downtown Kyoto so that he and his followers would have a base, and this is where Ittoen started. As to how he reconciled this home with homelessness, here are his words:

Although the need for nonpossession is for me absolute, I cannot shirk my responsibility when I am entrusted with anything, and I do not say it is wrong to have possessions. I only say it is not necessary to own anything at all. Because it is not wrong to possess things, I must show in practice how one must handle what one is entrusted with. I have not retired from the life of the world, but I have ceased to depend upon it. I may not enforce my way of life upon others, but also I may not be a coward when called upon to perform some worldly duty. I should be like a wooden gong that sounds only when it is struck and otherwise is silent.*

This transition has occurred in many faiths. The earliest devotees often have no place to lay their heads, so they are forced to be both physically and spiritually dependent on God. Gradually the group acquires possessions. In the end, those in the group have a life of more security that most other people, because they live in a community where no one is trying to possess anything for himself or herself.

Tenko San waited ten years for his wife to find Light and join him. She did not do so and in 1913 he married a member of Ittoen. He had no children from his second marriage but his two sons did eventually join him and his grandson now heads the community.

In 1919, in an effort to maintain something of the original spirit, Tenko San started the Rokuman Gyogan movement. *Roku* means "six," referring to the six paths of Buddhism toward enlightenment: giving alms, keeping the precepts, perservering, training hard, keeping equanimity, and attaining wisdom. *Man* means "10,000." Gyogan means "a prayer." Tenko San asked his followers to go out into the community 200 days a year for ten years and request permission of five households to clean the toilets. This is symbolically the most menial form of service and its performance helps people to remember their principles.

In 1921, Tenko San's first book, *Life of Penitence,* was published to

---

*Tenko San, *A New Road to Ancient Truth* (New York: Horizon Press, 1972), 57.

popular acclaim. It went through 301 editions and sold over 600,000 copies. The book was influential in attracting many new people to Ittoen. Tenko San also organized an association of lay disciples called the Friends of Light. As his fame spread, he was invited to lecture abroad. He visited Taiwan in 1924, Manchuria and Korea in 1925, and the United States in 1927.

In 1928, 25 acres of land on the hillside above Yamashina, a suburb of Kyoto, were donated to the movement and a new base was created there. The small house in Kyoto that the group had been using was taken down and reerected on the hillside. A year later the organization was incorporated as the Kosenrin Foundation. The community gradually grew with new members and with the birth of children.

The printing department started in 1927, initially to print the movement's own books and magazines. A drama troupe—which is still going strong—was organized in 1931. A primary school was established in 1933, followed by a junior high school in 1947, and a senior high school in 1952.

Tenko San was elected to the Japanese House of Councilors in 1947 and served six years. His ideas were too radical for his fellow members, however, and so after some early proselytizing efforts he did not speak.

After Tenko San's death in 1968 at the age of 96, the administration of Ittoen passed to his grandson, Takeshi Nishida, a man now in his fifties. Spiritual leadership was assumed by the oldest man in the community, Tanino San, who had formerly been a priest at a large Jodo Shin Shu temple.

From the Shinomiya station, 12 minutes from downtown Kyoto, it's just a short walk through the village to Ittoen, which now occupies 60 acres. The community outskirts begin along both sides of a tree-shaded canal with a wide path for walkers, hikers, and joggers. The community land is relatively flat at the base, then ascends a narrow defile and includes much of the hill on either side. At its base it is hedged in by a few houses owned by outsiders and by a cemetery that predates Ittoen. Above it are woods. Ittoen comprises more than 50 buildings, some modern masonry ones built to a very high standard, and some small older wood ones built in the best tradition of Japanese domestic architecture. Many of the latter were moved to Ittoen from original sites elsewhere and were owned by important disciples of Tenko San. One beautiful house, recently moved to Ittoen, is used by its owners when they visit the community. At other times it serves as a house for important guests.

The community is physically divided into two parts. The buildings of its various businesses, including a large primary school for outside children, are clustered around the canal at the bottom of the hill. Above these a large stone-and-wood gate leads into the more private area of

residences and Ittoen's school for its own children. These smaller buildings are grouped along a beautiful path that winds its way up the hillside, accompanied by a meandering stream flowing down the hillside,
which occasionally breaks into small waterfalls and ponds. The path is
edged by bonsai trees and flowering shrubs. It is a captivating place.
When we finished our visit at Ittoen we went back to savor this hillside
garden for a while longer.

Many in Western intentional communities are unconcerned with esthetics. Not so those in most Japanese communities, who have a long
tradition (drawn particularly from the Zen influence) of living life
beautifully. The apparent simplicity of this thoughtful and beautiful
way of life is the fruit of centuries of the most intense study into the
inner nature of things. The importance Ittoen places on esthetics is
evidenced by the fact that its gardener is one of the most highly paid
outsiders employed by the community.

In the center of the residential area is the worship hall, where a service is held for the adults every morning at 6:00 and every evening at
5:00. The hall consists of two tiers (one for each sex) at either side of a
large open floor with an altar at one end. Participants kneel on their
heels in the Japanese fashion while one of the elders leads the congre-
gation in chants or prayers accompanied by the beat of a drum or two
percussive sticks. Over the altar is a circular window through which
members can worship Light by looking out on a view of trees, plants,
and a stone lantern. Overhead is the Ittoen symbol—a sun with 12
points of light, a Buddhist swastika bent into a circle around it, and a
Christian cross in the center.

Worshipers chant Buddhist *sutras* (aphorisms or verses that express
Buddhist principles) morning and evening, and each morning they also
recite a passage written by Tenko San called "One Fact of Life." It
summarizes the teachings of the community, reading in part:

A man is standing at the roadside. Although he is an ordinary man he seems to
be illuminated by Light. At times he holds his hands prayerwise as if worship-
ping the Invisible. At other times he enters homes to straighten the footwear at
the door, sweep the garden, clean the toilet, or tidy the storeroom. . . .

Unless he cannot avoid it he never accepts any favored treatment. When people
want him to do so he stays in their homes and does whatever work may be asked
of him. In these homes he treats all with equal respect and gratitude and works
diligently and with gratitude for the blessings received. . . .

When asked about life and death he smiles but does not answer. When asked
who he is he holds his hands prayerwise and then turns to sweep the dust from
the road. When one who believes in him asks the way to trust, he answers that
he is ashamed because of his lack of virtue. When pressed for a fuller answer he
replies that he is led by Light and walks and acts in accord with the Formless
Form.

He does not believe exclusively in either God or Buddha or Confucius but regards all three as within the ... Light of Oneness....

Gentle, modest and diligent, he has no desire to compete with others, neither has he desire for possessions though he delights in producing plenitude. He neither affirms nor denies any of the world's ideologies, but with innocent heart trusts all things to the operation of natural law.

A mortal man? The Light Itself? Or maybe an idiot. He himself does not know. How much less do others? Nevertheless, here is one fact of life.*

A number of other religious buildings and shrines are scattered through the community. One of these is the Hall of Light, with an altar in the center and flags of all nations painted around the Ittoen symbol on the ceiling. Another building is a replica of the temple in which Tenko San received his enlightenment, in which there is an eternal flame. Tenko San brought it from one of the oldest Buddhist temples in Japan, where similar flames have burned for centuries. High on a hill is the mausoleum for the ashes of deceased members of Ittoen and Friends of Light, and below this is a small shrine with life-sized statues of Tenko San and his second wife going out to perform their humble service.

At present Ittoen has about 270 members, down from 300 a decade ago. As Ittoen has prospered (and as the world has changed) it has had somewhat less attraction for people from the world outside. The members have fairly typical Japanese backgrounds, except they have slightly more education. Most have a high school education; some are university graduates. The members—all Japanese—live mostly as families, though single people of all ages live there also. About 40 old people who are judged too elderly to care for themselves live in their own building with a nurse in attendance. Except for the senior high school students, who live in a dormitory, the children stay with their parents. Singles, couples, or families usually have their own private quarters, typically consisting of a six-tatami mat room (about 9 feet by 12 feet) for living and sleeping, plus a small kitchen and toilet. Baths are taken in the communal bathhouse, which has separate soaking tubs for men and women. The tubs are filled every other day, but showers and buckets of hot water are available in the summer. Lunch and dinner are eaten communally in a large, modern, newly built dining hall. Members have their own bowls and chopsticks, which are wrapped in a cloth between meals and kept on a shelf at the entrance. Members may obtain food for breakfast and snacks at the dining hall and take it back to their own quarters.

In addition to receiving food and housing, each member of Ittoen—

*Ittoen leaflet, n.d.

including children, even infants—receives $36 a month for incidental expenses. This largely goes for clothing, reading material, cigarettes, and television sets. Most Ittoen families have their own television sets. Japan has twice as many television sets as households, and the people of Ittoen are not immune to this national addiction. Members may also accept small gifts from friends and relatives. Ayako Isayama, the English teacher who showed us around, had a television set that had been given to her by a friend. She makes a yearly visit to her family in Tokyo, which they pay for.

Ittoen offers a monthly four-day course on its way of life; attending it is the first step for anyone interested in joining. After that, prospective members are invited to stay on, and after several months they may be accepted as associate members. Facilities for visitors cost about $8 a night. At the edge of the grounds is a shelter where any homeless person can stay and receive three meals a day. At the time of our visit it housed one man who had lived there for three years; it was expected that he would live out his life there without becoming a member of Ittoen.

Those who sincerely want to become members stay on at Ittoen for about a year, participating in its activities so that the members can get to know them well and judge their suitability. The final decision is made by Takeshi Nishida and, if appropriate, a ceremony of acceptance is held. Ittoen gets few applicants for membership from the outside these days. Sometimes an outsider employed by one of Ittoen's businesses decides to join and sometimes someone joins because he or she wants to marry one of Ittoen's young people. After the young people from the community graduate from high school, about 30 percent to 40 percent leave. These losses, and the deaths of old people, account for the very gradual reduction in members. Virtually no adult members leave otherwise.

By Japanese standards, the governing of Ittoen is not terribly hierarchical. Originally the administration of Ittoen's various activities was conducted by a committee of leaders appointed by Tenko San which met twice a week. After he died, however, a more democratic system was gradually worked out, since no one in the community was invested with the degree of authority that he had exercised. At present, all the fathers—about 50—belong to the fathers' group, which meets twice a month with Takeshi Nishida to talk about community administration. The mothers' group, which concerns itself with women's matters, elects two mothers each year for a two-year term to participate in the fathers' group. The fathers' group is organized into four committees: education, training, business, and daily life. Each committee has two administrators, chosen by the fathers' group, usually men in their early thirties. All eight of them meet with Takeshi Nishida as an executive committee.

Takeshi Nishida and Tanino San, the spiritual leader, have two assistants who are also chosen by the fathers' group. Despite this governing structure, the tendency, as elsewhere in Japan, is for the members to accommodate their views to their perceptions of the desires of the leaders.

As mentioned earlier, Ittoen has its own educational system for the children of members—from nursery school through senior high school. The nursery school is in a small, separate wood structure, but the other schools share a large, modern, three-story school building, constructed of masonry, as well as a playing field, tennis court, and Olympic-size swimming pool. At the time of our visit 10 children were in the nursery school, 25 were in the elementary school, 15 were in the junior high, and 26 were in the senior high. Some 20 teachers from Ittoen teach in the schools, and 21 teachers from the outside come in to teach special subjects.

The school day starts with a children's service in the worship hall at 8:00, followed by exercise and cleaning of the school until 9:00. The regular classes and club activities of the elementary and junior high schools run from 9:00 to 5:00 and follow the curriculum established by the Ministry of Education, though with an Ittoen orientation. The children take part in the work and spiritual life of the community and the girls learn a variety of household skills by the time of adolescence.

The high school operates differently. Believing in the primacy of work, high school students work till noon and begin classes at 3:00 in the afternoon. They are assigned work in agriculture, animal husbandry, carpentry, construction, printing, nursing, care of small children, food preparation, or maintenance. They usually hold a job for six months or a year, then move on to another one. In this way they learn useful skills and also find out what sort of work they enjoy and what department of Ittoen they may wish to work in when they finish their education. If they want to continue their education outside Ittoen, the community will pay for it. At the time of our visit, one student was learning to be a gymnastics teacher, another was studying to be a mathematics teacher, and a third was training to be an acupuncturist. All expected to return to Ittoen when they completed their studies.

While Ittoen does receive occasional gifts or bequests of money or buildings, at present virtually all of its support comes from its various highly successful business enterprises. The oldest of these is the printing department, begun in 1927. Though the intention was merely to print Ittoen materials, outsiders soon asked them to print other things, so the operation took on other business. Now, although it continues to print a monthly magazine with a circulation of about 1600 among the Friends of Light, as well as other Ittoen publications, most of its business is from the outside, providing one of the principal sources of income for the community. Downstairs in its large two-story building are its offices and five modern presses capable of doing high-quality four-color work. Upstairs is the composition area. Most of the work is set by hand from lead type, and since the Japanese language has about 7300 characters, merely storing all this type in the many sizes required is a major undertaking. The printing department now has one photo-typesetter, and this too is much more slow and complicated to use than those in the West, since it requires keyboarding those same 7300 characters. The printing department has produced many books, including some beautiful full-color art books, as well as posters. Of the staff of 29 people, half are members of Ittoen; the rest are hired from the outside.

The drama troupe was started in 1931. Tenko San loved drama, having participated in a children's kabuki (a traditional form of drama) theater group when he was young. In 1929 a famous kabuki actor joined Ittoen and inspired the formation of a drama group. At first it just performed plays in the community, but as its work became known it was asked to perform elsewhere. It soon began operating on a professional basis and has continued with great success for more than 50 years. The troupe is now led by the son of the kabuki actor, and it has its own quarters. Currently the troupe has about 25 members, half from the outside, as well as a dozen apprentices who came to learn the craft. It spends most of its time traveling, giving some performances in large halls, but performing mainly in schools. Its repertory includes both religious plays and Japanese or Western stories, as well as plays for children, such as *Snow White* and *Pinocchio*. The custom of the troupe is to chant *sutras* at the beginning of each performance, and to clean the theater and its toilets after the performance. In the course of this, it collected about 1500 handkerchiefs over the years, dropped by audience members. These were laundered and sewn into a large curtain, which is still used occasionally when the group performs in a large hall in one of the major cities. At times the troupe has gotten as much publicity for its curtain as it has for its performances! Because the members live simply, the troupe is able to contribute a considerable amount of money each year to the support of Ittoen.

The agriculture department employs 40 people; 14 from Ittoen and 26 from the outside. Its major business is the sale, primarily by mail, of more than 60 varieties of rice seed. About 450,000 pounds a year are shipped in from growers all over Japan who produce it for Ittoen. It is then put into 2.2 pound plastic bags that Ittoen sells for about $3 each. The agriculture department also imports and packages under its own label a plant food that is sprayed onto the leaves of vegetables and fruit trees. Other products packaged there are mushroom spawn from Shītake mushrooms, comfrey tablets, and royal jelly. It operates a retail store at the edge of the community that sells these products, as well as ginseng, vegetable seeds, sprayers, and other products for farming and gardening. The department is not oriented toward organic methods.

There are a number of large greenhouses in the community (made of plastic on metal frames as is usual in Japan) in which the agriculture department raises a variety of vegetables—some of them hydroponically—for Ittoen's own use and for outside sale. They also have a large bamboo grove from which they harvest the shoots for sale every spring, and a large shītake mushroom operation that occupies several sheds on top of the hill. These mushrooms are a famous Japanese delicacy (imported into the United States as dried mushrooms) and they are grown on four-foot oak logs. Small holes are bored in the logs, the spawn is dropped in the hole, and a plug is inserted over it. The logs are piled up and kept suitably damp and warm for about six months until they start producing mushrooms. The Japanese government prohibits the export of the spawn in order to maintain its near monopoly of this healthful and highly prized delicacy. The department also operates a beef cattle farm in Kyushu (the next island to the south) with about 150 head.

Another large business is the construction department, which employs 27 people, 11 of whom are community members. Four of the members are licensed as first-class designers, capable of designing any type of structure. In addition to the buildings and other construction undertaken in the community, the construction department does a great deal of outside work, ranging from a multi-story apartment building to a variety of private homes and even a small, finely detailed teahouse.

Another income-producing business is the Ittoen training program in selfless service. This has its own quarters, including separate living and eating facilities for the approximately 100 people who take the four-day course each month. Most of these people are sent by their employers or potential employers who pay forty dollars each to have them learn humility. This training program, which started before World War II, is one of many in Japan to which employers send workers or managers in hopes they will develop useful attitudes from them.

In the Ittoen training the students hear lectures on the history of the community, nature of its rituals, and meaning of penitent service. The students learn by doing labor for the community and by going out to do selfless service for people in the nearby suburbs. One morning they are sent out to scrub toilets in the homes of strangers; the next day they are sent out alone to aid anyone in need, in imitation of Tenko San's original acts of service. For decades the trainees have been descending into Yamashina at the same time each month, wearing dark blue jackets and inscribed headcloths. Some Yamashina families save up odd jobs in anticipation of this free labor.

An academic who took the course out of curiosity reported that most of the trainees who were sent by their firms to learn humility were not in the least interested in the lofty aims of Ittoen and wished only to get through the course and back to their accustomed way of life as soon as possible.* Nevertheless, it is quite possible that some of the training will linger with even the most reluctant participants.

The large nursery school at the edge of the property is another business bringing in a substantial income. It is housed in an attractive two-story masonry building, with a playground, fish pond, and wading pool. About 170 Yamashina and suburban youngsters, ages 3 to 5, attend this school, which is owned by Ittoen and staffed almost entirely by Ittoen members. The children are usually brought to school in the morning by two school buses that Ittoen owns and operates. No effort is made to preach the Ittoen principles at this school, though the spirit of loving service is present in everything that members do, and doubtless is part of the parents' attraction to the school.

So Ittoen is a community in its maturity that has developed a number of successful businesses and an apprentice program for training its young people to perform many of the key functions in them. Only one person works on the outside—a nurse who works in the Kyoto University Hospital. She turns over all her pay to the community, but does receive a larger allowance than the others because her expenses are greater. On the other hand, Ittoen does employ quite a few people from the outside, so that it is by no means self-sufficient in labor. As previously mentioned, its beautiful gardens are maintained by an outside gardener who is highly paid. Medical care is provided by a nearby doctor who is a member of Friends of Light. Several of the community's own students work in her clinic and help her family. If a medical problem is serious, a member may be sent to one of the local hospitals.

Despite their spiritual orientation and their somewhat ascetic way of life, the people of Ittoen are by no means cut off from the world outside. Each department has two or three cars or other vehicles that are available for business purposes, but not for personal ones. There is really no need for personal vehicle use, however, since Japan has a fine rail system and the nearest station for the street railway to Kyoto is close by. Each department also subscribes to one or two newspapers, and many members have their own subscriptions as well.

The members are in occasional contact with other communes in Japan through attendance at meetings of the Japanese Kibbutz Association, and with other religious groups through organizations such as the World Conference on Religion and Peace. Two members attended that

---

*Moshe Matsuba, ed., *The Communes of Japan* (Hokkaido, Japan: The Japanese Commune Movement, 1979), 63.

organization's Princeton, New Jersey, meeting in 1979, and one of the them stayed on to travel around the United States, performing selfless services at many homes and farms.

Ittoen maintains a remarkable balance between its spiritual commitment and the practicalities of carrying out worldly duties. As one member put it, "Ittoen is a cart with two axles, material and spiritual. If too much weight is put on either axle, the cart cannot run smoothly." We hope that Ittoen's cart will continue to run smoothly for many decades to come.

Flower gardens at Yamagishi-kai for the use of members, with children's center in the background. Behind it are the homes of neighboring villagers.

CHAPTER 19

Yamagishi-kai: A Japanese Kibbutz

"I, a part of nature, do my best to prosper with all men, the sun and the soil."

—SLOGAN AT THE ENTRANCE TO TOYOSATO

Kai means "association" and this is the story of the association of followers of Miyoso Yamagishi, a chicken farmer who developed his own philosophy about personal development and social relations and gave birth to a movement that includes about 1500 living in communes and perhaps 30,000 more supporters throughout Japan.

Yamagishi was an expert chicken farmer in the area of Japan where the cities of Osaka, Kyoto, and Nara are located. He was acquainted with Tenko San and he is thought to have studied Chinese philosophy, nonviolence, Zen Buddhism, Marxism, and anarchism, making a unique amalgam of them all. In his writings he stated: "The world of Yamagishiism is the world of truth and sincerity . . . and . . . from the bottom of my heart I want to realize a socialistic society of love, rich both materially and morally."*

An Israeli member of Kibbutz Dalia, Isaiah Charash, studied Yamagishiism and wrote:

At the root lay his utter faith in man and his ability to reach full expression of his inner strength; and through inter-communication and persuasion on a mutual basis, he believed that it was possible to create a new social climate and, in consequence, a new world without violence and without private ownership of any sort of material or spiritual possessions—which would gradually become the general rule. . . . He suggested security of the collective farm; a fight for peace and understanding, the creation of internal harmony between man and his surroundings—a plan basically atheistic, but rooted in tradition and therefore comprehensible to the peasant.

Yamagishi chose a highly unusual way of getting his ideas across. He sent out a call to the peasant farmers of his district to come and learn new methods of

---

*Quoted ibid., 144.

chicken raising. The farmers duly came, and during the study days devoted to methods of increasing laying in the chicken run, they also received a handsome ration of the new plan. "The reality of my," "the instincts and how to restrain them," "Anger, the enslaver," "Co-operation, the liberator"; these were some of the subjects explained. The new concepts, the discussion and the careful attention paid, the vibrant atmosphere, the flight from the troubles of daily life, and, above all, the hope of some security in the future—all these played their parts and got results. The first nucleus-groups of the movement were formed.*

That was in 1953. Three years later, Yamagishi held the first in a continuing series of seminars to train his followers in the principles of what he called "Kensan." Kensan, his major contribution, combines a philosophy of how to live life, with a method of how to put this philosophy into practice. It might be compared with est or some of the other programs that seek to change attitudes through concentrated group activity. Almost any problem can be dealt with in a Kensan—a meeting utilizing this method.

In 1958 a Yamagishi-kai center was inaugurated with the opening of a large chicken farming commune at Kasuga, near the ancient Japanese capital of Nara. Gradually other communes were started elsewhere in the area, and also north of Tokyo and even in Hokkaido, the large island at the far north of Japan. Yamagishi died in 1961. For six weeks following his death his followers argued about how to interpret his philosophy in making future policy. Many members left as a result of the conflict, but a core group remained and the original population of 300 was eventually restored with the arrival of new members. Nearly 100 of the people had left with Yamagishi's wife to form a rival commune nearby. This commune is still in existence, though it now has only about 50 members. Another commune, whose members had dropped out of the movement after Yamagishi's death, rejoined several years later when its leadership concluded that its members were losing all spiritual drive and declining into superficial materialism.

As new people join the Yamagishi-kai, new communes are started, drawing on experienced members from the older communes to help get them going. At present about 30 communes are in existence, ranging in size from 4 to 400, and averaging about 25. The size of each commune is controlled only by its available land and economic base. Members would like to see their movement spread throughout Japan—and the whole world, for that matter.

The largest of the communes, and the one we visited, is called Toyosato, which means "rich village." It is the ancient name for the area. Located 20 minutes from Tsu, the capital city of Mie prefecture, it houses and employs about 400 members, including children, on about 110 acres. Before discussing Toyosato, let us examine the prin-

---

*Ibid., 145.

ciples and practice of Kensan—the system on which the whole movement is based.

The initial one-week Kensan training course, costing $65, is regarded as fundamental: one cannot be a member or registered outside supporter of Yamagishi-kai without participating in it. In fact, Yamagishi refused to talk to people about his philosophy unless they had taken the course. It covers six subjects: (1) things and thought; (2) anger and how to avoid it; (3) society as a single unit (everything in the universe is one); (4) the body and spirit of the individual; (5) property; and (6) sharing. A full day is devoted to each subject, with continuing discussion and a five-minute break every hour. In the last day of the course, those taking part, one after another, aim at reaching the "zero point," a kind of trance in which they become detached from their material surroundings and personal problems and soar to spiritual synthesis with the group. Those at the zero point supposedly can observe, consider, and inquire into all things completely impartially, without preconceptions based on past experience or education.

Two or three leaders are assigned to each training group. They are charged with guiding the group through the agenda and bringing it to the zero point. Course participants live communally in a hall in an isolated location. This serves to minimize the trainees' habitual behavior and to maximize their reliance on the training program. Among the other elements of control are the great length of the discussions and the Spartan arrangements for eating (two meals a day) and for washing and sleeping. The leaders explain that the living arrangements and the course format are set up so as to disabuse people of their notions regarding personal needs. Trainees are urged to speak openly, but not to read or write during sessions, except when the Kensan book is being read aloud by the group. Leaders sometimes draw sketches on the blackboard that are then discussed by the group, and a painting by Yamagishi's son is hung on the sixth day and trainees are asked to interpret it. Trainees may sit or recline in any position they wish and may drink tea or smoke when they care to, but they cannot leave the room without permission and must always face the discussion circle.

Here is an example of a discussion on equality, reported by Dan Sachs, a Western participant in one of the courses. A tomato had been placed in the middle of the hall. In the morning most of the participants had spoken a few times each, and now they were getting near a stage of summing up:

Leader. "We are dealing with the question of how to behave in equality when dividing up the tomato."

A. "We first find out who is interested in getting a part and then we divide it between these interested people."

B. "Let us divide it in a spirit of honesty. . . ."

C. "Let's cast lots. . . ."

D. "We shall divide it according to the actual needs of those present."

E. (tries to sum up what has been said): "Equality is the condition wherein there are no complaints. . . ."

Leader. "My thought is different from your thought. Let us read from the book."

The Kensan book is opened and one member reads: "Equality is a poor thing when it gives everyone the same thing. Besides, this is not possible in actual life; not everyone can eat the same quantity. Correct equality is that which gives to everyone the possibility of attaining his desires. There is great inequality today in modern life; so hopes of equality are important."

Leader. "Different things are heard at every Kensan meeting; this time appropriate things were said and interesting opinions expressed. But we have not really got down to the heart of the problem, so you have not understood the essence of equality. You discovered how to divide up something; but that is not the same thing as the concept of equality. What is important is the equal possibility for everyone of getting the tomato. When everyone has equal hopes of attaining the desired object, one can practice Kensan and decide how to go about it. If anyone is worried about eating it himself for fear he may deprive others, that too is a sign of inequality. It is true that even in Yamagishi-kai there is sometimes a lack of equality. But anyone who starts from the basis of how to divide can never solve the problem of equality."

F. (a peasant woman, about fifty, from a neighboring village): "Very often the children want apples or tomatoes or bananas. I have not enough to give them all the same thing so I give one an apple, another a banana, and so on. . . ."

Leader. You can give them all the fruit available and let them divide it up between them. . . . We are in the habit of taking sweets to the children's house and the children arrange a sort of Kensan and decide. Sometimes they give all the sweets to one child, and this, too, is equality. Once we had a Kensan meeting here of secondary school students. We put a watermelon in the middle of the hall. They discussed it for a whole day, and in the end no one ate the watermelon at all . . . (general laughter). One must liberate oneself from the idea of division and stick to equality itself."

G. "The matter is not clear to me. If there are many hungry children and only one sweet, what about equality?"

Leader. "Perhaps they will discuss the matter among themselves and come to a decision. I should ask who is the hungriest. For I certainly could not divide one sweet among all of them. I was once sitting with some students and we had one biscuit. The youngest suggested that the oldest eat it. I was the oldest; I was very pleased, but I suggested that the youngest eat it. There was a very long discussion, and in the end the youngest did eat it. This was equality."

H. "Perhaps one should appoint someone who will divide up according to his judgment of the situation."

Leader. "I propose we conclude this part of the discussion. From now on we shall continue to discuss matters with the help of a leader taking over from me in turn, and I shall take part from the ranks. Real equality" (laughter).*

From this extract we can see that Kensan is not a pat formula of questions and answers, but rather a process of explaining a philosophy through discussion. It belongs to that class of guided discussions that are intended to bring about changes in participants' beliefs and actions such as an encounter group or a Chinese communist "struggle" meetings. Groups of varied composition are preferred, as they provide more interesting conversations. Anyone of junior high school age or older may participate. Trainees are expected to be eager to erase their "fixed ideas" and thus learn to see "reality." They are promised that through Kensan they can achieve in seven days what it took the Buddha seven years to achieve. According to the leaders, the best trainees are younger students and less educated people, who have fewer fixed ideas. The poorest prospects are those who are devoutly religious, highly intellectual, or strongly self-confident.

In addition to the goals of changing participants' beliefs and actions, the seminar aims at producing people who are interested in living in communes. In this it has obviously been successful, judging from the number living in Yamagishi-kai communes. Becoming a member of a Yamagishi-kai commune cannot be undertaken lightly. Members are required to dedicate their property and abilities to the commune. They are expected to voluntarily offer their minds, bodies, property, and everything else, material and spiritual, and operate their daily lives by the principle of respecting individual opinion as well as obeying the collective will. A central coordinating committee considers all applications for membership, classifies them, and then assigns people as it deems appropriate to the various movement communes and institutions.

Let us now look at the life and operation of Toyosato, the largest commune in the Yamagishi-kai movement.

We took an early morning train from Kyoto, via Nagoya, arriving at Tsu around 10:00 A.M. We were met at the station by Tsunehiro Nakayama, a handsome young man of about thirty who had spent several years in Europe and had developed fluency in English. Nakayama had been a university student in Kyoto in the late 1960s, but had dropped out along with many other Japanese university students who were rebelling, like their fellow students in the West.

As we made the 20-minute drive from the prosperous provincial capital city of Tsu, we passed not only the ubiquitous rice fields but also

---

*Quoted ibid., 170–172.

a great many nurseries growing shrubs and trees to grace gardens all over Japan. This commune is not in an isolated or depressed area. Just off a superhighway we saw its many long buildings capping a small hill. As our car continued up the curving road to the top of the hill, we found ourselves in the middle of a large agricultural-industrial settlement. It didn't have the look or feel of most of the spiritual communities we had visited, where the economic activities are seen as a means to achieve a spiritual goal. Here it appeared as if agricultural production were the goal. And yet we knew from our previous reading that there was more to it than that.

We stopped first at the office, where we met one of the leaders with whom we would talk later, had a drink of fresh milk, and looked at some of their publications, lavishly illustrated with pictures of happy members working on the farm. Then Nakayama took us for a walk around the commune.

Toyosato occupies about 110 acres, 66 of which are at the base of the hill and are rented, primarily to grow fodder for the cattle. The commune has gradually grown from a much smaller area on top of the hill as it has bought up bits and pieces of land from neighboring farmers. One slice of private land still exists; located in the middle of the commune, it is filled with large ornamental rocks. It belongs to a nursery that stores them there and sells them as elements of Japanese gardens.

The long one-story buildings (about 30 feet by 300 feet) are built of wood or metal and house chickens, pigs, cattle, and people. Many of these buildings have been erected, since this is a large community, with some 50,000 chickens, 4000 pigs, 1000 cattle, and 400 people. Each kind of animal is housed in a homogeneous way that expresses the community's views as to what is scientifically right and necessary for its well-being.

There is a certain drabness about Toyosato, less of a feeling for esthetics than was evident at Yamatoyama and Ittoen. And yet, while this reflects the lower value placed on esthetics at Toyosato, it is also a function of the members' priorities—the emphasis has been on economic success. Toyosato, only about 15 years old, is the youngest of these three communities and only recently has it begun to pay attention to form and beauty. At the center of the community on top of the hill, some of the original small wood buildings stand side by side with large new ones constructed of masonry in traditional Japanese style. The largest of these is the dining hall, a bright, airy, cheerful building with a curved green tile roof, in which the members enjoy their two meals of the day—brunch about 11:00 and supper about 6:00. Next to it is a large, two-storied hall, the newest of the public buildings. Beyond this is an attractive bathhouse, finished inside in wood, stone, and tile. It houses two large baths in separate rooms for each sex, plus two smaller private ones for old or sick members. The bathhouse shares hot water with an adjoining laundry. The members bring in their clothes, with their names on them, and leave them to be washed by the laundry workers. When the clothing is done, it is neatly folded and left in small cubicles to be picked up by its owners.

One of the older buildings houses the commune's shop and common room. The shop is a room about 20 feet by 30 feet, stocked with various necessities: cleaning supplies; basic clothing; buttons and thread; soap and towels; coffee, tea, and sugar; and sake and vodka (but no beer). No money is used in the commune and all of these items are available for the taking. Members who need something not carried in the shop, write their request down on a slip and put it in a special box. Periodically these requests are considered by a Kensan and, if the Kensan agrees, the item is bought. Next to the shop is a room that contains a large selection of better clothing, available for members to borrow for visits outside the community, for example, to attend a wedding.

At the other end of the building is the common room. It is flanked on one side by a barber shop and beauty parlor, each with two chairs. The shops are operated by commune members and are open in the evening. On the other side are two small rooms, without furniture, where members can visit privately, stretch out for a nap, meditate, or watch videotapes made of Toyosato activities. The common room has chairs and benches, and members can talk or read the several newspapers to which the community subscribes. There is no library or adult education program of a cultural nature, and most members do little reading beyond the newspapers and a few magazines.

The six long, barracks-style communal houses lie at the foot of the hill. They are side by side and about 25 feet apart. Each has a long hallway along one side, with room after room opening onto it, and an area in the center with washing facilities and nonflushing toilets. Each room is about 12 feet by 25 feet in size, including closets, and is occupied by a couple or by two or three singles. The rooms are sparsely furnished, in the Japanese style. A few have TV sets that have been bought by the commune for those who request them. Most don't. Up to the age of six children stay with their parents. Then they move to the children's house, where they live with their peers. The children's house is at one end of the housing area, alongside a two-story preschool.

As we ascend the road, going up the hill from the housing area to the community center, the road straightens out at a certain point, allowing us a lovely view of the valley. Several benches have been placed here so that members can sit and enjoy the view. In the foreground is a large flower garden, from which members can pick flowers to take to their rooms. Although the garden is laid out in straight nursery rows, its very existence testifies to a love of nature and beauty. Beyond it is another long, low building that houses the children's day care center, and in the background are the vegetable gardens, behind which are the neighbors' farms. It is a pleasant vista that enables one to relax and to look beyond the work and cares of the moment.

The 300 adults and 100 children are divided into six groups called "families," and each family is as heterogeneous as possible, with a balance of ages. All of the members are Japanese (though two Swiss and two Bangladeshis live in other Yamagishi-kai communes). About 50 of the members are single. The average age of the adults is about 30. About 15 are older than 50; the oldest is 81. Men slightly outnumber women. As we have previously mentioned, the first members were mostly farmers. Many of those members around 30, like our host, Tsunehiro Nakayama, were university students in the late 1960s and early 1970s. By now a good cross-section of educational and socioeconomic backgrounds exists. Two members are doctors who work outside the commune. The membership is quite stable. Few adults leave the commune, except to move to other Yamagishi-kai communes. New members join as land is bought and facilities are expanded.

The situation with children is rather different. After preschool, all children go outside to the public schools. The result is that they absorb the values of the larger society and most of the young men choose to leave when they finish school. They feel that the material and cultural opportunities at Toyosato are insufficient for them. On the other hand, most of the young women stay on, which probably reflects the culturally prescribed role of Japanese women more than anything else—unmarried women live at home. The commune tries to integrate school experience with community life by holding Kensans each day after school for returning students. At these meetings they talk about what happened during the day at school. The basic idea inculcated is that no one can teach anyone anything; each of us must learn for ourselves what is true from our own experience.

In the early 1970s an effort was made at the nearby Kasuga commune to start a school for the Yamagishi-kai. The primary instigator was a 12-year-old girl who had read about Summerhill, the famous school in England started by A. S. Neill at which students were free to attend classes or not as they chose. She begged to be allowed to attend the school. Her father, a professor of Chinese literature and a supporter of the Yamagishi-kai adopted from Summerhill the idea of a home-atmosphere school for the movement's children as a way of solving his own problem of finding a satisfactory school for his daughter. He published an article entitled "Paradise for Children," and organized discussion groups all over the country. He was finally able to obtain a nearby farmhouse complex rent-free, where he began the school in 1974 with 12 teachers and 13 young students. The plan was for everything to be run autonomously, according to movement principles, leading to rich experience and creative activity. The professor left Yamagishi-kai after several years for personal reasons, so the school struggled on without him. It now has about 20 adults and 30 children but has developed into a small community rather than a school.

The governing of Toyosato, like other Yamagishi-kai communes is a matter of constant experimentation, in keeping with the scientific orientation of the movement. At present, the basic governing groups are the "families" of about 60 people each, already mentioned. Each family holds a "being a good friend" Kensan twice a month. Each family also elects two members to the life operating committee.

Parallel to the families are the operating departments. These are: cattle breeding, divided into milking, beef cattle, and fodder; pig breeding, chicken raising, divided into eggs and broilers; transportation; construction; life, divided into welfare, food, and children; and human affairs, divided into marriage, education, and health. Each department elects two members to the work operating committee.

The life operating committee and the work operating committee elect the ten managers. Currently one, the human affairs manager, is a woman. In accordance with the original design, committee elections are held twice a year, so that every term of service ends automatically after six months, ensuring that no one has time to acquire undue power or prestige. There is thus considerable change in the composition of the two operating committees, which deal with general philosophical and management concerns. The operating details are left to the managers, who have their own committee. And there is very little turnover among the managers. Once in the job, most people, stay on year after year. Because of the way in which the commune is functionally divided up into separate families and departments, decisions usually are made at the top by the managers. The system might be thought of as a form of democratic centralism, that is, the leaders are elected, but they have a great deal of power. No single charismatic leader has replaced Yamagishi. The basic principles and methods of Yamagishiism are sufficiently clear and effective that the movement has been able to survive his death and to grow in relative harmony.

In addition to this formal structure, a great many special Kensans are held. Any member can call a meeting and propose its theme. And members are encouraged to take follow-up training courses in Kensan ideology each year so that they stay in tune with the rest of the commune members.

Economically, Toyosato is joined with the other Yamagishi-kai communes in a network to produce, distribute, and sell a variety of agricultural products. In addition to the producing communes, more than 20 small urban communes of 4 to 30 people serve as supply centers to distribute these products. The Toyosato transportation department, with 80 to 90 cars and trucks for use inside and outside the community, moves the products from the community to the supply centers. The supply centers then distribute them to consumer cooperatives of householders interested in Yamagishi-kai products. These are made up largely of urban members of the association. Some people join the cooperatives just because they like the products—such as the fertile eggs—and they go on to develop an interest in the organization, eventually taking a Kensan training course.

About 70 percent to 80 percent of the food eaten at Toyosato is produced there. The agricultural methods are not organic, though some alternative agricultural practices are employed. Yamagishi-kai communes have experimented with two kinds of chicken farming: the "industrial" kind using the battery system of birds in individual cages, and the "socialist" kind in which the chickens are free to run around in large rooms. We saw only the latter at Toyosato. The individual rooms were about 12 feet by 25 feet, with two lights, a fan, roosts, and an enclosed cabinet for laying. Each accommodated about 100 hens and 5 roosters.

Most of the commune members work 9 to 11 hours a day, seven days a week. Members take a rest when they or their colleagues feel they need it. One man, interviewed during Richard Fairfield's visit to Toyosato, said:

You see, we have decided that work is our whole life. When we eat it is for the sake of working the next day, when we sleep it is for the sake of working, and so on. We do not have any special Sunday or other day off. When we are tired we rest. Then, rested, we can go back to our work. You see, our idea of rest is the same as work. We do not differentiate between the two. Through Kensan we decide when to rest.*

We were not at Toyosato long enough to draw many independent conclusions about it; we did conclude, however, that life there is mostly work and little play. When we asked Tsunehiro Nakayama if he had any hobbies, he replied that his only hobby was his work. Members engage in no organized sports and few recreational and social activities. A chorus sings traditional Japanese music and folk dances are held occasionally. Two festivals are held each year: one to celebrate spring, and one to mark the anniversary of Yamagishi's death. Other functions are arranged when members feel like it, perhaps to honor the New Year, moon, flowers, or snow. Marriages are performed according to a special ceremony and are attended by members of the couple's families, both inside and outside the commune.

*Richard Fairfield, *The Modern Utopian: Communes, Japan* (San Francisco: Alternatives Foundation, 1972), 52–53.

Beyond the commune, some of the people at Toyosato have friends among the neighbors. Some of the neighbors are worried by the rapid growth and expansion of the community. One older member specializes in cultivating the neighbors' friendship and in trying to persuade neighboring farmers to sell land to the community. Recently many of the members have gone out among the neighbors to knock on doors and explain their ideas and methods to them.

Most of the outreach, however, is through the efforts of the Yamagishi-kai, whose headquarters are at Kasuga, a few miles away. Its formal planned framework includes the Yamagishiism Inquiry Institute, the Secretariat, the Experimental Institute of Human Principle, the Experimental Institute of Social Principle, and the Test Field of Industrial Principle. But most of these grandiose schemes have yet to be realized, because of the pressure of too few people trying to do too much on too limited a budget.

Yamagishi-kai's publishing department produces a monthly newsletter, and a theoretical journal called *Rags and Water* is published irregularly. The title comes from one of Yamagishi's articles in which he put out this call: "All those who are ready to work for nothing, wearing rags and with only water, come to us." Every summer the association sponsors a children's camp, called Children's Paradise, which attracts about 200. About 800 people take the week-long Kensan training course each year. These average 30 to 40 participants in each course, with an average age of about 35. Most are held in the summer and they attract many housewives and teachers—more women than men. Occasionally they are given in English or taken to Korea or Switzerland. A commune was established in Switzerland by a Swiss who had spent time with the group in Japan, but it didn't last.

When we asked a couple of the members of Toyosato what they saw happening in the world in years to come, they answered in terms of the spread of Yamagishi-kai communities in other countries. Yamagishiism is a remarkable movement that has had substantial success in Japan. We suspect, however, that it is one Japanese product that will not prove to be exportable to the West.

Part VII

NEW ZEALAND

Members of the Riverside Community tamping down dirt to build a rammed earth house.

CHAPTER 20

The Riverside Community: A Group in Transition

In 1941, World War I veteran Hubert Holdaway and his wife, Marion Holdaway, together with a small group of young New Zealand Christian pacifists, started the Riverside Community. Dedicated to the repudiation of war, abolition of private ownership and private profit, and limitation and equality of income, the first few years of the community's existence were a terrible struggle. New Zealand had been involved in World War II from its inception, and most of the men were jailed for draft resistance. Under Hubert Holdaway's leadership, the job of clearing the land and creating the physical beginnings of this farm community fell mainly on the women. The neighbors were intensely hostile to this group of "communists" and pacifists. The group was poor and faced with challenges on all sides, but the members persisted.

Their idealism and commitment paid off. With the end of the war the men returned and new members joined the community. Gradually the farm expanded, homes were built, friends were made in the surrounding community. Today, more than forty years later the Riverside Community has a population of about 70 people and 520 acres of farm and village with a net worth of around $1 million. The neighbors' hostility has given way to pride. The community is a public attraction about which the local tourist brochures wax eloquent. Riverside Community is the oldest, largest, and most stable intentional community in New Zealand.

But 40 years is a long time in the life of a community. Most of the people who started it have died; others have retired. The issues that were of burning importance in the 1940s and 1950s seem irrelevant to the younger members. The founders were all teetotaling Methodists who emphasized Christian commitment and practice. All members were expected to attend church. Those who did not were not allowed to play any sport or go anywhere in a community vehicle. But as the years went by, and public attitudes changed, the community found that it attracted few new members. It was forced to drop its requirement that persons wishing to join be both members of a church and of the Christian Pacifist Society. The community settled for an affirmation of Christian belief, as the applicant understood it, without denominational strings. Even this proved too restrictive, and in recent years both Jews and atheists have become members. The Methodist church, which was built in the 1950s on property donated by Riverside, is no longer used for services, and the few practicing Christians drive into town on Sunday mornings. Many younger members live together in what are called "de facto marriages," drink wine and beer in public, and smoke marijuana in private. Certainly these changes have not occurred without friction. Some of the oldtimers—and younger people as well—have left, convinced that Riverside has given up its ideals. But most of the members have adjusted gracefully, if not always enthusiastically, to these changes.

Today the Riverside Community is in a state of transition. The old is not yet dead; the new has not yet fully arrived. It is a comfortable, economically well-off place in which to live. Yet unlike many of the communities we have studied, it lacks both a charismatic leader and clearly defined goals and practices. How it fares under these circumstances is the story that we will tell here.

At the north end of New Zealand's South Island lies the province of Nelson. With the Tasman Bay on one side and sheltering mountains on the other, Nelson enjoys a mild, sunny climate. The beaches are popular with vacationers, the towns abound with artists and craftspeople, and the fertile soil supports many of New Zealand's fruit orchards as well as crops of tobacco and hops. Some 3 million boxes of fruit—mainly apples—are exported each year, and in the late summer and early fall the population swells when 3000 or so young people arrive to help with the picking. The Riverside Community is located in an idyllic setting, 30 miles from the town of Nelson and 5 miles from the smaller town of Motueka, along the highway that connects the two towns.

The bus stops at the entrance. The village consists of about 20 houses, a church, a hostel that accommodates about 30 guests or temporary workers, a community hall, and several buildings for offices, woodworking and engineering shops, and storage. The houses are substantial and comfortable and would fit in well in any middle-class suburb in New Zealand. Some are of timber that was logged on the farm. The windows and doors are made in the community's own woodworking shop. Several of the houses, including one under construction while we were there, are made of fortified rammed earth. In this process, 15 parts of subsoil are mixed dry with 1 part cement, then poured in a thin layer into a form that can be moved along the wall, and carefully tamped down before the next layer is added. Fortified rammed earth makes very strong, homogeneous, adobelike walls that grow stronger as they age. After they are plastered inside and outside to protect them from the elements, they are indistinguishable from more conventional walls. The process requires few purchased materials but involves a good deal of labor, though it is not highly skilled labor. For these reasons it was promoted by the United States Department of Agriculture during the Depression, and is today being taught in various developing countries. The Riverside Community is proud that it is a pioneer in the use of rammed earth construction in this part of New Zealand, and invites others to visit it and observe the process.

The village also includes tennis and volleyball courts, a crafts building for basketry, weaving, and so on, and carports for the vehicles. These consist of three vans, three sedans, and two trucks. Members may use the vehicles to go to church and also to go shopping three times a week, at no charge. They can also use them for other personal reasons at a cost of 8¢ a mile, which includes gas and oil.

On their 520 acre farm the main source of income is the orchards—mainly apples—but the community also produces boysenberries, pears, beef, mutton, timber, wool, and milk from its herd of 140 cows. The milk is sold in bulk. The community uses some of this, but buys mostly pasteurized milk for its members. Health department regulations permit single families to drink the raw milk of their own cows, but do not advise this for communities.

The emphasis at Riverside is on economic success, but not necessarily self-sufficiency. Vegetables grown for the members' own consumption are organic, but the commercial crops are not. The community markets its products through a variety of cooperatives, including a dairy cooperative, sheep marketing cooperative, wool marketing cooperative, and the New Zealand Apple and Pear Board, which is a growers' cooperative that is in partnership with the government. It purchases supplies from the Fruit Growers Federation, another cooperative. The community had originally hoped to combine farming with the running of small industries, such as an engineering workshop, printing, fine woodwork, and weaving. Because so much labor was needed in the orchards, however, these were never established as businesses, although Riverside has its own woodworking and engineering workshops. At one time the members kept about 100 bee colonies, selling honey and beeswax candles. They dropped this, however, both because the demands of other operations (particularly the orchards) didn't leave enough time for beekeeping, and because they came to feel that candles were a luxury item. This illustrates the mix of idealistic and economic considerations that have influenced production decisions. Early on, members decided not to grow hops or tobacco, since they felt that neither made a constructive contribution to human well-being. And Riverside buys eggs and cheese and other foods, because members believe that producing them would be an uneconomic use of their energies.

How has Riverside managed to achieve this affluence? The community was begun on land owned by one of its first members. It was a productive orchard that provided immediate income. Fruit growing is an activity that can provide a fairly high return per acre, but is labor intensive, particularly at harvest. Thus the average grower is dependent on hired labor, which currently costs more than $4 an hour, including accommodations and other labor costs. A community with its own supply of low-cost labor is at a considerable economic advantage. If it can maintain a modest standard of living over a period of years, as Riverside has done, it can amass a substantial surplus of funds.

Riverside was originally set up as a limited company on land owned by one of the members in partnership with his brother who owned adjoining land. A problem arose when the brother decided to move, and the community had to raise the money to buy his land. Members canvassed supporters throughout New Zealand for loans and donations. After several years the company was closed out and the entire operation became a charitable and religious trust. Six trustees are elected by community members. The trustees' only role, however, is to sign documents, since decisions are made by the community as a whole. Now that the community is a trust profits may be made and retained, free of tax. The only taxes paid are on members' earnings, and these are minimal since their earnings are so small.

Partly because its profits are tax-free, but more because of members' beliefs, it is Riverside policy to contribute to worthy, often unpopular, causes. Such contributions, along with Riverside's involvement in various protest movements, are a vital part of its *raison d'être*.

After buying the brother's land, the community was able, over the first decade, to buy a number of adjoining parcels at prices that seem very low today. About a dozen different purchases were made to create the present 520-acre spread. The community has also obtained some capital from members, because they are required to donate whatever capital they have to it.

In one instance a retired couple wished to move to the community. They had a considerable amount of savings but also three grown children, and wanted to leave some money to them. A compromise was struck, whereby the couple entered as associate members, a special category just for them; this means they cannot vote. They built their own house, which will eventually pass to the community, but did not donate the rest of their capital. This arrangement displeases some community members, who dislike the idea of a special category of membership, so the arrangement is not likely to be repeated. A retired Dutchwomen lives in the community and pays $10 a week rent for a small house, but she is not a member.

Growth during World War II was slow. At the beginning of 1947, three families and one single person lived in the community. The fourth family, who came that year, was that of Jan and Arch Barrington. Arch Barrington was one of the national leaders of the Christian pacifist movement in New Zealand. Now 77, he no longer plays a role in governing the community, but until recently was its secretary and accountant. Several years ago he was vice-president of the Methodist Church in New Zealand, thus helping to keep Riverside before the public eye.

Except for the Holdaways and the Barringtons, all the original members were in their twenties when they came to Riverside. The growth and age distribtion of the population can be seen from this table:

	1942	1952	1962	1972	1982
Children	3	19	24	8	23
Age 15 – 30	6	15	8	7	7
Age 30 – 60			16	11	14
Age older than 60	0	0	1	7	6
Total	9	34	49	33	50

These figures include only full members and their children. They do not include probationary members and others who live in the community but are not members. Frequently, the community has taken in a few people who had physical or mental handicaps or difficulties of one sort or another. It seems to have a capacity to absorb and help such people in small numbers.

As the preceding table helps to show, Riverside continued to grow until the early 1960s, but then declined in the early 1970s, prompting the community to relax its rules in order to attract new members. Most of the children of the original members left the community when they grew up. The original members were mostly self-educated people of strong conviction. They wanted their children to do better than themselves, not materially, but professionally. Their children went off to university or teachers training colleges, and in most cases were lost to the community. The exception was the Cole family. Norman and Joy Cole, now in their mid-sixties, have six children. One is still at university; the others went away to university but eventually all but one returned to Riverside. One of them, Colin, is farm manager, with particular responsibility for the dairy, and his wife, Barbara, was at one time chair of the community.

Colin Cole recalled that at college he was more mature than most students, because of his community upbringing. He worked as a teacher for a couple years, but it didn't satisfy him. "While living away from home I felt I wasn't using my human potential. As a teacher I did just enough to get by. Now I feel that I am using my mind and my other abilities far more than I would elsewhere."

When an individual or a family applies to join the community, they may be accepted as probationary members for a minimum of one year before they can apply for full membership. It's not hard for newcomers to become probationary members if they exhibit no obvious behavior problems. Most probationary members had heard about Riverside and wanted to try community life. Some probationary members just happened by as casual workers during harvest time, liked what they saw, and stayed. When people become probationary members their assets are "frozen" and they are treated like regular members. If accepted as full members, their assets are transferred to the community. The only possessions they may keep are personal items, such as clothing and furniture.

All members are provided with free housing, electricity, and telephone service; free fruit and vegetables in season; five eggs per week per person; and subsidized meat and honey. The weekly cash allowance is forty-eight dollars and fifty cents for a couple, forty dollars and fifty cents for a single householder, thirty-two dollars for a single person, and one dollar and fifty cents to five dollars for a child, depending on age. Medical, dental, and optical expenses are paid by the community. There are also allowances for weddings, higher education, and vacations. Members are given a vacation of three weeks a year. They can borrow one of the community cars for it and pay 8¢ a mile, or they can take public transportation and be reimbursed for the cost, minus 8¢ a mile. The community also has a "love fund," which members can dip into for special needs like film.

Mothers are not expected to work outside the home, although many do volunteer work. Children age ten and older may work, if they wish, at graduated pay rates depending on age.

The governing of the community is largely through consensus. A community meeting is held weekly. Two out of three are general meetings; the other is a work meeting to plan both community work schedules and individual schedules. An annual meeting that lasts for several days is held at the end of the picking season. A community chair is elected at this meeting, and he or she usually serves for a year or two. By and large, it is not a job that is sought after and it usually is accepted with some reluctance. In a typical meeting, after a full discussion has been held, the chair states his or her understanding of the consensus reached. If no one disagrees, that's that.

Each morning an informal meeting is held at which decisions are made about the day's work. People congregate in the yard or workshop, discussing the upcoming day's tasks. All the members participate in managing the farm to the extent that their experience and judgment enables them to do so. At the same time, members recognize that some have a specialized knowledge, and the specialists' opinions usually carry extra weight.

Working hours are about the same as for farmers elsewhere in New Zealand. Members have one hour for lunch, and usually return to their own homes for their meal. Communal meals are held four times a week and on special occasions such as Christmas. By and large, people at Riverside live a pretty ordinary family life, and they display a considerable range of values and interests. Voting is an individual matter, though most usually vote for the Labour party. Most younger members are more liberal than most older members, and the lack of strong common ideals is a source of regret for some.

At the time of our visit, one couple who had been members for three years, Gordon and Sharon McFadyen, were getting ready to leave to join a community run by Catholic Social Services for delinquent boys. Gordon said:

We feel that Riverside doesn't have a goal. People are just working for the community. It is so successful economically that it can afford not to be concerned with its ideals. We don't see any unifying force or ideals. We were told this was a Christian pacifist community, but we found kids playing with guns and older people helping them make the guns. We also found that women followed traditional roles, which we didn't want. Riverside has let down its standards too much to get new members. Now there is nothing that the whole community shares.

We spoke to another couple, Rick Wiseman and Leslie Barry, probationary members considering applying for full membership. Wiseman was on the building team, doing mostly maintenance. He liked the fact that he could change jobs easily when he wished. Wiseman's view was different from McFadyen's.

We thought Riverside would be far more community oriented; we found it is very family oriented. But we like having the older generation around. We like the philosophy: the pacifism, the equality of income, the lack of emphasis on materialism. We've been through the rat race and are delighted to give it up. We like sharing meals, working with people. We've worked harder in the last ten months than ever before. Joining the community is a life commitment, like marriage. We hope it will work out, but we really don't know what's around the corner.

While some members see the changes as aimless drifting, or as a necessity to maintain the community, Chris and Jean Palmer, who've been at Riverside since 1952, feel good about the changes. They feel that Riverside is moving with the times. The churches are now less rigid about who is a Christian. Why not be flexible? They note that Riverside didn't do any better in the past in attracting stable, community-minded members.

Now the community accepts the different value systems of younger and older members. Although the older members sometimes find it hard to adjust to this change in the community, they go along with it. The members believe that the community has a valid way of life that enables people to work through the conflicts of living and survive differences of opinion.

Although generational differences are handled fairly easily, in an atmosphere of tolerance, issues of community direction are more difficult to handle. These issues frequently cut across generations. Rick Wiseman would like to see Riverside move from using tractors to using horses; from employing electric heat to employing wood fires. Many older members don't want to go "back" to that sort of thing. The issue of raising organic crops versus raising commercial crops is a continuing one. And younger members who advocate homeopathic medicine and other alternative approaches to health care often find themselves arguing their position with older, more traditional members.

Colin Cole, who is both young and an oldtimer, had this to say:

We're getting out of this place what we can for ourselves, and trying to share it with others. Right now, we find it hard to see what lies ahead. As we become a community of younger people, we're becoming more like a typical commune. It's the way things are done that's changing, not what is done. There's more job sharing, more role sharing. We used to be more committee oriented. Now we work for consensus. We think changes will be slow enough that people will be able to handle it.

Is the Riverside Community a successful one? Certainly. That it lacks the driving idealism and commitment of its youth is not surprising. Such a change in the life of a community is probably as normal as it is in the life of an individual. Riverside's affluence—the result of years of dedication and hard work—gives people time and emotional energy to pursue individual goals without threatening the stabilty of the community.

Let Barbara Cole have the last word: "Radicals look on communities as a means to an end. We look on it as an end. We're not trying to achieve women's lib or political regeneration. We're just trying to live together successfully."

Part VIII

SOUTH AFRICA

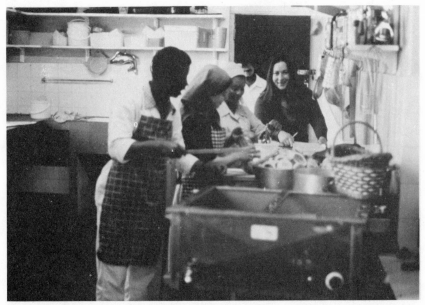

In the kitchen, community members of the Hohenort Hotel work interchange-
ably with local staff.

CHAPTER 21

The Hohenort Hotel: Undermining Apartheid with Love

We left the lovely city of Capetown, South Africa, behind and followed the highway along the shoulder of Table Mountain to Constantia—a beautiful and elite suburb of spacious estates perched on a hillside with a breathtaking view of Table Bay. The homes and ambience reminded us of Beverly Hills, though the vegetation was lusher. Could a wealthy suburb such as this nurture and be nurtured by a hotel run by a spiritual group? This is what we were to find out; the year was 1978 and the hotel had been managed by the group for about six months.

We had phoned ahead that morning for a room, purposely not stating our intention of writing about the group. We wanted first to see the community as it was and not as the members might want us to see it. The 27-room hotel which had once been a private mansion, is set on 7½ acres that includes a swimming pool.

The warmth and openness with which we were greeted would have made us wonder if we had not known something of the nature of the management. Elsewhere in South Africa we had been greeted by negative, arrogant whites or powerless, obsequious blacks. Here we felt the difference immediately. The blond young woman behind the desk at the Hohenort Hotel greeted us with a wide smile and sparkling eyes. Nearby were a number of other young women, all with the same glow. They asked if we would be dining there that evening. We explained that we were vegetarians and they said they would gladly fix a special meal for us. They particularly wanted us to join them that night because it was Thursday, the night they held a special feast in front of the fireplace with entertainment by folksingers that often lasted until the wee hours. People came over from all over Capetown just for these events. We accepted their invitation gladly.

That evening as we enjoyed the banquet and the music, we explained to the manager, Valerie Morris, that we were writing a book on intentional communities and said that we would like to write an article about the hotel and the community. Her response was very cautious. Morris said she was not sure the community wanted any publicity, but she would talk to the others and let us know in the morning. We assured her that our book wouldn't be out for a long time, said that probably few people in South Africa would see it, and pointed out how others could profit from their experience.

Morning came and we were told that Rupert Maskell, the group's leader, would be glad to talk with us. Maskell is a handsome Englishman in his early forties who lived in South Africa as a boy, returning in 1970. In his twenties he managed the London office of an American real estate company. But though he had outward success, he felt no sense of inner peace. He discussed his feelings of emptiness and dissatisfaction with a friend who had visited the Canadian headquarters of the Emissaries of Divine Light, in British Columbia. She told him that their path was what he needed. But Maskell was 28 and still very caught up with the material world. It took another year for the seed to sprout. Finally he flew to Canada, very apprehensive. Once there, he realized that he had found his way. A year later he went to Sunrise Ranch, the Emissaries' center in Colorado, for a five-month intensive course, attending classes in the morning and working on the Emissaries' ranch in the afternoon.

The message of the Emissaries is that people must look beyond the material world to what is real—that is, their spiritual reality, their carrying of the life force, their oneness with the universe. The teachings of the Emissaries are intended to bring people into harmony with their own spirituality. Only as individuals change for the better, will this world change for the better.

Lord Martin Cecil, leader of the Emissaries of Divine Light, has this to say:

In order to leave the self-centered state, some other state must be known; there must be movement from one state to another. This other state may well be described by the word *integrity*, the state of integrity, integrity which places primary value in spiritual things rather than in material things. . . .

My own personal concern for many years has related to this matter of integrity, and there are those who have recognized this to be true and who have therefore shared this attitude with me. To the extent that we have done so, we have found ourselves to be integrated, not because we chose each other particularly, but because we all chose integrity. . . .

It is surely far more creative and constructive to give value to what is right, to recognize that true values are spiritual values and to behave as though one recognized that this was the truth. Those who aspire to spiritual experience so often do so on the basis of the fact that they have given so much value to material experience. They think they have to get away from the material experience in order to find spiritual experience, as though here were two separate things. . . . This is an entirely false view because the fact of the matter is that heaven and earth are one; it is only human beings who are so dumb that they don't know it, and their dumbness is proclaimed by the way they behave. . . .

The most futile of undertaking, as we well may see, is this: to try to cause the world to be anything else than a reflection of the people who live in it. We can't fix the world up to be a Utopia while less than Utopian people compose it—a very simple truth, seemingly, but virtually unrecognized, apparently, so that almost all human effort is given, individually and collectively, to fixing the world up so we may live in peace and prosperity, enjoying happiness and fulfillment for ourselves without in the least being concerned with respect to our own characters and the quality of our own living. . . . Unless there is a different quality of human beings present on earth there will not be a different quality of world, so let's leave the world alone and concern ourselves with human beings. Human beings—plural? There is only one human being at the center of our world and that is the person who may refer to him- or herself as "me."*

After the course was over, Maskell visited his parents in South Africa before returning to England. Old friends noticed changes in him and asked about his experience in Colorado. He gave a number of private, informal talks and found a responsive audience. Back in England the interest was not so great, so he wrote to Cecil and said that he felt his true work was in South Africa; could he move there and form a group? Permission was granted, but once Maskell was in residence, those whose enthusiasm had drawn him back to South Africa were no longer in evidence. During the first year, only two or three people came to his weekly meetings. Gradually he developed a small following and then gave a few public talks. After about 18 months, he had attracted five other Emissaries. They lived and worked together, supporting themselves by running a small health food store. The group continued to grow and they bought a small farm about 30 miles from Capetown. Eventually 14 Emissaries lived on the farm—the maximum number the land and housing could support—and auxiliary groups formed in Capetown and Johannesburg. The farm gave the Emissaries the necessary environment for internal and group growth without outside distraction. Running the farm was hard work, and each Emissary received only a little more than $5.00 a month spending money, plus room and board. Still, the experience welded them together as a group, giving them a focus and providing a place for nonresident Emissaries to come on weekends.

By 1978 there were more than 100 Emissaries in Capetown, and Has-

---

*Martin Cecil, *On Eagle's Wings* (New York: Two Continents Publishing Group, 1977).

kell realized that the farm was becoming a limiting factor. It was too far away for city people to come regularly for classes, and too small for all the Emissaries to meet together. At the same time, the rent on the group's health food store had risen, so they had decided to give it up. The Emissaries needed a way to generate income as well as have a center for their community. Haskell thought of buying a hotel or apartment house, and started perusing the classified ads. He had known of the Hohenort Hotel since childhood and had watched its progressive deterioration after one wing was destroyed by fire. It had developed a bad reputation but the most recent managers had made many improvements. On a hunch he went to the hotel and asked at the desk if it was for rent. A surprised clerk replied, "No, indeed!" But that night Haskell saw a classified ad describing a lease for sale on a hotel that he was sure must be the Hohenort. He went to see the realtor and found that he was right. A true case of manifestation or synchronicity! He put the farm up for sale and, despite a terribly depressed land market, sold it within three weeks.

The group bought the lease on the hotel for $70,000 in 1978, and signed a new ten-year lease, with an option to buy. Its total value, with its 7½ acres of land, is probably about $300,000. Another stroke of good luck came a few weeks later when Rupert saw another ad for the house next door to the hotel. He bought this large house with 2½ acres for $75,000—an incredible deal by American standards. Rupert and his wife Tessa plus several of the group moved in. The house also provided a place away from the hotel where they could hold classes.

Moving to the Hohenort Hotel meant being uprooted from a pastoral and independent environment. When the group took over the hotel it included an existing staff of 15, a rowdy bar, and a noisy discotheque that was the local teenage hangout. After six months they converted the discotheque to a dance hall with live music, and began to attract a more mature crowd.

When the Emissaries first took over the hotel, the manager was so uncomfortable with them that he left halfway through the first day—leaving them in the dark about where the keys were, how the heating system worked, and all the other basics of a hotel. They had to learn the hard way. About seven of the remaining staff were coloreds (persons of mixed race), and the rest were blacks, whites, and Indians. The Emissaries kept them on, firing only two staff members—both because of alcoholism.

The local staff seemed to us to be much happier than most of the employees we'd seen at other South African hotels. They exuded pride and looked patrons in the eye, the way we'd seen employees do in hotels in black Africa. As Haskell said, "We relate to them in a different way, so they're learning to relate to people in a different way. They've changed a lot. Some are thrilled. The oldest employee [he'd been there seventeen years] told the landlord that we were the only people who really took care of the place." The local employees and the Emissaries work together as equals in the kitchen and bars and it is apparent that the Emissaries do not take all the best jobs for themselves—though only Emissaries handle the money and work the front desk.

Community members never announced to the local staff or patrons that they are members of a spiritual group. They feel that the essential thing to do is be who they are and let their light shine, allowing people to ask questions if they are curious. When people do ask questions, they try to answer honestly and at the depth that seems most suited to the questioner's intent. If people express further interest, they are invited to the group's Sunday meetings when they get together to discuss a theme, listen to tapes, or watch videotapes of talks by Sir Martin Cecil. A number of the employees attend these meetings also, though none is an Emissary.

At the time of our visit 26 Emissaries lived in or around the hotel; 16 worked there, the other 10 worked outside. The manager was a woman, Valerie Morris. She made the work assignments, usually checking out her decisions with Haskell when he was around. Morris formerly managed a large Transcendental Meditation hotel in New York state. Haskell told us he had been uncomfortable with a female manager, but Morris was the only member with the necessary experience and business acumen. The Emissaries favor traditional sex roles. Haskell said

Women are generally more yielding and responsive than men. Men are generally more stable emotionally. Women naturally respond to men and therefore they are more able to be, and men are more able to achieve. There are not too many true men around, however, because most have been sexually and emotionally controlled by women and have lost their centering. Part of the Emissary work is to clarify the distinct male-female roles, and to strengthen members of each sex in their proper role.

To this end, men and women hold separate meetings twice a week.

The income from the hotel ranged between $20,000 and $25,000 per month, with a profit of about $2000. Part of this was being set aside in a fund to buy the hotel at the expiration of the lease. All Emissaries working at the hotel got $100 per month, except for Rupert Haskell, who drew only $75 because he had private resources. The other employees were paid between $25 and $80 a week, plus room and board. We asked Haskell why he didn't staff the hotel entirely with Emissaries and he explained that working with the local staff is an important part of the community's outreach program.

Incomes from outside and personal possessions are a personal matter. Members who have outside incomes tend to donate to the Emissary fund but it is not required. A number of privately owned cars were loaned out rather freely. A few weeks before we were there, one of the group had nearly demolished a fellow Emissary's car, and he was expected to pay for all repairs. The group feels that personal responsibility for possessions is the only way in which they will be taken care of. Haskell cited the two vehicles that belonged to the hotel as examples. These belonged to no one in particular, and therefore were not very well cared for.

As part of their outreach program, the Emissaries hold a number of one-week and two-week classes each year. The classes cost $75 per week, including food and lodging. The weekend following our visit to the Hohenort a meeting of more than 50 Emissary group leaders from all over South Africa and Rhodesia was held. All were lodged at the hotel, filling it to capacity. In addition to the money they make at the hotel, the Emissaries receive contributions from nonresident members, and this money is used for paying outside consultants to the community and for travel expenses for resident members. The day we were there, a Canadian arrived for a two-month stay. He had extensive experience running kitchens and was there to advise members on running theirs. In 1979 the community paid the expenses of four of its people to go to Sunrise Ranch in Colorado for extended classes.

No specific vacation time is given, but members sometimes go away for a few days at a time to a beach cottage owned by one of the Emissaries. Everyone has one day off a week. On weekends they often work 12 to 14 hours a day, but the schedule is much more lighter during the week.

We asked Haskell about the philosophy and structure of the group. He answered that:

The Emissaries of Divine Light exist to provide a point of spiritual orientation for people to show that it is not only possible but practical to live a different life from the way it is usually experienced. There are no group exercises and we don't advocate any particular techniques. The expression of right spirit is what counts with us.

When we pressed him to be more specific, he replied

It involves being noncritical and nonjudgmental, and giving without concern for results. The key is the development of the ability to be thankful for all things at all times. Not to judge or to react—simply to see any happening as the opportunity for true expression of self. True cause brings true effect. The whole of one's life is given over to this practice and the key is finding attunement with life. Life has certain characteristics and qualities. There is a design in life and inherent within this is control. If we are correctly attuned with life we find that a design appears. It's not haphazard, not just loving everybody. The important thing is seeing that one's capacities for expression are under control of right spirit. We always seek to offer into any situation the right and fitting thing.

About 200 Emissaries live in South Africa and several thousand live around the world in a couple hundred centers. The Capetown group is predominantly young; most members are in their late twenties or early thirties, and a few members are in their fifties or sixties. There are no membership requirements. People either believe that they are Emissaries or they don't. The Emissaries in Capetown are mainly South Africans of English heritage. A few are Afrikaaners, English and Americans. About half are college graduates and most are from middle-class backgrounds. Since they started the hotel, few Emissaries have dropped out of the movement. And Haskell believes that those who dropped out were never really Emissaries. "If you truly have the experience, it is something you have always."

The Emmissary community is run in a somewhat authoritarian way. Rupert Haskell is the head focalizer, responsible for making all final decisions. A community member is appointed as manager in charge of each area of importance. All decisions relating to the hotel and the group's activities are discussed in twice-weekly meetings. Guidance on personal matters is never imposed, and is offered only if requested. The group has no rules about eating or drinking, but stresses moderation in all things. There were no vegetarians in the community at the time of our visit. Those who came into the community as vegetarians gradually gave it up since there was no internal reinforcement and meat was served at every meal. Members believe that humans are the capstones of creation, transmuting meat into a higher energy when it is eaten.

With so many unmarried young people living together, one might expect a great deal of pairing. In fact, little of this had occurred. Unmarried couples were not encouraged to have sex and were never put into the same room. There had been a few "sexually predatory" people of both sexes, but they tended to mellow out as they became more conscious. There were four married couples in the group—but all of them came into the group as pairs.

With only three preschoolers, the question of education had not yet come up. Each Sunday there was a junior training school for these three and twelve other young Emissaries from outside the hotel.

Haskell discussed the community's philosophy about world events.

Very obviously, events in the world are moving to a point of climax. Forces put into action by man's wrong identification with the material, rather than the spiritual, plane will overwhelm the present structure. Tremendous changes are to come. A significant number of people are beginning to find themselves in right orientation. This causes turmoil and upheaval. In recorded history there has been no large-scale right being. This increasing right spirit increases the pressure on what isn't based on right design. Nothing can stand in the way of the power of spirit—it sweeps everything aside. This is apparent on earth in an increasing degree, loosening up people and society so that they can participate in the ongoing creation. When light comes, darkness disappears. Our concern is to keep the light shining so that what has to work does work. We need to keep a steady current of right expression and find people able to maintain stability when the boat begins to rock—because rock it will.

Our visit to the Hohenort Hotel was in 1978. Six years later the hotel and the community had continued to develop. After its first year in operation, the South African Hotel Board advanced it from one-star to two-star status, noting that its friendly service deserved five-star plus status! A year later the community initiated Sunday evening classical dinner concerts, drawing in more customers and establishing a reputation for innovation. For about four years the community has also run an à la carte restaurant called the Plum, rated in many of the guidebooks as one of the better places to eat in Capetown. Over the years revenue from liquor sales has dropped sharply, while income from accommodations and food sales has risen accordingly. The hotel continues to make a modest profit each year, and in 1983 the community arranged to extend its lease in exchange for having contributed to the construction of a new staff accomodation wing and adding a number of bathrooms in the main building.

The Hohenort Hotel has been granted international hotel status which permits it to serve patrons of all races. It attracts a number of large international companies, who bring them quite a bit of in-residence seminar business, which is a boon in the off-season months. It also plays host to many New Age groups, including Transcendental Meditation and est, who hold their own classes at the hotel. In 1982 the hotel hosted weekend seminars for both Carl Rogers and Paul Solomon; Rogers celebrated his eightieth birthday there. The Emissaries are pleased to provide a facility that is equally appreciated by large corporations and spiritual groups.

As for the Emissaries themselves, the community has spread out a bit with the purchase of several nearby houses, but the immediate community continues to number about 30 people because the amount of accomodation they have suits that number of people. Over the years many people have come and gone, usually maintaining close links after they have left. Some have gone on to start their own Emissary communities elsewhere. A large live-in community that rents out space as a conference center has been established on the outskirts of Johannesburg, and a 40-acre farm has been started about half an hour's drive from the city of Durban. Valerie Morris, the hotel manager, moved to England to manage a hotel that the English Emissaries purchased in the Cotswolds.

The somewhat rigid attitudes we observed have softened. Haskell now says, "The Emissary ministry isn't a bunch of rules and views, but a group of individuals who must think and act for themselves." In matters of sexual mores, it's now very much up to individuals to make their own choices. Premarital sex is not frowned upon although not promoted either. Space allowing, people have their own rooms and are able to choose how they conduct themselves. The same goes for food. There are vegetarians in the group these days and when people choose not to eat meat the group ensures that proper alternatives are offered.

Some of the black and colored local staff have, over the years, expressed considerable interest in finding out more about the Emissaries and regular meetings have been instituted to share views and experiences. The Sunday meetings have become far more multi-racial in recent years. The Emissaries also now have a close rapport with a black spiritual community in Zululand.

Many people think of South Africa as an international pariah and imagine it is the last place in the world to find a New Age consciousness. After visiting the Hohenort Hotel, our conclusion was that we could think of no better or more important place for a spiritual community. Their location in a hotel and their constant interaction with the public, rather than being hidden and isolated on a farm, seem ideal. While they make no political statements and are, in fact, apolitical, they accomplish the purpose of helping to undermine the apartheid for which South Africa is famous by the quality of their interaction with both the perpetrators of the system and its victims.

Conclusion

We have roamed the world, across five continents and eight countries, visiting twenty-one intentional communities. These communities are not a cross-section, nor are they a statistical sample, and there certainly are a lot of other successful and important communities we haven't discussed. Nevertheless, we think that a close look at these groups can tell us something about the impulse toward community, and about the elements that make for success.

Among the twenty-one communities, six—Renaissance, Community of the Ark, Yodfat, Ittoen, Yamagishi-kai, and Riverside—are fully communal in the sense of joint ownership of virtually everything. At the other extreme, three—Stelle, Dartington, and Ein Hod—are almost marginal as intentional communities, with people living their own lives in a middle-class style very much as their neighbors do, devoting only a small part of their energy and attention to the community. The other twelve have strong community ties, but people keep their own financial resources, outside the control of the community.

There are community movements but there is no one community movement. The most significant are the Israeli kibbutz and *moshav* movements mentioned in Chapter 15. A kibbutz movement exists in Japan, but as far as we could tell, it has little influence and is primarily the vehicle of a few enthusiasts. In the United States the Federation of Egalitarian Communities is an important community organization; the two principal communities in this organization are Twin Oaks in Louisa, Virginia, and East Wind in Tecumseh, Missouri—both inspired by B. F. Skinner's book, *Walden Two*. *Communities* magazine, of which Twin Oaks is one of the main producers, represents a larger spectrum, but its range covers primarily secular communities.

In our visits we found that most communities are interested in what other communities are doing, but few visit other communities or carry out joint activities. Perhaps this is because many of the communities we studied are oriented toward their own spiritual concerns and community life is merely a means to an end. A few—Ananda, Findhorn, Homeland, and Riverside—are quite interested in contacts with other communities and in promoting the idea of community life.

One of the purposes of this book has been to examine what seems to work best in making communities successful. Let us look briefly at a number of the aspects we examined—membership, values, way of life, economic base, and governance—and see what conclusions or generalizations we can make.

Membership

Most of the communities draw heavily on relatively well-educated, predominantly middle-class people as members. Except for Findhorn, most communities are largely limited to citizens of the country in which they are located. This has more to do with national immigration regulations than with the attitudes of the communities. They are, on the whole, quite international in their outlook, following Hazel Henderson's dictum to "think globally; act locally."

Many of the communities we visited have little turnover, because they follow a spiritual path that members usually adopt for a lifetime. If they leave the community, it is to continue on the path elsewhere, perhaps in other communities of the same organization. By contrast, nonspiritual intentional communities usually have a much higher turnover, frequently 25 percent or more a year. In these cases, the individuals may regard living in a community as an educational experience; when they have gotten what they want from it, they leave. Findhorn and Homeland have a large turnover by design, while Stelle and the Abode of the Message have had a large turnover because of member disillusionment or lack of careful screening.

Screening is important, because no community can be stronger than the members who compose it. In his wise little book, *Cooperative Communities: How to Start Them and Why,* Swami Kriyananda said of communities: "There can be no 'perfect' system, for its members will always be the determining factor in its performance. . . . A system can facilitate the expression of goodness in people; it cannot create goodness."* To assure that its members have that quality of goodness, most of the communities have elaborate selection procedures, involving trial periods running from weeks up to several years, frequently with increasing levels of commitment, and sometimes with a period away from the community to give the applicant perspective. Communities that take care in screening potential members seldom find it necessary to expel members.

Values

The essence of a spiritual community is that each person is engaged in inner work for self-betterment. We believe that this, and the commitment to shared ideals, are very important factors in helping members get along with others. In a secular community people are more likely to project their inner turmoil onto the environment around them, and the

---

*Kriyananda, *Cooperative Communities,* 44.

community can then become the scene of interminable debates about power, equality, women's and men's roles, consciousness raising, gay liberation, and so on. General agreement on values, therefore, is one of the keys to a harmonious community. A community cannot be all things to all people. As Mary Robinson at the Universal Brotherhood said, "the world is made up of chords. . . . If people do not fit in here, they should leave and try to find a chord with which they are in harmony."

On the issue of communal ownership of all property versus individual initiative, we have reached no conclusion. Our own bias, as businesspeople, leads us to favor permitting individual initiative and making no rules about private property. Such a policy will attract more people with initiative and property. Some communities—such as Ittoen and the Community of the Ark—that ask all members to take a vow of poverty, are remarkably successful. But The Farm which was probably the outstanding examples of this, found it didn't work and, in 1983, began a shift away from communal ownership of everything. There is a place for both forms of organization: people will gravitate to whichever they find more attractive.

Way of Life

We observed a considerable difference in ways of life, ranging from the middle-class, gracious living of Stelle to the "third-world" living of the Farm. In almost every community, illegal drugs are banned—more successfully, we think, than in the society outside—and alcohol consumption is usually minimal. Sexual mores range from the conservative to the free. The vast majority of communities, however, agree that members have the right to handle their sexual needs in their own way. In every case, communities emphasize that sexual relationships should be responsible and nonexploitative. Stable, loving relationships are encouraged, but most communities do not insist that couples be married.

These communities are concerned with what people are, not who they are or what they have. This, of course, is made easier by the fact that in many cases everybody has about the same number and kinds of possessions and not much of them at that. But this is a strength; not a weakness. A life that is not devoted to the accumulation of possessions leaves a lot more room for the accumulation of friends and good times.

In most of the communities a strong concern is exhibited for the environment, reflected in their efforts at energy conservation, organic gardening, healthy diets, and avoidance of waste. This sometimes extends to social action outside the community, although a number of the communities shun politics in the interest of avoiding controversy with their neighbors.

Voluntary simplicity is a way of life that is consciously followed to some extent by millions in North America and Western Europe who are appalled by the wasteful excesses of their countries' economies. This way of life requires cooperation with neighbors to jointly accomplish what each individual or family used to do for itself. And here the intentional communities are way ahead of the rest of us; they already have the structure for the flowering of voluntary simplicity.

Economic Base

Possibly the single most difficult problem for the intentional communities as a whole has been how to make a living. In part this is because many of their members turned away from what they had been educated to do, starting out as pioneers with few material resources and little relevant training. Remember the 270 people who went on the caravan with Stephen Gaskin and ended up on a farm in Tennessee. Only one of them had any farming experience. They thought they might have to work a day a week to get by, but quickly learned that being pioneers isn't easy.

A great many business failures have occurred among the communities, at probably a higher rate than in the larger society. This stems from their shortage of material resources and training, and also, in many cases, from an antiprofit mentality. And few have the drive to succeed that so strongly motivates many entrepreneurs. As a result, a number of communities, such as Ananda, the Zen Center, Stelle, the Abode of the Message, and Yamatoyama, have developed mixed economies, in which community businesses and private businesses operate happily side by side. These communities have a pragmatic approach, free from economic dogma about how things ought to be.

The one element that has been advantageous for the communities in their businesses is their low labor costs; If they had to pay prevailing wages, more of their businesses would have failed. On the other hand, at the Rochester Folk Art Guild, low labor costs have also made it possible to use more hand labor and achieve a higher quality than is generally possible in other businesses.

Many of the communities have achieved a considerable degree of self-sufficiency or, at least, a local sufficiency between themselves and their neighbors. This usually reflects an expectation of future economic or other disruptions in the outside world. If these expectations come to pass, the people living in these communities will be able to survive better than most of us. And if they don't come to pass? Well, as Tim Wilhelm said at Stelle, "Everything we've been doing makes this a better place to live and improves our lives and our children's lives. That's enough justification."

Governance

Most of the communities are remarkably democratic. Where the communities have a spiritual leader, he frequently stays out of the day-to-day decision making. Most communities govern by consensus rather than by vote. This, of course, underscores the importance of careful selection of members and the members' commitment to common ideals. At the same time, most communities recognize the need for strong leadership. We observed nearly everywhere that there is little politicking for positions of leadership. The communities seek out the people they regard as the best-suited for these jobs and often have to convince them to take the positions.

Swami Kriyananda urges that rules be kept to a minimum. "It is far better to establish general customs than hard and fast laws. Even if everyone follows a rule, that fact that it is a rule makes it fertile soil for gossip and suspicion. It acts as a narrowing influence upon the mind, where simple customs might only help everyone to grow harmoniously."* Recall that Findhorn, for example, has only two rules—no smoking in public places and no illegal drugs—and everything else is a rhythm. In small communities such as these, the informal and often unspoken social controls are strong enough to make most rules superfluous.

As we said in the introduction, communities go through a variety of stages: birth, youth, maturity, old age, and eventually death. What counts is the quality of the community's life while it is alive. Community life, like any other life, is full of problems and hard work. For some people a cooperative life can be a difficult one because society has trained them for competition and individual success. On the other hand, cooperative living can result in many economies since each individual or family does not have to duplicate many of the tools of everyday life and there is little conspicuous consumption. In fact, one of our most profound impressions—and something we hadn't thought much about before we began this study—was of how good the quality of life can be in a cooperative community despite a very low cash income.

This may be one of the most significant ways in which intentional communities are "seeds of tomorrow." We live in a time when the cash economies all over the world are in trouble. Taxes are high, unemployment is high, national debts are mounting, the banking system appears to be threatened with collapse. Some people are rioting or revolting or sinking into apathy; others are transferring more and more of their energies to the noncash economy, the activities that don't enter into the Gross National Product or get taxed. They are helping each other, bartering, making many things that they used to buy. And here, intentional communities are a good model. Some, such as the Rochester Folk Art Guild and Ittoen, enjoy a material quality of life that many highly paid people might envy, although they are below the official poverty line. While these models are not for everyone, because of the character de-

---

*Ibid., 47.

mands they make on their members, probably millions of people in the United States alone could adapt to communal life. We hope that one of the values of this book is to show what this alternative is about and to help people reach their own conclusions as to whether it is right for them.

Our job is done. We've tried to present these twenty-one communities to you as we see them. It has been a wonderful experience for us personally, because we have met many fine, loving, committed people. If any of our readers get discouraged by the pettiness and greed and hypocrisy that sometimes seem rife in society, we invite you to visit a community or two. The pioneer spirit is still alive. May these seeds of tomorrow continue to sprout and grow.

Appendix I: Addresses

While most of these communities welcome visitors, each has its own arrangements and charges. Never drop in on a community; always write in advance and wait for an invitation.

Ananda Cooperative Village
14618 Tyler Foote Road
Nevada City, CA 95959
   (916) 265-5877

Zen Center of Los Angeles
905 South Normandie Avenue
Los Angeles, CA 90006
   (213) 387-2351

Stelle Group
Stelle, IL 60919
   (815) 256-2200

Renaissance Community
Box 112
Turners Falls, MA 01376
   (413) 863-9711

Abode of the Message
Box 396
New Lebanon, NY 12125
   (518) 794-7659

Rochester Folk Art Guild
RD 1, Box 10
Middlesex, NY 14507
   (716) 554-3539

The Farm
156 Drakes Lane
Summertown, TN 38483
   (615) 964-3574

Universal Brotherhood
Box 21, Balingup, WA 6253
Australia
   Tel: Bal. 62

Homeland
Thora, NSW 2492
Australia
   Tel: 066 558514

Community of the Ark
La Borie Noble
34260 Le Bousquet d'Orb
France

Domaine du Bonfin
83601 Fréjus Cedex,
France
   Tel: (94) 40.70.22

Dartington Hall Trust
Elmhirst Centre
Dartington Hall
Totnes, Devon
England
   Tel: Totnes (0803) 862223

London Buddhist Centre
119 Roman Road
Bethnel Green, London E2
England
   Tel: 01.981 1225

Findhorn Foundation
Cluny Hill College
Forres
Scotland IV 36 ORD
   Tel: Forres 72288

Moshav Shitufi Yodfat
DN Bik'at, Beit-Kerem
Israel
   Tel: 04-912-028

Ein Hod
Israel
  Tel: 02-278-111 (Ministry of
Education and Culture)

Shorokshinto-Yamatoyama
12-13 Takinozawa, Sotodoji
Hairauchi-cho, Higashitsugaru-gun
Aomori-ken 039-33
Japan
  Tel: 01775-7-2241

Ittoen
Shinomiya, Yamashina-ku
Kyoto 607
Japan
  Tel: 075.581.3136

Yamagishiism Seikatsu Toyosato
Jikkenchi
5050 Takano, Toyosato-cho
Tsu-shi, Mie-kan 514-22
Japan
  Tel: (0592) 30-1151

Riverside Community
Lower Moutere (near Motueka)
New Zealand
  Tel: Motueka LMO 792

Hohenort Hotel
Constantia, Cape, South Africa
  Tel: 74-1027

Appendix II: Selected Bibliography

Aïvanhov, Omraam Mikhaël. *The Universal Great White Brotherhood.* 105 pp. Fréjus, France: Prosveta, 1976. This is a bilingual (French-English) transcription of lectures by the leader of Le Domaine du Bonfin. (Aïvanhov also published a whole series of additional books.)

Balado, J. L. G. *The Story of Taize.* Photographs, 128 pp. New York: Seabury, 1981. In this book Balado, a Spanish journalist, describes the history of Taize—a large French Christian community—from its beginnings in the 1940s to the present days.

Ball, John. *Ananda: Where Yoga Lives.* Photographs, 232 pp. Bowling Green, Ohio: Popular Press, 1982. This subjective look at Ananda and its founder, Swami Kriyananda, provides a detailed survey of the community's history. Ball is a follower of Kriyananda.

Bennett, J. G. *Needs of a New Age Community.* 99 pp. Sherbourne, England: Coombe Springs Press, 1977. This is a collection of talks on the title theme by a leading follower of G. I. Gurdjieff.

Blair, Don. *The New Harmony Story.* 71 pp. New Harmony, Ind.: New Harmony Publications Committee, n.d. This is an official history of this important nineteenth century community.

Case, John, and Rosemary C. R. Taylor, eds. *Co-ops, Communes and Collectives: Experiments in Social Change in the 1960s and 1970s.* Notes, index, 329 pp. New York: Random House, 1979. The editors have compiled a collection of generally radical papers and reports of experiments in progress. Some of the most perceptive activists and critics of the movement provide thoughtful insights into the successes and failures of the period and the new social mosaic many of them see forming.

Cecil, Michael, ed. *Spirit of Sunrise.* 192 pp. Loveland, Colo.: Sunrise Ranch, 1979. This collection of talks provides an introduction to the spiritual teachings of the Emissaries of Divine Light.

Clark, David. *Basic Communities: Towards an Alternative Society.* 239 pp. London: SPCK, 1977. Clark presents an academic survey of the communitarian movement in the United Kingdom today. He focuses on Christian communities, though he does include a few of the more important non-Christian ones. The analysis is descriptive and many case histories are included.

Coates, Gary J., ed. *Resettling America: Energy, Ecology and Community.* Index, 576 pp. Boston: Brick House, 1981. This collection of 22 articles ranges from popular accounts of contemplative communities, such as the San

Francisco Zen Center, to theoretical pieces on the politics of scarcity, urban decentralization, and neighborhood revitalization.

Fairfield, Richard. *The Modern Utopian: Communes, Japan.* San Francisco: Alternatives Foundation, 1972. This is a somewhat scattered account of visits to several Japanese communities by someone with a strong commune orientation.

Findhorn Community. *Faces of Findhorn: Images of a Planetary Family.* Photographs, 177 pp. New York: Harper & Row, 1980. Members of the community share a history of Findhorn's recent developments and their own experience of life in the community.

Findhorn Community. *The Findhorn Garden.* Photographs, 180 pp. New York: Harper & Row, 1975. The authors present an early account of the development of Findhorn and the philosophy that sustains it.

Fogarty, Robert S. *Dictionary of American Communal and Utopian History.* Bibliography, index, 297 pp. New York: Greenwood press, 1980. The first half of this scholarly reference work is devoted to biographies of individuals who played significant roles in the communal movement in the United States from its inception up to the twentieth century. The balance is a summary discussion of many communities.

Foster, Lawrence. *Religion and Sexuality: Three American Communal Movements of the 19th Century.* Many notes, index, 374 pp. New York: Oxford University Press, 1981. Foster provides a thorough analysis of the origin, early development, and institutionalization of three communal religious groups that rejected existing family and sex role patterns: the Shakers, the Oneida community, and the Mormons. Much of the book is based on primary documents. Case histories describe the development of each group.

Fracchia, Charles. *Living Together Alone: The New American Monasticism.* San Francisco: Harper & Row, 1979. 186 pp. This is a journalistic exploration of 12 contemporary American communities with religious roots. The bulk are Christian, though Hindu and Buddhist communities are also included.

French, David, and Elena French. *Working Communally: Patterns and Possibilities.* Notes, bibliography, index, 269 pp. New York: Russell Sage Foundation, 1975. The authors provide an examination of communal work situations in Europe, Israel, and China. The book includes indications as to the elements that are transferable to the United States combined with a study of past American communitarian movements, and the nature and limitations of American community experiments of the 1960s and 1970s.

Freundlich, Paul, ed. *A Guide to Cooperative Alternatives.* Index, 184 pp. Louisa, Va.: Community Publications Cooperative, 1979. This guide was put together by the editors of *Communities* magazine, a bimonthly journal that provides the most up-to-date information on communities in the United States. This book, like the magazine, focuses on social action communities, referring only occasionally to spiritual communities.

Hawken, Paul. *The Magic of Findhorn.* Illustrations, 261 pp. New York: Bantam Books, 1975. This personal account of Hawken's impressions following his visit to Findhorn is the book that put the community on the map, awakening broad public interest.

Horgan, Edward R. *The Shaker Holy Land: A Community Portrait.* Illustrations, notes, index, 246 pp. Boston: Harvard Common Press, 1982. This book probes the actual life of two Shaker communities, detailing the histories and personalities. The communities studied—Harvard and Shirley—were founded by Ann Lee herself and were the site of much of her life's work.

Hostetler, John A. *Communitarian Societies.* 65 pp. New York: Holt, Rinehart & Winston, 1974. Hostetler's sociological text focuses on the Oneida community and the Hutterites, two of the most significant nineteenth-century American communal movements.

Hostetler, John A., and Gertrude Enders Huntington. *The Hutterites in North America.* Bibliography, 119 pp. New York: Holt, Rinehart & Winston, 1967. This is an extremely thorough anthropological analysis of the Hutterites of the Dakotas.

Institute for Community Economics. *The Community Land Trust Handbook.* Illustrations, bibliography, index, 239 pp. Emmaus, Pa.: Rodale Press, 1982. This book offers case histories of ongoing land trusts, along with practical advice on setting one up.

Kateb, George. *Utopia and Its Enemies.* Index, 244 pp. New York: Free Press, 1963. Kateb evaluates the main contemporary currents of attack on the utopian ideal and offers an analysis of modern utopian thought.

Kidel, Mark. *Dartington.* Exeter, England: Webb & Bower, 1982. In words and pictures Dartington Hall's interpretation officer has captured the spirit and flavor of this community.

Kriyananda, Swami. *Cooperative Communities: How to Start Them and Why.* Photographs, 118 pp. Nevada City, Calif.: Ananda Publications, 1968. Kriyananda offers his thoughts on successful cooperative communities and includes details on Ananda.

Kriyananda, Swami. *The Shortened Path: Autobiography of a Western Yogi.* 209 pp. Nevada City, Calif.: Ananda Publications, 1981. This is a shortened version of the life story of the founder of Ananda, covering his years as a student of Yogananda and the inception and development of his community.

Kueshana, Eklal. *The Ultimate Frontier.* Index, 337 pp. Stelle, Ill.: Stelle Group, 1982. This book presents the story of the founding and development of the Stelle community and the historical rationale for its existence.

Matsuba, Moshe, ed. *The Communes of Japan.* 247 pp. Hokkaido, Japan: Japanese Commune Movement, (Kibbutz Akan, Shin Shizenjuku Nakasetsuri, Tsurui Mura, Akan Gun, Hokkaido, 085-12), 1979. Matsuba presents a collection of lengthy narratives describing the leading Japanese communities.

Melville, Keith. *Communes in the Counter Culture: Origins, Theories, Styles of Life.* Bibliography, 256 pp. New York: William Morrow, 1972. Melville relates the communes to the revival of the anarchistic tradition, to the search for alternative social structures that satisfy the needs for interdependence and closeness, and to a rebellion against the middle-class. Case histories are included.

Morgan, Griscom, ed. *Guidebook for Intentional Communities.* 43 pp. Yellow Springs, Ohio: Community Services, 1977. Community Services is one of the most active communal organizations in the United States today.

They run conferences on small community issues, have an up-to-date bibliography, and issue a regular newsletter.

Renard, Pierre C. *The Solar Revolution and the Prophet.* 193 pp. Fréjus, France: Prosveta, 1980. This is the most thorough English-language presentation of the initiatic teachings that are the basis of Le Domaine du Bonfin. Details on community life are also included.

Robertson, Constance Noyes, ed. *Oneida Community: An Autobiography, 1851– 1876.* Photographs, bibliography, 380 pp. Syracuse, N.Y.: Syracuse University Press, 1970. In this compilation from Oneida community newsletters, the men and women of the community describe the way they live; how they work and play; and their views on child rearing, personal relationships, education, and religion. The editor provides introductory material.

Sangharakshita. *Peace is a Fire.* 127 pp. London: Windhorse Press, 1979. This is a topical selection from the writings and sayings of the founder of the Friends of the Western Buddhist Order.

Spangler, David. *Vision of Findhorn: Anthology.* Illustrations, 92 pp. Forres, Scotland: Findhorn Publications, 1977. In this a collection of essays, Spangler seeks to clarify the vision of the New Age and relate that vision to the realities of the world today.

Spiro, Melford E. *Kibbutz: Venture in Utopia.* Bibliography, indexes, 327 pp. New York: Schocken Books, 1970. This is a revised and updated edition of the standard work on Israeli collectives. It is a sociological study that focuses on one kibbutz, examining its daily life, and attitudes and problems of its members.

Subhuti, Dharmachari (Alex Kennedy). *Buddhism for Today: A Portrait of a New Buddhist Movement.* 205 pp. Salisbury, England: Element Books 1983. An account by one of the leaders of the Friends of the Western Buddhist Order of the movement and its principles.

Tazawa, Yasusaburo. *My Response to the Challenge of Peace.* Illustrations, 64 pp. Aomori, Japan: Yamatoyama, 1980. This book combines a statement of the approach of the leader of Yamatoyama with a brief history of the community and the movement throughout Japan.

Tenko San. *A New Road to Ancient Truth.* Glossary, 183 pp. New York: Horizon Press, 1972. Tenko Nishida was the founder of Ittoen. In this book he presents, through parables and anecdotes, the inner meaning of the movement. He also includes case histories and a bit of material on the community.

Tod, Ian, and Michael Wheeler. *Utopia.* 160 pp. New York: Harmony Books, 1978. The authors present a pictorial study of utopian ideals and those ideals as put into practice throughout history, from earliest times to the present day.

Vasto, Lanza del. *L'Arche Avait Pour Voilure Une Vigne.* 273 pp. Paris: Editions Denoel, 1978. This French book covers ten years of Lanza del Vasto's life after *Return to the Source* was published, and contains all the rules that govern del Vasto's Community of the Ark.

Vasto, Lanza del. *Return to the Source.* 232 pp. New York: Schocken Books, 1968. This is an autobiographical account of the life of the founder of the Community of the Ark. Included are vivid accounts of del Vasto's discipleship with Mahatma Gandhi and his pilgrimage throughout India.

Veysey, Laurence. *The Communal Experience—Anarchist & Mystical Communities in Twentieth Century America.* Notes, index, 508 pp. Chicago: University of Chicago Press, 1978. Most of this book consists of comprehensive studies of four little-known communities, two of them religious and highly structured and two anarchistic. Veysey also provides general information on communities.

Weisbrod, Carl. *The Boundaries of Utopia.* Notes, index, 320 pp. New York: Random House, 1980. Weisbrod's book is an imaginative work that surveys the nineteenth-century utopian communities' relationship with the larger society, focusing on the legal aspects of that relationship.

Young, Michael. *The Elmhirsts of Dartington: The Creation of an Utopian Community.* Notes, index, 381 pp. Boston: Routledge & Kegan Paul, 1982. This is a thorough biographical study of the Elmhirsts. Combined with the life stories is a great deal of information about Dartington and its innovations.

Zablocki, Benjamin. *Alienation and Charisma: A Study of Contemporary American Communes.* Tables, notes, bibliography, indexes, 479 pp. New York: Macmillan, 1980. Zablocki provides the most comprehensive sociological study of communes published to date.

Zablocki, Benjamin. *The Joyful Community: An Account of the Bruderhof, A Communal Movement Now in Its Third Generation.* Notes, bibliography, index, 362 pp. Chicago: University of Chicago Press, 1980. The Bruderhof is one of the most successful Christian communes. This balanced sociological account is based on the author's firsthand investigation.